BATTLETECH:
EMBERS OF WAR

JASON SCHMETZER

BATTLETECH: EMBERS OF WAR
Cover art by Victor Manuel Leza Moreno
Design by Matt Heerdt

Published by Catalyst Game Labs,
an imprint of InMediaRes Productions, LLC
PMB 202 • 303 91st Ave NE • E502 • Lake Stevens, WA 98258

THE CHAOS MARCH

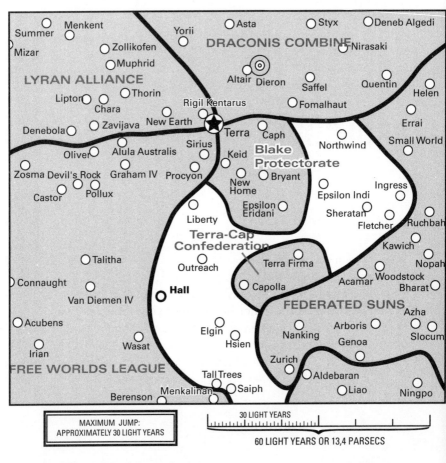

| Summer | Menkent | Yorii | Asta | Styx | Deneb Algedi |

DRACONIS COMBINE

Mizar · Zollikofen · Nirasaki · Muphrid

LYRAN ALLIANCE

Altair · Dieron · Saffel · Quentin · Helen

Lipton · Thorin · Rigil Kentarus · Fomalhaut

Chara · Zavijava · New Earth · Errai

Denebola · Terra · Caph · Northwind · Small World

Oliver · Alula Australis · Sirius · Keid

Blake Protectorate

Zosma · Devil's Rock · Graham IV · Procyon · New Home · Bryant · Ingress

Castor · Pollux · Epsilon Indi · Sheratan

Epsilon Eridani · Fletcher · Ruchbah

Liberty · Kawich

Terra-Cap Confederation

Talitha · Outreach · Terra Firma · Acamar · Woodstock · Nopah

Connaught · Bharat

Van Diemen IV · **Hall** · Capolla

FEDERATED SUNS

Azha

Acubens · Elgin · Nanking · Arboris · Genoa · Slocum

Irian · Wasat · Hsien · Zurich

FREE WORLDS LEAGUE

Tall Trees · Saiph · Aldebaran · Liao · Ningpo

Berenson · Menkalinan

| MAXIMUM JUMP: APPROXIMATELY 30 LIGHT YEARS |

30 LIGHT YEARS

60 LIGHT YEARS OR 13,4 PARSECS

THE INNER SPHERE

LEGEND
1 - Draconis Combine
2 - Federated Suns
3 - Capellan Confederation
4 - Free WorldsLeague
5 - Lyran Alliance
6 - Clan Wolf
7 - Clan Jade Falcon
8 - Clan Ghost Bear
9 - Magistracy of Canopus
10 - Outworlds Alliance
11 - Taurian Concordat
12 - Marian Hegemony

Coreward

Anti-spinward · Spinward

Rimward

© 3067 **COMSTAR CARTOGRAPHIC CORPS**

PROLOGUE

It felt unnatural, watching a mountain fly through the air with giant war machines leaping out of it.

Adele Estwicke blinked, pushing down the sense of awe that warred with the worry in her heart. The flying mountain was a matte-gray DropShip with an orange tiger's snarling face painted on the side; the war machines were BattleMechs making a combat drop. Behind her, the small crowd in the field tent cheered.

The tiger's face meant this was the Stealthy Tigers, the mercenaries Emperor Baranov had hired to help him put down the rebellion on Hall. Or at least, that's what the newscasts said. Estwicke wasn't about to argue.

Not when the emperor was about to win.

Because beneath the dropping mercenaries was the gathered force of Count Radcliffe McNally, the emperor's fiercest opponent. His 'Mechs and tanks had been evenly matched against the emperor's Fourth Republican. With what looked like at least a battalion of mercenary 'Mechs falling at him, he was doomed.

Hence the cheering.

This could be it, she told herself. *The culmination of my mission here. The fulfillment of the years of work the Word of Blake has put into Hall.*

The Word of Blake, the holy order devoted to communications and the preservation and control of knowledge, had been the core of the communications conglomerate known as Com-

Star for centuries. A decade ago, during the height of tensions with the Clans, and while the Federated Commonwealth was distracted with breaking into two realms, it had struck, reclaiming Terra from its ComStar custodians and establishing, finally, its own legitimacy.

Estwicke wasn't a soldier, but she'd been a part of Operation Odysseus. She'd been among the first to put her feet on the holy soil of sacred Terra. She'd felt the spirit of Jerome Blake himself reinvigorate her soul as she had done so. That vigor had sustained her for a decade, and she'd spent those years working toward a mission like this one.

When Precentor Blane had sent her here from Terra three years ago, she hadn't actually believed she'd be able to pull her current mission off. The Word of Blake had been consolidating its hold on the worlds around Terra, laying the foundation for what had become the Word of Blake Protectorate; a barrier of worlds around Terra, all allied to the Word. She'd heard some call it a new Terran Hegemony, but Estwicke dismissed those people. The Terran Hegemony was ancient—and tainted—history. Until the Clans were dealt with . . . she sniffed.

The first Tigers BattleMechs landed, crashing to the ground in *thuds* Estwicke could hear and feel from kilometers away. Those with integral jump jets landed and immediately moved toward McNally's shocked force; the others, wearing detachable thruster packs, shed their wings and followed.

Excitement tingled in Estwicke's fingertips. She'd accompanied the Fourth Republican into the field to get a better appreciation of the reality of the emperor's fighting forces. She didn't trust the sycophantic reports that came back to Harney, the capital, from the front. If those reports were true, word for word, then McNally would have been dead years ago.

But he might get killed today, Estwicke realized. She had enough experience to recognize that. The Tigers BattleMechs, humanoid war machines up to twelve meters tall, moved in tight, synchronized groups with no fear. Body language didn't translate directly, but Estwicke had seen enough 'Mechs on the march to recognize nervous MechWarriors in the cockpits. The Tigers were not nervous.

The McNally MechWarriors, however, were terrified.

Estwicke couldn't help it. She thought about the future.

With McNally dead, the emperor's hold on Hall should be all but ironclad. The nobleman had been the largest thorn in William

"Bud" Baranov's scheme to seize ultimate power since the Federated Commonwealth broke apart a decade ago. The two had been sparring ever since, neither able to land a decisive blow against the other.

Until, perhaps, now.

Estwicke looked up then, across the low valley toward the fight. Lasers flickered, red and blue and green. Missiles smoked and swarmed. PPCs flashed blue-white. Cannons hammered. Even this far away, she could hear the pounding of weapons against armor, the *crash* of overstressed metal collapsing, the manmade thunder of energy weapons drilling holes in the atmosphere. She felt like she was watching an action holovid: the fate of a world, being decided right in front of her eyes.

Her mouth was dry. She coughed and worked her tongue, tried to swallow.

"Look at those suckers go!" one of the Fourth Republican officers behind her shouted. She looked back and forth, and saw a lance of four Stealthy Tigers 'Mechs drive straight through the encampment the Republicans had told her was the count's headquarters.

"We should get out there," another Republican shouted. There were sounds of agreement. "We don't want to miss this."

Estwicke ignored the rush past her. She wasn't a MechWarrior—there was no tall 'Mech for her to rush off to. Instead, she watched the battle. It was as one-sided as anything she'd ever seen on the HV.

The Tigers methodically worked their way across the field, firing at and crushing every McNally 'Mech and tank in their way. Still, the McNally forces weren't giving up. Both sides were firing, and here and there a Stealthy Tigers 'Mech fell. Several of them got back up. At least three did not, but the losses weren't enough to stem the tide.

The Tigers were more numerous and better organized. Estwicke watched one McNally 'Mech, then another, turn and try to run away. Past the fight, the Tigers lance that had overrun the count's headquarters was moving slowly, firing at the ground at figures that were little more than specks to Estwicke's eyes.

People, she realized. She turned and looked behind her, and up.

The Republican *Centurion* was tall, about eleven meters. Estwicke recognized it from training years ago. It stepped closer to her, every footfall shaking the ground. To her, standing unarmored and alone on the ground beneath it, it was as tall as the sky and as heavy as the earth. She licked dry lips and looked from it back toward the fight, unwillingly imagining what it must be like for the people in the count's camp.

She shivered.

The *Centurion* stepped over her like she wasn't there. Its footsteps quickened as it accelerated, every step shaking the ground. Estwicke shivered again and wrapped her arms around herself.

How could anyone survive that? she wondered.

Then she shook herself and blinked several times.

She smiled as she watched the huge 'Mech stomp off toward the battlefield.

If he's dead by the end of the day, she told herself, *then the Blessed Blake's plan for this world is one day closer to completion.*

"Where were these mercenaries a month ago, when it might have mattered?" asks an anonymous McNally supporter.

"We went out in the south and asked the people there what they thought of the arrival of the Dismal Disinherited, mercenaries under the illegal auspices of the Allied Mercenary Command. Here's what they said:"

"Who?"
"I mean, the fighting is over, isn't it? McNally is dead? Baranov won?"
"Does this mean Wolf's Dragoons supports the emperor?"

"No matter where you stand on the rebellion launched by the late Count McNally against the emperor, it's clear that no one wants the AMC on Hall."

–From the *Harney Morning Edition*,
Harney HV Channel Six

CHAPTER ONE

10 KM SOUTHEAST OF HARNEY
HALL
THE CHAOS MARCH
18 JANUARY 3067

When he knelt and touched the loose soil, Ezra Payne breathed in the cloying scent of wet earth and dust. He rubbed the coarse brown dirt between his fingers, looking down, eyes half-closed. His other hand, resting on his knee, twitched.

When he closed his eyes, he could smell more: sweat and hot circuits. Overheated lubricants and the sinus-tearing taint of missile exhaust. Ozone. Wood smoke. And beneath it all, the burned-meat stench he recognized from a dozen other worlds.

Ezra opened his eyes and stood. He wiped his hands against each other and looked toward the horizon. At a discreet throat-clearing behind him, he sniffed and turned around. Eleven men and women stood in front of him.

"It was right here," he told them.

And then for a few seconds, he said nothing. He wanted to see how they would react. Only one of them—Sergeant Major Robert Halleck—had been here before. And Ezra knew he could trust the sergeant major to keep his mouth shut until the proper moment.

The assembled MechWarriors didn't move, but he saw their eyes moving. A couple of them frowned, looking back and forth. The after-action reports were available, of course. It was a famous battle already, on Hall. Even in the Tigers' own lore, it wasn't every engagement that ended a civil war. Ezra knew the sergeant major had checked to see which of the MechWarriors had reviewed

the reports. Ezra hadn't checked, and he hadn't asked Halleck. He preferred to find out himself.

Besides, he told himself, *how many times have you heard—or said!—that the map isn't the ground?*

"Who can tell me why we're out here?" Ezra asked a moment later.

No one spoke.

"Sergeant Major?"

Halleck didn't turn his head. "Talb. Answer the captain."

One of the MechWarriors blinked. She was tall, with thin, blond hair and gray eyes. A scar ran from her temple back into her hair, and unless you were looking you didn't notice that she stood with a slight lean. "This is where the regiment won Hall, sir."

"Wrong," Ezra told her. "Who else?"

No one spoke. Sergeant Major Halleck growled low in his throat.

"This is where Major Calhoune died," MechWarrior Tima Zan said.

"Correct," Ezra said, "but not the reason we're out here."

Zan frowned, but didn't say anything more.

Ezra waited another handful of heartbeats, then looked at Halleck. "Sergeant Major?"

"This was our last fight, sir," the short, solid, black-skinned man said.

"Right in one," Ezra said. He looked at the MechWarriors, trying to see if any of them grasped the significance. He didn't expect them to. They didn't know each other well enough—they were too new. Some of them new to the Stealthy Tigers, and some of them new to his company.

Instead of speaking, he turned back and looked across the field. It had been a few months, and Hall's native ecosystem had attacked the battlefield with a vengeance. New-growth grasses and brush dotted the field, glowing a lighter shade of green than the mature plants around them. Each place marked a spot were the turf had been torn or broken.

Sometimes it had burned.

"This is where we dropped to kill Count McNally," he said quietly. "We didn't plan to kill him—only to stop him. But sometimes stopping people means killing them."

He blinked, and it was like he was there again. He felt the jolt as his *Crusader* touched down, felt the shuddering ripple as he fired his missiles. He heard the sounds of combat and the crowing triumph of Major Markoja when her 'Mech crashed through the count's field headquarters.

Ezra blinked again, and it was gone. He reached up and rubbed his hand across his brush-cut brown hair. Then down across the short stubble on his face. He hadn't shaved to the skin since December. He wasn't sure he wanted to ever again.

"Until a couple of weeks ago, you'd have been right, Talb," he said. "With McNally dead, there's really no one left to oppose the emperor." He turned back to face the MechWarriors. "Until a couple of weeks ago. When . . . Zan?"

"The Dismal Ds landed," Zan replied.

"The Dismal Ds landed," Ezra repeated.

The Dismal Disinherited were among the elite of the mercenary regiments of the Inner Sphere. Three full regiments strong, they had thrown their support behind Jaime Wolf's Allied Mercenary Command almost immediately. One of those regiments—the Third—was here, now, on Hall. "Checking for signs of Blakist aggression or coercion."

Ezra felt his lip curl. Those had been the Dismal D colonel's words when he'd landed.

The emperor's media machine had immediately condemned the AMC's presence, and that condemnation carried a lot of weight—even without the pushing of the local media, firmly in Baranov's pocket after ten years—with a lot of people. The Allied Mercenary Command was an abomination, so far as Ezra and a lot of the Stealthy Tigers were concerned.

Mercenaries fought for a contract. It didn't matter why they had become mercenaries in the first place. It didn't matter what side they fought for. It didn't matter what the reporters said, or the pundits. It didn't matter if they were a lone platoon of infantrymen or a full-size regimental combat team. Mercenaries were a way of life in the Inner Sphere. Centuries of constant warfare ensured that there were always men and women trained to fight, and that same warfare meant there were also just as many men and women becoming disenfranchised with the reasons they'd begun fighting in the first place. Mercenaries had earned a place in almost every conflict across the Inner Sphere. Often they were too skilled to be left out.

But they didn't fight because they *wanted* to. Because they found some policy or group they *objected* to.

They fought because they'd signed a contract that stated they would. Because they were professionals. Because when you went into combat without the weight of a national government behind you, all you *had* was professionalism.

Which brought them back to this field of grass.

"Right now the Dismal Disinherited are unloading. They're setting up their patrol routes, looking at combat zones, and doing all the firsthand intelligence gathering they can fit into every hour of the day." He looked down the line of MechWarriors. "In short, they're doing everything we would be doing on first landfall of a new contract."

Ezra looked at Sergeant Major Halleck. Then he glanced down the line again and nodded. "I brought you out here today," he said, "to make this point: it's important to win. Winning is everything, even when winning means simply not losing. But the reasons we fight—the reasons we win—aren't because of the rightness of our cause, or because we're destined for victory, or because anything else." He licked his lips.

"We fight because we're professionals. We fight because we have a contract, and because we *keep* to that contract. That is where *our* honor lies."

Bringing his hands out from behind his back, Ezra reached up and tapped the small pin on his lapel. It was an enameled black pin with a white tiger's head in side-profile on it. "This is a Raider pin." He didn't ask if they knew what that meant. They were Stealthy Tigers. They knew.

"You can't buy this pin," he said. "You can't be promoted into it. The sergeant major can't give you one. I can't give you one. Even the colonel can't give you one. You have to earn it, and earn it in the eyes of every other Tiger who wears one." He dropped his hand.

"You earn it by doing your job." He looked up and down the line again. "It's that simple. Do your job. Do it well, as best you can. Not because you want this pin, or because you want a promotion, or you're trying to get laid." He ignored the smirks.

"We only have one philosophy," Ezra said. He half-turned and swept his arm across the field. "Every Tiger who fought here did so for one single reason: because it was their job, and because they did that job to the best of their ability."

"If the last time the Tigers had fought in open combat had been a skirmish where no one did anything more than scratch each others' armor, I'd have brought you there today. I'm not trying to impress upon you the glory of combat. I'm trying to impress upon you the exact opposite."

Unbidden, Ezra's mind showed him Major Calhoune's *Huron Warrior* crumpling under the sustained fire of two McNally Demolisher tanks while a soot-charred *Firestarter* blasted his 'Mech with plasma-powered flame. The commo had cut out before the screams could have began, but Ezra knew—he'd seen it too many times, on other worlds—the regiment's XO had died screaming, baking, or melting as he succumbed to heat and fire in his cockpit.

He sniffed. He smelled the burned-meat smell in his nostrils, even though the air was clear.

There is nothing glorious in combat, he told himself.

Except we keep going back to it, over and over again.

A chirp from his pocket made him grimace and look down. His comm was set on private. Only a handful of people could override that setting and make his personal communicator signal. He pulled it out and looked at the screen.

RTB Bravo soonest. Return to base—Bravo Base, in this case—as soon as possible.

It was slugged Tiger Six—the regimental commander. The colonel.

Ezra looked at the sergeant major. He held up the comm. "RTB."

Halleck nodded and spun. "All right, boys and girls. Back on the bus. Playtime is over."

Ezra looked back down at his comm, sent an acknowledgment, and frowned.

The meeting must've been moved up.

By the time Ezra and the sergeant major made it back to the base, the meeting had already begun in the small room off the colonel's office. Ezra led the way through the door and then held it for the sergeant major. Four people looked up from the table as he came in.

"Captain." Colonel Yuri Rauschenbusch nodded at him. He was a fit man in his eighties, just beginning to show signs of slowing down. His hair was short and white, and you had to look to see the permanent circles under his eyes, or the way it took him just a little longer to catch his breath. Ezra hated to notice those things, but he couldn't not notice them. He'd known the colonel for too long.

Yuri Rauschenbusch had commanded the Stealthy Tigers for more than three decades. It was his personality that was imprinted on the regiment. It was his personality that drove their quest for excellence and professionalism. It was he who had taken Ezra Payne under his wing when Sergeant Aster Payne and her husband had been killed by a terrorist bomb in the Free Worlds League. He was, in every sense except the legal, Ezra Payne's father.

And he was getting old.

Across the table from the colonel were two people of Ezra's age, a man and a woman. Mason and Kirsten Markoja were twin brother and sister, and both wore the rank of major on their khaki day fatigues. Mason, older by a few seconds, commanded First—Panther—Battalion, while Kirsten commanded Second—Leopard—Battalion. Of all the Stealthy Tigers, only those three people outranked Ezra Payne. Sometimes that thought made him proud, and sometimes it scared him. Proud, because he was a Stealthy Tiger to the core. He wore a Raider pin.

But scared, because of those three, he only respected the colonel.

The majors Markoja he despised.

Mason, who was chocolate-skinned with a shaved head and thick eyebrows, rode the knife's blade between respect and sycophantism with Colonel Rauschenbusch more adroitly than Ezra had ever imagined anyone could. He was the odds-on favorite to replace the colonel when he finally retired, and that thought terrified Ezra. Mason Markoja was a competent tactician and a gifted combat commander, but he couldn't think more than ten minutes into the future. He had absolutely no gift for strategy, no ability to not say the wrong thing around current and potential employers. *He is,* Ezra thought, *just a brute.*

Kirsten Markoja was a few centimeters taller than her brother, and more slender, but never weak. Her eyes flashed in any light, and her hair—jet-black, straight, and fine—was never out of place. She wore little, if any, makeup, and she was master of at least four martial arts that Ezra knew of. She said little in these meetings, often just listening. That didn't mean she wasn't smart. Most of the Raiders agreed that Kirsten had gotten all the brains Mason could spare in the womb. She was sneaky.

And, excepting duty in the field, the two were never, ever apart.

Neither of them wore Raider pins.

And neither of them ever would, so long as Ezra Payne and Robert Halleck were around.

The fourth person at the table, Colonel Jasper Richmond, wore the field-gray camouflage the emperor's officers wore as duty uniforms. Ezra nodded to him as he took his seat, careful to keep his face expressionless.

Jasper Richmond was a joke of a man in every sense of the word. He'd been a leftenant when the ball went up on Hall. A rear-echelon leftenant. Not even a MechWarrior. Now he was a colonel. He never appeared in public in anything other than the comic-opera dress uniform the emperor's officers had adopted, and always insisted on being addressed by his rank.

Always. Ezra sometimes wondered if he wore his dress uniform into the bathroom.

"Colonel Richmond was just about to lay out the emperor's position," Rauschenbusch said as Ezra and Halleck sat down.

"Yes," Richmond said. "As I was saying before we were interrupted . . ."

The colonel frowned almost imperceptibly at Richmond's choice of words.

"The arrival of the Allied Mercenary Command is distressing," Richmond went on, "but ultimately futile. Their mandate is only against the Word of Blake. They have no grounds for actions against us or the emperor's rightful campaign against insurrectionists."

"A very reasonable position," Colonel Rauschenbusch said.

"Very," Mason Markoja agreed.

Ezra said nothing, though he was relieved. There had been talk that the emperor would order the Tigers to attack the Dismal Disinherited, which would have been at best illegal and—at worst—suicidal. The Dismal Ds had landed with a full regiment—three battalions—of BattleMechs and battalions of supporting armor and infantry. The Stealthy Tigers, after a decade of hard fighting, could mount a few 'Mechs more than two battalions for combat. There were more machines in various states of repair, but funds and parts were tight on Hall. And Ezra knew—because his own Jaguar Company was built out of it—that even if they found the parts and the money, MechWarriors who could fight to the Tigers' standards were even scarcer.

"Therefore," Richmond continued, looking pained for a second. "The emperor would like you to place a liaison officer with the Disinherited."

Mason Markoja made a dismissive sound, but his sister merely raised an eyebrow. Neither Halleck nor Ezra himself said anything, and Rauschenbusch leaned back in his chair. "Interesting," he murmured, looking at the ceiling.

Ezra considered the idea. It made a lot of sense, after a moment's reflection. The Dismal Ds could treat with a Tiger as a fellow professional. They'd accept a fellow mercenary where they may not one of Baranov's men. They'd expect another mercenary to know what was important to notice and what wasn't.

If it was the right officer, of course. Without meaning to, he looked up and met Kirsten Markoja's gaze. She was already watching him, and it took everything he had not to flinch. Instead, he raised a questioning eyebrow. He'd be damned if he'd back down before that snake.

She looked away.

"We'll send Captain Payne," the colonel said a moment later.

Which explained why Kirsten Markoja had been watching him. She'd already known—or at least suspected.

"Sir—" Mason started, but Richmond cleared his throat and cut him off.

"Sir," the Hall colonel said, "I wonder if perhaps a more senior officer would be more appropriate. One of the majors, here, perhaps?"

"Sir, Colonel Richmond may have a point," Kirsten Markoja said, speaking for the first time. "We don't want to send Colonel Marik-Johns the wrong message."

Ezra felt more than saw Sergeant Major Halleck's hand curl into a fist below the level of the table, but ignored it. He wasn't surprised to hear either of the majors trying to get the posting. It was as high profile as anything on this contract, and whoever got it would gain a small bit of clout in the emperor's court, to boot.

Not that Mason Markoja would make that connection. Ezra looked at the polished tabletop. The *chair* was more likely to make the connection before he did.

"You don't think they'll take a captain seriously, then?" Rauschenbusch asked. He was looking at Richmond, but Ezra knew he was asking the entire room. Except him. He knew his place.

Richmond smiled placatingly. "Would you, if the positions were reversed?"

Kirsten Markoja looked down at the tabletop.

Sergeant Major Halleck's cheek twitched toward a smirk.

Ezra kept very still. He knew—they all knew—what was coming. It would have been the same if the colonel had said "Captain Hargood" or "Captain Wa." It didn't matter that it was Ezra Payne. Inside, he was grinning. *It didn't hurt, though.*

Colonel Rauschenbusch leaned forward suddenly, grabbing the edge of the table to stop himself. His knuckles were white from the strength of his grip.

"Of course I would," he said, holding his stare until Colonel Richmond looked away. "Captain Payne is one of the finest soldiers in my regiment." He looked at Ezra. "You will accept this assignment?"

Ezra nodded. "Of course, but I have a company in training . . ."

Rauschenbusch looked at Halleck. "Sergeant Major?"

"It's taken care of, sir," Halleck said.

Rauschenbusch let go of the table and leaned back. "Excellent. What else does the emperor's staff have for us this fine day, Colonel?"

Richmond blinked. And said nothing.

The meeting broke up a few minutes later. The Markojas stood to escort Colonel Richmond out of the building, but Ezra stayed behind with the colonel and the sergeant major. Once the door closed behind them, Rauschenbusch blew a breath out between his lips and sat back in his chair.

"That could've gone a lot differently," he said.

"Too right, sir," Halleck said. He looked at Ezra. "You did good, sir. Keeping your mouth shut."

"Hard to get in trouble when you don't say anything," Ezra said, leaning back in his chair. "I was worried they were going to say attack."

"I was, too," the colonel said. "I even had Kirsten working on plans, just in case."

Ezra frowned. "You're kidding."

"Of course not. Planning is cheap, son." He shared a grin with Halleck and laughed. "Always be ready. Remember that."

Ezra nodded and then looked down. "Thank you for this."

Rauschenbusch waved the comment away. "Nonsense. You're going to be a major soon enough."

Halleck grunted. "Not soon enough, from where I sit."

"How's the training coming?"

"Good, I think," Ezra said, glancing at Halleck, who nodded. "We need to get them in the field more, but I think with the sergeant major running them into the ground day and night while I'm off 'liaising,' they should come right along."

"Good." Rauschenbusch crossed his arms. "I want you to pay close attention to the Dismal Ds," he said. "Not just for the contract. They're pros. Pay attention to how they do things. Maybe there's something we can learn there."

Ezra nodded. If the colonel—and, by extension, the regiment—had one article of faith, it was that learning never ended. New ideas were encouraged and rigorously tested. If they were successful, they were added to the Tigers' doctrine.

If they weren't, they were discarded.

When he thought about it, Ezra considered that as close to a religious belief as he'd ever felt in his life.

"I just don't see why we have to put up with them being here," is what Alistair Kung told us here at the *Harney Morning Edition*, speaking about the arrival of the Dismal Disinherited on Hall. *"They don't even have a contract. Doesn't that make them pirates?"*

"To answer that question, we asked the experts at the Harney Judicial Center. Speaking on condition of anonymity, one jurist told us yes, in some cases, mercenaries acting without contracts are considered pirates. But the Disinherited, acting under the banner of Jaime Wolf's Allied Mercenary Command, are technically under contract to the planetary government of Outreach."

"Don't make no difference," Mr. Kung told us when we explained that to him. *"The emperor will see them off, too, just like he did with that traitor McNally and the rest of them mercenaries."*

– From the *Harney Morning Edition*,
Harney HV Channel Six

CHAPTER TWO

BRAVO BASE
HALL
THE CHAOS MARCH
18 JANUARY 3067

The door of Colonel Richardson's hover limo had barely closed before Kirsten Markoja heard her brother curse under his breath. They stood near the sentries at the entrance to Bravo Base. The sentries were braced to attention, but the majors were not. As soon as the limo's muted lift fans engaged, they turned away. Mason turned, she was sure, like anyone would, to keep the dust from blowing into his eyes.

That was why she turned, also. But it wasn't the only reason, or even the main one. Mostly she turned away because she didn't want to look at the toad of a man the emperor had set on them anymore.

"Not here," she told Mason. Nodding to the sentries, she led him back into the building and toward her battalion's offices.

The regimental headquarters for the Stealthy Tigers—on any world they served on—was called Bravo Base. It didn't matter if it was a cubbyhole in a planetary defense headquarters or a field tent on the windswept plain of a barren world. It made for a sense of continuity for the regiment's soldiers. Many mercenary regiments had similar traditions. Mercenary soldiers fought where there was fighting, and unless they were hired for that purpose, they didn't spend a great deal of time in garrison. It was hard to put down roots when you're always moving.

Hence, Bravo Base.

On Hall, Bravo Base was a row of low buildings on the edge of Fort Decker, fifteen kilometers northeast of Harney. Fort Decker was a sprawling military reservation that served as the capital's garrison and military station. Unless there was a frontline regiment on-world, it was maintained by the planetary militia. Under Emperor Baranov, it housed the Fourth Republican—the former Federated Commonwealth troops who'd stayed loyal to him when he'd declared himself emperor a decade ago—and his closest supporters, including the Stealthy Tigers.

The offices of Kirsten's Second Battalion were near the center of the headquarters building. Her office was at the center of that mess, accessible via either a private, heavily-secured corridor that led out the back of the building, or through an orderly's office. She nodded at her orderly, Sergeant Bush, as she went past. Mason followed her into the office, closing the door behind them. He flopped down onto the low couch across from her desk while she went around the desk and sat down.

"Well, that didn't work," he said.

"No, it didn't," Kirsten said. She keyed her desk terminal live and punched in the access codes for her private files. While she did that, an automatic data security check ran and showed her green codes: no one had attempted to access her files. The codes were always green, but she still always ran the check.

Kirsten Markoja had not risen to her present position by trusting that people were honest.

"How are we going to get around this?" Mason asked her.

Kirsten blinked and looked up at her brother. He was her twin, and her only living relative. They had known each other literally since birth, and she loved him as much as she loved anything. They had been a team since they were old enough to know what the word meant.

But none of that meant that he wasn't, sometimes, exasperating.

"We're not," she said. "We're going to shift tactics."

"Tactics?"

"Tactics."

Mason stared at her. She could almost see the wheels turning behind his eyes, but he just shrugged. "Fair enough. What do you need me to do?"

Kirsten looked back at her screen. "I'm still figuring that out." She had counted on the colonel selecting Mason for the liaison role. He was the obvious choice: a senior officer, the heir apparent to the regimental command, and something of a dullard. He'd be both appeasing and nonthreatening to the Dismal Disinherited. They'd see him as another mercenary officer they could dismiss; skilled, polite, but nothing to be worried about. That would have been perfect. She was long accustomed to using Mason to manipulate people into doing what she wanted. And Mason—bless his heart—trusted her far too much to ask too many questions. She made the decisions. It had been that way since they were teenagers and had gone out on their own.

But the colonel—here, in her office with only Mason to see, she didn't bother to hide her scowl—had picked his pretty boy for it. Ezra Payne. Payne was like an itch she couldn't scratch. He was an annoyance that wouldn't go away. He was the colonel's favorite, and if things didn't move quickly enough, there was a real chance he could supplant Mason in the colonel's esteem.

That couldn't be allowed to happen. Things had progressed too far. Important things, far more important than who led a pissant mercenary regiment on a no-name world in the Chaos March.

She hadn't quite believed the activation code when it had pinged on her console, but after a year on Hall, she believed it. The deal she and Mason had made all those years ago had seemed like a pipe dream: after this long, she never expected to be called upon, but she had. On Hall, of all places.

To be ready to help the Word of Blake.

To help the Master.

She looked at her right wrist, where the scar she expected to see wasn't there. She flexed her hand. It moved naturally, like nothing was amiss. Like there weren't three bones missing and replaced with polymer, and the circuitry, and the other things she didn't allow herself to think about. Or hadn't, until the code came. And the orders.

She blinked and cleared her head. There'd be time to worry about that later. For now, she needed to see how she was going to deal with the wild card the colonel had dealt her. They wouldn't be able to deal with the Dismal Ds directly, which meant she'd have to work through other means.

She already knew she couldn't maneuver Payne.

That meant she had to take another tack.

She snapped her fingers. "Elly Burton."

Mason looked up, frowning. "We should've killed that bitch, too."

Kirsten ignored him. She typed a query into her system and then sat back in her chair, thinking.

When the Sarna March had collapsed into the Chaos March in 3057, and Baranov had made his bid for empire on Hall, Count Radcliffe McNally had been his principal opponent. His private army had been one of the few sizable formations on Hall, and as the Fourth Republican tore itself apart fighting between those who supported Baranov and those who didn't, he'd moved quickly. He'd grabbed defensible terrain, made a couple powerful alliances, and begun hiring mercenaries.

One of those mercenary outfits had been Burton's Brigade, a small, spectacularly uninspiring 'Mech unit. Over the years, they had manned their defense points manfully. They had kept to their contract.

And Elly Burton, the Brigade's founder and leader, had fallen in love with Count McNally himself. And bore him a son.

With McNally dead, Elly Burton remained a rallying point for anti-Baranov factionalism. None of the remaining nobles on Hall had the strength to stand against the emperor's forces, not with two battalions of Stealthy Tigers still on-world. But her son . . .

Kirsten smiled.

McNally had died without a clear heir, and Elly Burton still maintained her contract and her vigil for her son's inheritance.

"She's the key," Kirsten whispered.

"She's the what?" Mason asked.

"The key." Kirsten looked up at her brother. He sat slouched on the low couch, fingers spliced across his belly. He looked bored. She frowned and resisted the urge to sigh.

"We'll use Elly Burton," she told him. "To get the AMC fighting Baranov."

Mason frowned. "Why would the AMC fight Baranov? They're here looking for Blakists."

Kirsten carefully didn't react. "Yes, they are. And since we don't want them actually fighting Blakists—since right now *we're* the closest things to Blakists with 'Mechs on Hall—we need them to fight Baranov. If we can get them to attack that fool, public opinion turns against them. We can play that across the entire Protectorate—hell, the whole Chaos March."

Mason grinned. "And keep them from shooting at us."

"Right."

Kirsten's console chirped. Eyes narrowed, she scanned the

few lines of text. After a few seconds, she found what she was looking for. Her grin grew to a wolf's smile. She stood.

"Come on," she said. "We need to deliver a message."

Mason stood. "A message?"

"To a friend," Kirsten said. *Some might even say a sister*, she thought.

Because it wasn't part of either of the regular battalions, Jaguar Company's offices weren't in the main Bravo Base buildings. Ezra had placed them out on the edge, along the 'Mech bays that served the company as hangars. He would have told anyone who asked it was because he wanted his new charges nearer their 'Mechs, and it would have even been the truth.

But it wasn't the whole truth.

When he and Halleck entered his small office off one of the 'Mech bays, four men and one woman in Tigers khaki were already waiting there. Three wore officer's matte-black insignia on their collars; the other two were MechWarrior sergeants. They varied in age, from Ezra's to the sergeant major's. There was no similarity in hairstyle or skin tone. Three sat in the small chairs along the wall next to the office door. The other two stood, leaning against the wall, arms crossed.

All of them wore Raider pins.

"Well?" Captain Heather Hargood asked. She was the only other captain in the Raiders, and Ezra had her by date of rank.

Ezra looked at her and sat down behind his desk. It was the only chair left.

"Colonel's made him liaison to the Disinherited," Sergeant Major Halleck said. He perched on the corner of Ezra's desk, crushing his boonie cap in his hands, looking down at it.

"So we're not fighting them?" Sergeant Ervil Gam asked.

"They're not here for us," Ezra said. He resisted the urge to reach into his desk drawer and pull out the anti-listening device scanner he kept there. One of the other Raiders would have already swept the office before they got there. That was only smart.

Dumb people didn't get Raider pins.

"Like that matters," Gam muttered. "We weren't supposed to fight the Faithful on Caph, either, but that didn't stop us, did it?"

"No," Captain Hargood said. She was one of the ones standing.

"It's the AMC?" Lieutenant Branden Roth asked. "That's confirmed—they're not here on someone else's dime?"

"It's confirmed," Ezra said.

"So they're here for the Blakists," Roth said.

No one spoke.

Roth looked around, then sighed. "Well, are we going to tell them?"

Ezra chewed on his lip. "We are not."

The room reacted as he expected it to. It wasn't the first time they'd asked the question, but it was the first time he'd answered it definitively.

"It's why they're here," Roth said.

"It's not our place."

"Our *place*?" Roth looked like he wanted to stand up, to pace, but he was a big man—over two meters tall, well over a hundred kilos. There wasn't room for him to get to his feet without making Sergeant Major Halleck move.

And Halleck wasn't moving. Ezra wondered for a second if the wiley old noncom had planned it that way, then decided he probably had.

"Our contract is with the emperor," Ezra said. Several of the others, Captain Hargood among them, nodded.

"That's bullshit," Roth said. "Our contract is with the bloody Robes. You all know that. The money is coming from Terra, no matter what the contract says."

Ezra frowned, and Halleck grunted. "Think about what you just said, son."

"What?"

"The contract is *all* that matters."

Several of the other Raiders grunted, but Roth sat back in his chair and grimaced. "You know what I mean."

"Here's what I know," Ezra said. "Tomorrow I have to go play nice with the Dismal Ds. I don't know how they're going to react. We're not going to fight them, not unless they get a lot more active than they are now."

"If they hit us—" Sergeant Liam Porra muttered.

"Then we'll hammer them flat," Sergeant Major Halleck said. "That ain't going to happen."

"Right now, we're going to do what we're supposed to. I'm going to go make nice-sounding noises at the AMC. Halleck is going to pound my Jaguars into paste on the training fields. Heather—" He looked at Captain Hargood. "—I'd appreciate it if you'd be available if Bob needs a hand."

Hargood looked at Halleck and nodded.

"Good." Ezra looked at the others. "What else?" No one spoke. "All right. Get out of here." He pulled his noteputer out and activated it on his desktop while the others stood. He ignored the small talk until he heard the office door slide shut again. Then he looked up.

Two people were sitting in the chairs across from him. Sergeant Major Robert Halleck, and Lieutenant Charles Monet. Halleck was sitting comfortably, one booted foot up on his knee. Monet was sitting upright, hands folded in his lap. He was frowning, but he was always frowning.

"For a second, I thought Roth was going to hit me," Halleck said, chuckling.

"I thought so, too," Ezra said. He was looking at Monet. "Charlie?"

"His method of articulating it aside, he's not wrong," Monet said. He was a slender, dapper, soft-spoken man. His hair and face were perfectly groomed, and his khakis were tailored. If you hadn't seen him in a BattleMech, you'd have thought he was far too effeminate to be threatening.

Ezra Payne had seen him in a 'Mech. More, he'd been there when the man had earned his Raider pin on Caph.

Come to think of it, he'd earned it in that same skirmish Roth mentioned, with the Always Faithful.

"What do you mean?" Ezra asked.

"I can show you the transfers," Monet said. He pointed at the noteputer on Ezra's desk. "I *have* shown you the transfers. I can trace the money back almost to Terra, from the shell companies that get it into Baranov's treasury."

"Inadmissible transfers," Ezra said.

"Yes," Monet allowed. "But that doesn't make them false."

"No," Ezra replied, "it doesn't."

The Stealthy Tigers were, in the modern mercenary market, somewhat odd in that they were a pure BattleMech unit. Regiments like the Disinherited had battalions or even whole regiments of supporting forces: combat vehicles, infantrymen, aerospace fighters. The Tigers had none of that, nor even the large staff components that many regiments maintained. Most of their "technical experts" were MechWarriors who wore two hats in the regiments.

So, where the Disinherited might have an entire team intended for information security and hacking, the Stealthy Tigers had one man.

Charles Monet was the regiment's hacker. The colonel didn't always like to think about where the information Monet provided came from, but he never disputed its validity.

Not even all of the Raiders had seen the information Monet had gathered about the emperor's finances. Monet had gone to Major Calhoune before he died, and Halleck. After Calhoune died, Halleck had brought Ezra in.

Not even the colonel knew this yet. Because it didn't matter.

It was hardly the first time someone had subsidized mercenaries for someone else.

But. Monet was staring at Ezra.

Charles Monet hated the Word of Blake the way people hated child molesters and long waits at the doctor's office. It was one of the few things that brought the normally placid man to open, instant, and boiling anger.

"We can't tell them," Ezra said.

"Why?"

"Because we'd be stabbing our employer in the back."

"He deserves it."

Halleck set his foot back on the floor.

Ezra smiled tightly. "Maybe he does. But he still signs our checks."

"With Blakist money."

"It spends no matter where it came from."

Monet's mouth worked, but he said nothing. Pink appeared on his cheeks, and his knuckles, still in his lap, whitened with tension. He glanced at Halleck, getting nothing but a raised eyebrow in reply.

"They're here looking for the Word of Blake," Monet said carefully. "And we know where the Word of Blake is."

"Then they should hire us," Ezra said. It was pedantic, but it was also the core of one of the few belief systems he had.

Monet stood. "If you'll excuse me, Captain?"

"Of course, Charles."

Monet spun and walked out of the office without another word. Halleck let out a big breath when the door slid closed again. "I thought Roth was bad."

Ezra was still staring at the door. "Am I wrong here, Bob?"

Halleck leaned forward, resting his elbows on his knees. "No," he said.

Ezra looked at him for a few moments. "That's all you got?"

"You asked me a yes or no question, Captain."

"Come on, Bob."

"You're right. It's not our place to tell them. Right or wrong don't come into it. We took the man's money, and maybe he's a fool and maybe he's letting the scariest people since Stefan Amaris finance him, but the contract is valid, and we signed it." Halleck sat back upright and glared at Ezra. "But you knew all that."

"We don't always get to pick our employers," Ezra said.

Halleck snorted. "Of course we do. No one made us sign the contract." He shook his head. "Besides. You remember who pushed for this one, right?"

It was Ezra's turn to frown. "Kirsten Markoja."

"The missy major herself," Halleck agreed.

Ezra ran his hands up and down his face, sighing. Kirsten and Mason Markoja made his head hurt. He didn't trust her, but not even Charles Monet could find any reason to doubt her. She was ambitious, but hell—Ezra was ambitious. No one became a mercenary officer without ambition. Certainly no one made captain.

He dropped his hands. "Sixty-eight and we evacuate, right?"

Halleck nodded. "Sixty-eight, sir." He rubbed his hands together. "Now. What do you think I should put these kids through while you're off playing nice with the Disinherited?"

Ezra grinned and tapped his noteputer live. "As it turns out," he said, turning the screen to face the sergeant major, "I've already given that some thought."

"Officers of the Dismal Disinherited, the mercenary regiment sent here illegally from Outreach on behalf of Jaime Wolf's vendetta-crazed Allied Mercenary Command, again refused to sit for an interview with us. Rather, they insisted they're here to uncover the hidden Word of Blake influence behind the emperor's rightful assumption of power."

"That's just crazy, John, and we all know it. Just because other worlds near Terra have appealed to the Word of Blake for mutual defense treaties doesn't mean they're actively building a new nation in the Chaos March. I think this is just another ploy to keep our attention away from the real issue."

"The real issue?"

"The AMC has always supported Victor Davion in his rightful quest to unseat Katrina Steiner as the rightful ruler of the Federated Suns, and this is just another transparent attempt to keep our attention away from New Avalon."

"So you're saying this has nothing to do with the Word of Blake at all?"

"Of course it doesn't. Have you—has *anyone*—ever seen a single Word of Blake 'Mech on Hall? No. I mean, come on—they don't even run our HPGs! ComStar runs our HPGs—and whose army did Victor Davion lead before he abandoned that one too to chase his sister?"

"ComStar."

"You're damn right, ComStar."

> – From the *Harney Morning Edition*,
> Harney HV Channel Six

CHAPTER THREE

BRAMPTON
HALL
THE CHAOS MARCH
2 MARCH 3067

Sergeant Jacob Brim grabbed his nose and squeezed it between his thumb and forefinger as he walked outside. He already felt the sneeze building, but if he could just hold it—he couldn't. He sneezed. It was, like all the others, both a wet and dry sneeze, the sneeze of sinuses tortured by the pollen of a new world.

He stepped aside, out of the path of the others walking. "Damn it," he muttered. He looked at his fingers, but they were clean. *At least I'm getting good at this.*

"Still bad?" asked a familiar voice.

"Go to hell," he snapped. Then he looked up. "Sir."

Ezra Payne chuckled and handed him a small white medicine bottle. "These helped me when we first landed," he said. "Allergies are just one of the wonders of star travel, don't you think?"

Jacob took the bottle and slid it into his pocket. "Makes me want to consider a filter mask." He stepped back onto the stoned path and into step with the Stealthy Tigers officer. "What's new today?"

Payne shrugged. It was already a familiar gesture.

It had only been a couple of months, but already Jacob was used to seeing the officer around the Dismal Disinherited field base. The liaison officer had gravitated toward him almost immediately, for obvious reasons. They were the only two soldiers not wearing the gray battledress of the Dismal Ds. Payne wore the khaki duty uniform of the Stealthy Tigers, and Jacob the blue duty jumpsuit of Wolf's Dragoons. They were both outsiders.

Jacob and his team filled out the Allied Mercenary Command component of the AMC mission to Hall. He and his squad—six other Dragoons—were seconded to the Dismal Ds from Wolfnet, the Dragoons' intelligence operations arm. Five of the six other Dragoons were technicians, not combat troops. They were data miners, computer hackers. One, Dooley, was a forensic accountant. Only Jacob and his team second, Sergeant Carlsson, were former combat soldiers.

Unconsciously, Jacob reached up and rubbed the stylized "7" on his shoulder patch. He didn't like to think of himself as a "former" combat soldier. He was only thirty-two years old. He wasn't a "former" anything.

"Another day, another briefing," Payne said.

Jacob laughed. "Major Fletcher?"

"Is it Tuesday?"

"It's Tuesday."

"Then Major Fletcher." Payne looked at him and grinned, but kept walking. Jacob grinned back, then twitched as he felt a twinge in his nose. He held the sneeze down and kept pace.

Major Kellen Fletcher was the Dismal Ds' intelligence officer. It was rare for mercenary regiments to maintain full time staff officers, but apparently the Disinherited were large enough that such chaff was worth the expense. Fletcher was a former MIIO operative from the Federated Suns, but that didn't cut him any slack with Brim. If the Davion intelligence agency—which maintained a respectable reputation among the spooks of the Inner Sphere—had employed Fletcher long enough for him to earn a pension, there was a serious flaw there.

It wasn't that Fletcher wasn't smart. He was very smart. But he was also very divorced from reality—what Jacob's instructors at Wolfnet had called ground truth. He came to every situation with the preconceived notions of right and wrong, truth and falsehood, that he'd learned on New Avalon.

He made Jacob shake his head in wonder.

And not in a good way.

"I hear the colonel will be in today," Jacob said as they approached the prefab building that stood as the Disinherited's central headquarters on Hall. The Third—John's Hostile Hellraisers, unofficially—had arrived and set up a base camp thirty klicks south of Harney, near the small village of Brampton. The building—all the buildings—had come out of the DropShips.

"Really?" Payne asked.

"Yeah. Something's broken loose." Jacob watched Payne carefully. Over the last few weeks, he had made himself close to Ezra Payne. Initially it had been because the liaison officer from the Stealthy Tigers was an obvious source of information. If Payne had been an idiot, prone to talking to prove himself smart, he could have been a gold mine. Jacob would have had to be an idiot—or Kellen Fletcher—to ignore him.

Two days had been long enough for Jacob to realize that hope was groundless. Ezra Payne was many things, but prone to talking wasn't one of them. He was friendly enough, always ready with a quip or a bit of banter. He was funny. But he rarely said anything of real importance.

After those two days, Jacob had stayed near him for two reasons. First, even if Payne wasn't a fount of information, he had still been on Hall for more than a year. He was a wealth of local knowledge, even if he was only willing to talk about the weather and the desert formations that gave Hall its name.

And second, because he was a fellow professional—and Jacob met few enough of those as it was.

But now he was watching to see if Payne would betray any interest. Saying "something's broken loose" was one of the best ways to pique anyone's curiosity. If Payne's mission here, as liaison with the Dismal Ds, was anything other than it was supposed to be, then now would be a good time to discover it.

Jacob Brim was too much a professional not to trade on the friendship he'd built with Payne. The answer he found might disappoint him, but he'd have the answer nonetheless.

Payne just glanced at him, sideways to keep the rising sun behind his head. He grinned and bounced his eyebrows at Jacob. "Can't wait," he said.

They reached the door and halted in front of the two infantrymen standing sentry outside.

"Corporal," Jacob said to the senior of the two. He nodded in greeting and used the motion to eye the guards' kit.

Each of them wore the gray-on-gray battledress of the Disinherited, with body armor and load-bearing harnesses. They had slung AX-22 assault rifles, with no magazine in the well, but full ones in bandoliers across their bellies. Each one wore a buckled helmet. Their gear was worn, but well-maintained. The corporal's nametape read *MATHER*.

"Sergeant," Corporal Mather said, inclining his head in return. "Your pass?"

Jacob grinned and displayed a chip to the noteputer in the corporal's hand. A chirp signaled acceptance of the codes on it.

"Thank you, Sergeant," Mather said. He turned to Ezra Payne. "Sir? Your pass?"

Payne slid his own chip out of a breast pocket and presented it. The noteputer made an identical chirp, and Mather nodded.

"Thank you, Captain," he said, bracing and stepping back.

"Any time, Corporal," Payne said. He nodded to the silent private standing on the other side of the door as he reached for the handle. "Shall we, Sergeant?"

"Of course," Jacob said, grinning. He let Payne open the door for him, then stepped inside. The building air system was set a few degrees cooler than the outside air—Jacob shivered with a sudden chill. His sinuses felt immediately better, though. The cool air was drying.

"I can breathe," he said.

Payne sniffed. "Little chilly in here," he said.

"Pansy."

It was a short walk to the briefing room. By the time they entered, about three-fourths of the two-dozen chairs were already filled, all by men and women in gray-on-gray battledress. Jacob and Payne took two seats near the back of the room, side-by-side. Payne had a noteputer in a thigh pocket, but didn't take it out.

Jacob had learned not to bother with notes after the second day. The intelligence shop circulated the day's report after the meeting for "expansion and discussion." Fletcher just stood up and read the report aloud, every time.

The door behind them opened and a sharp voice called, "Tenhut!"

Everyone in gray snapped to their feet. Jacob grinned at Payne and stood as well, though not nearly so quickly.

Three officers strode down the narrow aisle toward the wide table at the front of the room. Jacob recognized Colonel John Marik-Johns, the Hellraisers' commander. He was a solid, fit man of just under forty years, with a full head of black hair and a stubbled chin. He walked everywhere like a man with purpose.

Behind him came the tall, stooped shape of Kellen Fletcher. Jacob didn't recognize the younger woman with them, but saw captain's insignia on her collar as she passed.

Marik-Johns went around the table and sat down without speaking. Once his companions were seated, he looked up.

"Sit," he said. Feet shuffled and chairs groaned as everyone sat back down. No sooner had Jacob's butt hit molded plastic than Marik-Johns spoke again.

"The daily intel brief is cancelled."

No one cheered, but Jacob doubted he was the only one who wanted to.

"We have a mission," the colonel continued.

Beside Jacob, Ezra Payne stood and cleared his throat. "Colonel?"

Marik-Johns looked at him without expression. "Captain Payne?"

"Would you prefer that I leave, sir?"

Jacob looked up at Payne, his estimation of the Stealthy Tiger rising a notch. By asking the question, he'd made it clear to the Disinherited that he recognized his role. A liaison officer was meant to keep both sides informed—not be a part of planning. Marik-Johns would be entirely correct to ask the Stealthy Tiger to step out of the room.

Waiting to be asked to leave would set a different precedent.

"Did your pass let you in here today?"

"Yes, sir."

"Then you're supposed to be here," he said.

"Thank you, sir," Payne said. He sat back down. Once he was settled, he leaned over toward Jacob. "Better me than them, right?"

Jacob grinned back.

"Thus far we have failed to bring the Word of Blake's involvement on Hall to light," the colonel said a moment later. "This means we're failing our mission. The commander sent us here to find the Robes, and that's what we're going to do."

Jacob nodded. He might quibble with the way they went about things, but he was fully behind the Disinherited—and the AMC—on this mission. The Word of Blake's growth among the worlds around Terra had to be stopped. He was a Dragoon, and Jaime Wolf said that was their mission.

That was all he needed.

"Our Wolfnet team," Marik-Johns went on, inclining his head toward Jacob, "is just getting its feet wet, but we can't wait for them."

Several of the Disinherited glanced toward Jacob at that comment. A couple sneered. Jacob ignored them. Good intelligence work took time.

"So, we're going to the source." He turned to the female captain with him. "Captain Ortiz?"

She nodded at the colonel and then leaned forward, hands clasped on the table. She was pretty, with short-cut brown hair and jade green eyes. Her skin was mocha-colored and smooth. "The late Count Radcliffe McNally was Baranov's chief rival on Hall for most of the world's independence," she said.

"You guys took care of that, right?" Jacob whispered to Payne. Payne only grunted.

"He was killed late last year," Ortiz went on. She looked at Payne, then looked away. "By mercenaries in Baranov's employ."

Jacob watched, but Payne didn't react.

"With his death, the coalition resisting Baranov collapsed." Jacob nodded. There were still pockets of resistance, but Baranov's Fourth Republican and the Stealthy Tigers were strong enough that it was only because they hadn't decided to destroy those pockets that the pockets remained.

"He did, however, leave behind a young son."

A screen behind the table lit with a flat image of a woman and a young child. "This is Captain Elly Burton, commander of the mercenary unit Burton's Brigade, and her son, Alexander Burton-McNally."

A sea of whispers swept the room, but Ortiz kept going. "She and her company, along with the remains of the count's forces, still hold his fortress at Deal. We're going to send a battalion to escort them here to Brampton."

With a frown, Jacob rose to his feet. "Captain, why not just send a team to her?" He ignored the sounds of consternation from around him. "I mean, yes—we should absolutely talk to her. McNally's network, if it hasn't imploded, would be invaluable. But why put a whole battalion out on the vine?"

Ortiz frowned and opened her mouth, but Colonel Marik-Johns held up a hand and leaned forward. "You have something that tells you we shouldn't move openly, Sergeant?"

"No, sir—"

"Then we're moving," Marik-Johns said. "It'll be good to get a battalion out to get a feel for the terrain, in any case." He looked at Jacob for a few more moments. "Anything else?"

Jacob shook his head. "No, sir," he said, and sat back down. Ezra Payne leaned over. "Why not go get her?" he asked. Jacob frowned. "It's thumbing their nose at Buddy Boy," he said, using the Wolfnet slang for Baranov. "They're saying 'Look, we can go talk to the woman who's been trying to kill you for a decade, and there's bugger-all you can do about it.'"

Payne offered a Gallic shrug. "I would have said your presence here already does that, wouldn't you?"

Jacob rolled his eyes. "Yeah, but once you've poked the boar with a stick, do you keep smacking it on the head?"

Payne leaned away.

One of the Dismal Ds was asking a question about routes, but Jacob tuned it out. It didn't matter which route they took to Deal. The mountain redoubt was about three hundred kilometers south, on the other side of the Helmand Desert. There wasn't anything but sand and rocks between them. All of Baranov's forces were north of them, and unless they had advance warning, they couldn't get in front of them if they wanted to.

Besides. If Buddy Boy was going to force a fight, he'd have done it already. They'd been down for almost a month.

"Captain Payne," the colonel said, bringing Jacob's attention back to the room. Beside him, Ezra Payne stood.

"Sir?"

"Would you care to accompany our column?"

Jacob blinked.

"I'd have to ask my colonel, sir," Payne said with only a moment's hesitation, "but yes—if he approves, I'd be honored to bring my lance along."

"Ask your colonel," Marik-Johns said. "I think in the name of transparency, it'd be a good idea to have observers along."

"Thank you, sir," Payne said, and sat back down.

Jacob didn't look at him. "You're crazy," he whispered.

"Maybe," Payne whispered back.

"You killed her son's father not three months ago."

"*I* didn't."

"You think she's going to look past the uniform?" Jacob knew the Burton's Brigade's ROMs would show the exact 'Mech that had killed their employer. Hell, it would be child's play to hack into the Tigers' own records and determine it. There was little chance it was actually Ezra Payne, but that didn't matter. It wouldn't matter to a woman grieving her son's father's murder. For her lover's murder.

"She's a mercenary. She'll understand. It was just a job."

Now Jacob looked at his new friend. For a moment he was one man speaking to another, not a fellow mercenary with a competing contract. "Maybe don't put it to her like that, okay?"

Payne didn't look at him.

The look Rauschenbusch gave Ezra when he told him the plan was at once considering and condemning.

"I think your spook friend is right," the colonel said. They were in his private quarters in Bravo Base. The colonel was sprawled on a low couch, with a glass of something gold-colored in his hand. He wore battledress pants and a tan undershirt. His hair was wet with sweat. Ezra's nose wrinkled with the scent of fresh exercise in such a small place.

"It doesn't matter," Ezra said. "He probably *is* right. But we have to stay in the loop, right?"

"You sure one lance will be enough?"

"It'll have to be. One 'Mech says I'm an idiot, but a full company says I don't trust them."

Rauschenbusch gulped half his drink. He glared at the glass for a moment, working the alcohol around in his mouth, before swallowing with a grunt. The he pointed toward Ezra with the empty glass. "Do you? Trust them, I mean?"

Ezra shrugged. "As much as anyone, so far."

"How're you playing it?"

"On the level."

"Hm." Rauschenbusch looked away, then back. "You think that was the right play?"

"I do."

Ezra could have gone to the Dismal Ds and played a role. He could have pretended he was a fop, someone to be dismissed. He'd seen—worked with, even—officers from employers that were like that. They weren't respected, nor taken into confidence. And, by extension, their units were disrespected.

Ezra had known as he'd driven up that he wanted the Disinherited to respect the Stealthy Tigers. The Ds were almost twice as large as the Tigers—it was imperative that they respect the smaller mercenary group. And when he realized the Dragoon assigned to nursemaid him around was a spook, and a former Seventh Kommando . . .

"I couldn't do anything else," he told his colonel, giving voice to his final thought.

"Doesn't matter now." Rauschenbusch glanced around, then lurched upright. He was still a strong man. When Ezra took his hand to steady him, he felt the strength of the colonel's grip, even if his skin felt a little looser, a little lighter, than he remembered.

"Which lance are you taking?"

"My Jags," Ezra said.

Rauschenbusch chuckled. "They'll be fighting to get out from beneath Bob's boot for a day," he predicted.

Ezra grinned. "Very likely."

The colonel reached up and stretched, rolling his shoulders first and then his head around on his neck. Hearing vertebra crackle and pop, Ezra tried not to flinch. It was one thing to do that with one's own head, but listening to someone else . . .

"All right," Rauschenbusch said. "Go. Pay our respects to Captain Burton. Keep doing your job. I'll see if I can't keep things calm here."

Ezra frowned. "Things aren't?"

Rauschenbusch laughed and clapped him on the shoulder. It was a solid smack. There was strength still in the old man. "Of course they aren't. We're less than a year from evacuating, our employer has a big, bad new problem, and the FedCom Civil War is winding down just when we need new work."

"Is—" Ezra started, but the colonel held up a hand.

"That's all for me to worry about," he said. "You go tomorrow. Do us proud." He stepped past Ezra, headed for the bathroom.

"We can use all the pride we can get!" he said over his shoulder.

"This morning, we were notified that a force of Dismal Disin-herited BattleMechs, tanks, and infantry departed their base at Brampton and moved south, into the Helmand Desert toward the rebel fortress at Deal. When queried, the emperor's press office declined to comment.

"We dug a little deeper, however. Speaking only on deep background, one source told us the emperor's staff doesn't care what the Dismal Disinherited do. *"If they want to wander in the desert, that's their business,"* the officer said. *"McNally is dead."*

"We'll keep you apprised of further developments as they happen."

–From the *Harney Morning Edition*,
Harney HV Channel Six

CHAPTER FOUR

HELMAND DESERT
HALL
THE CHAOS MARCH
4 MARCH 3067

It felt good to be back in a 'Mech, even if all the other ones around him were gray instead of desert-camo. Ezra Payne pushed his shoulders back against his cockpit seat, trying to scratch the itch between his shoulderblades, but his cooling vest was too stiff. The vest was a thick weave of narrow tubes that cycled liquid coolant around the core of his body during combat. It was made from ballistic fibers thick enough to qualify it as light body armor, and it kept him alive in the hellish heat of his cockpit during a fight.

But at that moment, it was annoying as hell because he couldn't scratch an itch.

Shrugging, Ezra leaned forward and slammed his back against the seat. The five-point restraints he wore to hold him into his seat didn't allow for a lot of movement, but that was a good thing. No one wanted to ride sixty-five tons of BattleMech all eleven meters to the ground unsecured.

He certainly didn't.

"Six, Six-four," Sergeant Jessica Roses signaled.

"Go," Ezra said. He looked at his holographic head's-up display for her *Hatchetman*. The medium BattleMech, with its namesake ax, was about 200 meters ahead of him in a break in the column. It had halted atop one of the windswept canyon walls that had given Hall its name centuries ago, and was looking back at him.

"No new contacts," Rose said. "Moving on to the next point."

"Very well," Ezra said. "Six out."

The *Hatchetman* raised its ax in salute and stepped down off the wall and out of sight. Ezra admired the forty-five ton 'Mech's movement for a second before concentrating on his piloting to guide his *Crusader* up and over another of the rock walls.

BattleMechs weighed from twenty to a hundred tons, and had been the preeminent tool of ground combat since their introduction nearly half a millennia ago. Every war of the preceding centuries had been fought by the heavily armed and armored behemoths. Equipped with missiles, rockets, lasers, autocannons, even particle beam weapons, a 'Mech feared nothing except another 'Mech. Just one of the machines, given enough time and ammunition, could lay waste to an entire city.

It was no surprise that the romance of piloting one of the monstrosities had, over the centuries, given rise to an entire social class of 'Mech pilots, the MechWarrior. Lauded as the elite, granted lands and titles, and immortalized in holovids and novellas across the Inner Sphere, the MechWarrior was the soldier every child wanted to grow up to become.

Balancing his *Crusader* as it started its descent, Ezra Payne grinned as he realized, not for the first time, that he was living one of his childhood dreams.

The Disinherited column had left Brampton just before the sun rose, moving at a sedate forty kilometers per hour. When Colonel Marik-Johns had said "a battalion," Ezra had imagined a full battalion of thirty-six BattleMechs. That's what it would have been in the Stealthy Tigers.

What he and his lance had found when they arrived, well before dawn, was a reinforced combined arms company. Two companies of BattleMechs escorted by a company of hovertanks and a company of infantrymen riding in tracked armored personnel carriers. A pair of VTOLs had linked up overhead just after sunrise. Ezra and his lance of four Stealthy Tiger 'Mechs had joined the center of the Dismal D column, near the headquarters group.

A major Ezra hadn't yet met was in notional command of the battalion, but he'd chosen to walk his *Crusader* next to the *Dervish* of Captain Nathalie Ortiz, from the briefing the day before. She marched a short distance away from the command group, and Ezra's battle computers noted her targeting sweeps as she washed the sensors directing her 'Mech's long-range missiles across the terrain all around them. A colored bar flashed across his HUD yet again as she swept his *Crusader.*

With a grin, Ezra keyed a discreet channel. "If you were a Tiger, Captain Ortiz, my sergeant major would be chewing your ass for sweeping active sensors across me like that."

There was a pause, and Ezra watched the *Dervish*'s head—with its cockpit—pivot slightly toward him. "You get a lot of accidental discharges in your regiment, Captain?" she asked. Ezra heard the smile in her tone. It reminded him of her eyes.

"No, ma'am," he replied. "My sergeant major sees to that with training."

She laughed. "Did you bring this sergeant major?"

"Someone had to stay behind and teach my company how to march," Ezra said.

"Pity."

Ezra looked at the *Dervish.* He hadn't studied the Disinherited enough to read the unit designators on Ortiz's 'Mech, but he recognized the identifier for the Hellraisers' Second Battalion, and what he thought was an award ribbon for 'Mech combat. That wasn't noteworthy in itself: almost any mercenary regiment saw much more combat than a regular state army command. Mercenaries went—were paid to go—where there was fighting. Few people paid the rates men and women demanded to fight and die just to watch them polish their 'Mechs in garrison.

Truth be told, few mercenaries worth their salt took those garrison posts. No one volunteered for mercenary work because they wanted to be bored far from home.

"Do you expect trouble today?" he asked her.

"I always expect trouble."

"That's why you brought so much force, then?" He made sure to put enough of a jibe into his voice to make it clear he was teasing.

"Nonsense," Ortiz said. "We're just here to protect you from the people your employer is oppressing." She said it with a smile he could hear, but Ezra Payne was a smart man. He heard the truth behind the words, too.

It had been a Tigers combat drop that had killed Count Radcliffe McNally during the last weeks of 3066. Baranov had hired them to end the decade-long conflict between himself and McNally's coalition, and they had done just that in a lightning attack on the count's exposed forces after drawing him out. That hadn't won the Tigers any admirers among the emperor's enemies, but it had fulfilled the terms of their contract.

"Sixty-eight," he whispered, too low for his microphone to pick up and broadcast.

The Tigers had taken to using sixty-eight in the same way other outfits used battle cries or refrains. It could mean "yes," or "you bet," or even "damn it," depending on the context. It grew from "Sixty-eight and evacuate," meaning the Tigers' contract with Baranov was up in 3068 and they'd be able to leave Hall for the next contract. With McNally dead, there was no one left to fight.

Except the Disinherited. And *no one* wanted that fight.

Except maybe Baranov.

Or his backers. Ezra frowned and worked his lips, wishing he could spit.

"I've studied your unit," Ortiz said. Ezra blinked and looked at her *Dervish*. "You were on Caph in 3057, right?"

"Yeah. On loan from the Free Worlds League to Sun-Tzu Liao." Ezra had to fight to keep the bitterness out of his voice. None of the Tigers had liked that mission. Ezra still remembered how the water had tasted in Aswan, the Tigers' base of operation on that ravaged world. Sweet and clean. He remembered because it was strange—he hadn't expected the water on Caph, of all places, to be clean.

Caph was an old Terran Hegemony world, long-since administered by House Davion's Federated Suns. It had been battled over by the Davions, House Kurita's Draconis Combine, and even House Liao's Capellan Confederation, for centuries. During the 3057 dissolution of the Sarna March and coincidental creation of the Chaos March, Caph had become a battleground once again. Local forces, much like those on Hall, had fought and held what they could. Mercenaries had aided both sides.

Mercenaries like the Stealthy Tigers.

Caph and the worlds around it had been fought over for centuries. The dissolution of the Star League in the twenty-eigth century had inevitably led to fratricidal fighting among its member-states that had raged off and on—mostly on—for centuries. History called those conflicts the Succession Wars, and the most recent, the Fourth, had changed the map of the Inner Sphere far more than any of its predecessors. The imbalanced realms of the Inner Sphere had tottered on the brink of war again for twenty years, until the Clans had arrived.

At once, the Clans had changed everything—and nothing. A martial society founded by the descendants of the vanished Star League Defense Force, the caste-ridden Clans had returned to conquer their lost homewards. It had taken all the Successor States, as the realms of the Inner Sphere were known, along with the massive army of ComStar, the communications giant, to stop them at Tukayyid.

And now, fifteen years after that fateful victory, the nations of the Inner Sphere were fighting again.

"Tough fight?" Ortiz asked.

"Not all of it," Ezra said, speaking without thinking, "but some of it."

Ortiz laughed. Ezra flinched, reacting to her laughter as if it were an attack, then realized that she'd taken his answer as flippancy.

"Most of them are like that," she said.

HARNEY
HALL
THE CHAOS MARCH
4 MARCH 3067

Kirsten Markoja hid her smile as she entered the bar. The sign read *O'Sullivan's*, but three of the neon letters weren't lit. It flickered in the bright daylight nonetheless. No one who knew her would ever expect to find her in a place like this. It made her skin crawl.

It was perfect for a meet-up.

Inside, the air was thick with synth smoke and old sweat. A battered bar stood along one wall. A woman in her forties or fifties stood behind it, tapping through images on her noteputer. She looked up when Kirsten entered, but when the mercenary strode toward the booths on the opposite wall, she looked back down and started swiping again.

Kirsten walked toward the line of booths until she found what she was looking for: a woman wearing a blue sweater with a red bracelet. That woman was sitting three booths from the back, holding a narrow-necked ale bottle in both hands and staring at the tabletop. She looked like the Platonic ideal of a woman with too little hope and too much weighing on her.

She didn't even look like she was paying attention. Kirsten was hurt for a moment—she'd put a lot of effort into her disguise. A wig, false nose, inserts in her cheeks to change the shape of her face, colored lenses in her eyes. It would take a full-on biometric scanner to ID her, and this part of town wouldn't host those.

Kirsten grinned as she slid into the booth. "That's a lovely bracelet."

The woman looked up at her with a frown. "It's all I have."

"You could have more," Kirsten said, completing the recognition signal. The other woman didn't react, but something in her eyes changed.

Kirsten's grin hardened down to a line. She set her satchel on the inside edge of the table as if she were reaching for the menu key.

"When?" the woman in blue asked.

"Tomorrow," Kirsten said. "When they return."

The woman shrugged, then looked down at her bottle. "Should be doable."

Kirsten shook her head. Her body language said *fine—don't take what I'm giving you.* She grabbed her purse and yanked it toward her. Half the contents spilled out. She cursed and half-stood, scooping the bag's contents—small packets, makeup kits, expired lottery tickets and a half-filled pack of synth cigarettes—back into it. Then she stalked out of the bar without another word.

On the street, she didn't bother to hide her smile. She felt the familiar anticipatory tingle of adrenalin coursing through her body. She tasted copper on the back of her tongue. There was every chance this was going to work.

Which meant it was time for to get back to Bravo Base and make sure Mason had his part of the plan ready.

She put a sway of her hips into the wave at an approaching taxi. The groundcar skidded to a stop quickly.

She smiled again as she climbed into the back.

Some things were so easy. She pulled her wig off and tossed it into the gutter. The rest of the prosthetics could wait until she got back to Bravo Base.

Adele Estwicke took another fifteen minutes to finish her ale before she stood. The rolled-up paper that had fallen out of the other woman's purse was in her pocket; if anyone had seen it, they'd think it was a C-bill. The color was the same. Who was she to turn down free money when a random woman left it on her seat in her rush?

Once outside, she walked back toward the safe house she'd set up in Harney. It was a little less than a kilometer, and the streets were mostly deserted at this time of day. A few late-eaters getting lunch after the rush. City workers maintaining the streets. No one would notice a run-down woman in a blue sweater walking like she carried the weight of the world on her shoulders.

That much, at least, wasn't an act.

Estwicke hadn't expected ever to see that activation code come through her coded communications. It was one of the few Sixth of June codes she had access to, and only then because Blane, her superior, had explained that in the most extreme cases he might be able to marshal resources outside of the True Believers' normal coffers.

Outsiders saw the Word of Blake as monolithic, but its adherents knew that couldn't be farther from the truth. All of the Blakists were united in their faith in the sanctity and rightness of the words of the blessed Jerome Blake, as passed down to his disciple Conrad Toyama just after the fall of the Star League. It was that very faith that gave them such zeal, and proved the rightness of their cause. But that faith was about all the various sects of the Word believed; after that, it came down to methods, and there the divisions were stark.

The True Believers were the closest in method to the old Com-Star, before the Schism that broke the holy order from the secular corporation that replaced it. They weren't pacifists, but recognized that only by bringing the disparate factions of the Word of Blake together could they gain the strength necessary to lead the Inner Sphere into the Third Transfer.

In contrast, the militant sects like the Sixth of the June or the Toyamas advocated direct action. The Toyamas were conventionally militant, claiming it was the Word's duty to conquer—if necessary—the Inner Sphere to bring about the new society Jerome Blake foresaw.

The Sixth of June, however, made the Toyamas look like pikers. The Sixth of June called for total war: either supplication to the Word of Blake, or eradication. They were assassins, intriguers, terrorists. If the nations of the Inner Sphere didn't recognize the rightness of the Word, then those nations didn't deserve to exist.

The other factions—the Shunners, the Expatriates, the other bands too small to rate a seat on the Word's Ruling Conclave on

Terra—were closer in politics to the True Believers, but Estwicke knew Blane himself considered them "the quiet bunch." They were too small, too passive to effect any real change.

She imagined the Toyamas and the Sixth of June considered them cowards.

It had been Blane and the True Believers that had brought the Word of Blake Protectorate into being. It had been agents like Estwicke herself, adepts sent on diplomatic missions, but with the wherewithal to call for military action if necessary, who'd brought in Keid, Caph, and Epsilon Eridani. Other missions were nearing their final stages. Estwicke knew it would only take another few worlds to build a critical mass, a momentum of Blakist hegemony that would sweep over the Chaos March and return those worlds to order.

She reached into her pocket and squeezed the paper.

The plans had been easy enough to set into place. She'd been stringing Aylmer and his idiots along for years, just for an occasion such as this. When the mystery woman had suggested the plan, Estwicke had agreed. If it worked, it would advance her plans with Baranov. And if it didn't . . . . Well, the Word had never had trouble capitalizing on unrest. All she'd required from the woman with the bag had been the final access codes to the funds.

Sixth of June funds.

It couldn't be anything else. Estwicke had access to all the public Word of Blake accounts on Hall, and all the hidden True Believer accounts. Blane had provided her with stolen accounts for the Expatriates and, if necessary, the Toyamas, as well, but none for the Sixth of Junes. She hadn't known these accounts even existed.

Estwicke squeezed the paper again as she reached the safe house. She keyed the lock without looking around and stepped inside. Then she stood at the viewport set in the thick steel door and watched to see if anyone showed any interest in the house after she'd entered. She gave her nominal tail three minutes to show up, then went upstairs.

Jurowicz, her acolyte, was waiting at the console upstairs. Estwicke pulled the paper out and handed it to her. "I want you to ID this account and any others like it you can find before we access the money."

Jurowicz was a small woman, about a meter-seven, but thickly built. She exercised every day, and muscles bulged beneath her tight clothes and tighter skin. Her cover was as a personal trainer here in Harney, and she took that role as seriously as her other duties.

Jurowicz took the scrap and flattened it on the desk in front of her. "What am I looking for?"

"Where the money came from," Estwicke said. "And if there's any more of it. I'm not handing a C-bill to anyone before we make sure it can't be traced back to us."

"I thought you said it's a Sixth of June account," Jurowicz said, already tapping console keys. Three of the six holographic displays in front of her burst into light and motion, though it looked like gibberish to Estwicke. "They'd cover their tracks, don't you think?"

"Usually? Yeah." Estwicke pulled the nasty blue sweater over her head and threw it in the corner. She wanted a shower, and now. "But with the AMC here, we need to be extra sure."

"And if it checks out?"

"Send the go codes," Estwicke answered while heading for the bathroom. "It's on for tomorrow."

"We have confirmed that the Allied Mercenary Command column has reached Deal. No one has commented on their purpose there yet, but no one can forget that Elly Burton, the late Count Mc-Nally's lover, and mother of his illegitimate son, remains with her mercenary company at the fortress.

"Unconfirmed reports have placed a number of Stealthy Tiger BattleMechs in the column. Neither the Tigers nor the emperor's press office have commented, claiming the travel is an "ongoing action."

"Which, as our savvy viewers will notice, is confirmation in itself. If there were no Tigers present, what action can be ongoing? You'll remember that it was the Stealthy Tigers, under contract to the emperor, that killed the rebellious Count McNally last year.

"Maybe they're at Deal to finish the job?"

–From the *Harney Morning Edition*,
Harney HV Channel Six

CHAPTER FIVE

DEAL
HALL
THE CHAOS MARCH
4 MARCH 3067

The courtyard of the fortress was far too small for the entire Disinherited battalion to fit inside. Only a handful of 'Mechs and the armored personnel carriers of the infantry actually came inside the walls, while the rest of the force bivouacked outside. Ezra kept his lance outside, on the edge of the Disinherited's perimeter. Captain Ortiz parked her *Dervish* nearby, as well.

Ezra parked the *Crusader*, setting it into a balanced stance and then locking the myomer muscles so it became an eleven-meter statue instead of a mobile war machine. He undid his restraints and racked his neurohelmet in the cubby above his command couch. Then he opened the hatch. He wanted fresh air for the next part.

Deal was on the edge of the Helmand Desert. Another dozen kilometers out of the hallways—the ancient arroyos that traveled for kilometers in places, giving Hall its name—would have seen them into the oasis of Kazan, a city of several hundred thousand people. The air that swept into the *Crusader*'s cockpit was dry and hot, and stank of burned lubricant and diesel exhaust from all the combat vehicles running around, but it was welcome nonetheless. It wasn't the recycled stench of Ezra's own sweat combined with that of the *Crusader*'s previous pilots.

From the compartment beneath his seat, Ezra pulled a clean, sealed set of Tigers khaki battledress and ripped it open. The pack contained a set of wipes, and he did the best he could to scrub the sweat and stink from his armpits and his chest. He dressed as quickly as possible in the cramped space, then climbed out onto the 'Mech's shoulder.

Disinherited APCs were already trundling back out through the gates to pick up the dismounts from outside. Ezra saw the other two MechWarriors he'd detailed to come inside with him already climbing down their 'Mechs. He did the same, moving carefully and trying not to scuff his clothes. A duty uniform or even dress browns would have been more appropriate for meeting Elly Burton, but that was impractical given the way they'd traveled. That in itself, Ezra knew, would be message enough.

There were worse first impressions the Stealthy Tigers could give than one of practicality.

By the time Ezra reach the sandy ground, his MechWarriors were already waiting. His fourth, Sergeant Roses, was still in her *Hatchetman*. She'd be relieved in a few hours, if all went well, but there was no way he was leaving four Tigers 'Mechs out in a desert with only the Dismal Ds to watch them.

In all likelihood, Roses would sit and watch empty sensors the whole time. Unless she didn't, which would make the entire exercise worthwhile.

He looked at his Jaguars. Sergeant Iqbal Akhtar, quiet and competent, stood to his left. Akhtar had joined the regiment just after Caph. He stood about two meters tall; thickset, but not fat. His hair was as dark as his skin was pale. He was a phlegmatic man, but a demon at the controls of his *Grand Dragon*. Ezra had his eye on him for a Raider pin someday.

Sergeant Aurel Hicks stood to Ezra's right. She was taller than Akhtar, with willowy brown hair that she wore in a ponytail and piercing brown eyes. Her left hand never strayed far from the pistol on her left thigh, and her eyes never stopped moving. She drove the *Centurion* in his command lance.

"Any problems?" he asked. Both shook their heads. "Good."

"Captain Payne?"

Ezra turned. Captain Ortiz was walking toward them. Like the Tigers, she also wore battledress, but in Disinherited mottled gray. The Dismal Ds favored a short-billed soft-cloth cap where the Tigers wore boonies. It had a matte-black Disinherited unit insignia in the center of the placard.

Ortiz smiled and jacked a thumb at the APCs rolling to a stop nearby. "Can I offer you a ride?"

"Thank you," Ezra told her. He glanced at his MechWarriors and jerked his chin toward the APC. Both of them nodded and headed that way in silence. Once they had, he fell into step with Ortiz.

"Nervous?" she asked.

"About Burton's reaction to us being here?"

"Yes."

"No." He looked at her. "I mean, yeah—she'll have a reaction. But I'm not nervous about it. It'll be what it'll be."

She regarded him for a second. "That's an admirably pragmatic outlook."

He laughed. "More or less."

They walked the next few steps in silence. "What will you do if she reacts badly?"

Ezra shrugged. "Whatever seems appropriate. If she wants us to leave, we'll leave."

"Be a long way to come for nothing."

He stopped. When she stopped too, he turned to face her. "Even that wouldn't be nothing. I'm not ignorant; we—someone wearing this uniform," he said, plucking his battledress, "killed her lover. Killed the father of her child. That's going to hurt."

He looked toward the APC. "But even if we weren't here, Mc-Nally would still be dead. We exist—both of us, Burton and the Tigers—in a universe where that's happened. It's fact. Nothing we can do now can change that."

Ortiz stared at him. Her eyes were narrowed, and to his surprise Ezra felt himself blush under her gaze. She must have seen it; she smiled and looked away. "Pragmatic," she repeated, and started walking again.

He fell into step with her again.

"Why did you come?" she asked a moment later. They were almost to the APC. In the distance, another one growled as its transmission engaged.

"Because you did," he told her. "The Disinherited."

"Just doing your job?"

"Part of it," he said, then stopped and waved her into the APC in front of him. She grinned and ducked under the hatch to enter the cramped fighting compartment. Ezra took a last look around, then followed her.

Deal was the military seat of a Davion nobleman, so of course it had an audience chamber. The room was grand, at least forty meters long and half that tall and wide. Fluted windows ran up the wall, letting in the desert light with only a slight shade of polarization. Ezra and his two MechWarriors entered the hall at the rear of the Disinherited delegation. The walls were already lined with McNally courtiers. Several wore uniforms of a sort. Ezra recognized them from briefings as McNally troops—a couple of the few remaining McNally Guard, a MechWarrior from the Achtung Eight, one of the count's mercenary hires, various others.

There had to be as least 200 people in the room, before the Disinherited—and three Tigers—entered.

Captain Ortiz walked with Ezra and his MechWarriors. Major Fletcher led the Disinherited delegation, as the senior officer. Alone among the mercenaries, he wore a gray undress duty uniform. Ezra felt his lip curl despite his control. Fletcher had ridden in a command APC, with cushions and air conditioning. Of course he wasn't wearing battledress.

"Captain Burton," Fletcher called when recognized.

At the head of the room was what could only be called the throne dais. The chair itself was unremarkable, but it sat a meter off the floor on a raised platform. Two armed infantrymen stood sentry in front of it. They carried their rifles at port arms, with magazines loaded. Ezra didn't doubt the magazines held live rounds, either.

On the dais sat two people: a woman in simple yet elegant court robes, and a young boy in formal dress. The boy sat in the center chair; the woman, to his side. Ezra recognized Elly Burton from file photos. She'd put on a bit of weight since the file photo had been taken; it showed in her cheeks and droop of her chin, but that was only noticeable after you recognized the pain the woman was in.

She was hurting. Even from a dozen meters the pain in her eyes was obvious.

Behind Ezra, Sergeant Hicks grunted softly. She saw it too. Burton's brown hair hung limply, and her skin was pallid. It was obvious she hadn't slept well in weeks. The signs of grief—of heartbreak—were clear.

So much for pragmatism, Ezra thought. He considered turning and walking out, but that would only draw more attention to them. And besides—the colonel had given him orders. He was a soldier. He carried out his orders, even the distasteful ones.

Burton looked at Fletcher as if she hadn't seen him walk in and blinked. "You're Major Fletcher?" she asked. "Your colonel said you'd be coming."

"I am, Captain," Fletcher said. "Thank you for allowing us to visit you."

Burton laughed. It was a high-pitched titter, right on the edge of hysterical. "Like we could have stopped you," she said, gasping.

The boy looked at Fletcher, frowned, then looked at his mother. "Are they here to help us with Daddy?"

Ezra licked his lips as the crowd around them erupted in furious whispers. He looked to his left and found an officer in Mc-Nally Guard colors staring at him. When Ezra met the man's eyes, he didn't look away. The soldier's expression was pure hatred.

Ezra blinked, then looked back at the dais. It wasn't anything he'd hadn't expected.

"No," Burton told her son. She opened her mouth to say more, then closed it and looked back toward Fletcher. "You're not here to help us kill Baranov, are you?"

Fletcher cleared his throat. "No, ma'am. That's not our contract."

"You're here from the AMC?"

"Yes."

"To look for a Word of Blake connection to Baranov?"

"That's correct."

Burton frowned. "And if such a connection exists?"

Fletcher coughed lightly. "Then we would be constrained to act." He stepped forward and spread his hands. "Perhaps, Captain, this conversation would be best tabled for a more private setting?"

Burton tittered again. She looked around at the room of people, down one wall and up the opposite. "These people, Major," she said, "have stood by Radcliffe." She stopped, swallowing. "By the count, and now the count's son—" She pressed her hand on her son's knee. "—for more years than he has been alive." She pulled her hand back. "They've earned the right to hear what is said between us."

Ezra's jaw clenched. He knew what Fletcher must be feeling. Putting them on display for the dead count's court made what should have been a simple conversation into a game of politics. It might have been possible to have a candid conversation between professionals, if it were just a few of them in a room.

In front of a hall full of angry, loyal feudal retainers? Impartiality in a crowd like that was only slightly less likely than Spherewide peace breaking out tomorrow.

"Then yes. If we discover a link between Baranov, we may be drawn into conflict with him. The terms of our contract obligate us to fight the Word of Blake. If the emperor—"

The entire room stiffened at the word. Ezra's palms began sweating, and he knew that behind him, Hicks' hand would be centimeters—millimeters—away from her pistol butt.

Fletcher continued as if he hadn't noticed. Perhaps he really hadn't, though that would indicate a disturbing lack of political awareness for an intelligence officer.

"—chooses to side with his benefactors, we could become entangled."

Burton was completely in tune with her court's—and it was her court now, Ezra knew—emotional tone. The smile she bestowed on Fletcher was as false as a politician's promise.

"Entangled . . ." she repeated, her red-rimmed eyes sweeping across the Disinherited delegation. "Such a small word—" she stopped speaking to stare at Ezra Payne.

Ezra stared back. He didn't care if it was impolitic.

Burton's mouth opened and closed. No sound came out.

Ezra took extra care to make sure that his frown wasn't showing, then began to move forward through the ranks of Disinherited officers. He made a small motion behind his back for his Mech-Warriors to stay where they were.

"You didn't—" Burton whispered. The entire room had gone quiet enough that Ezra could hear her whisper. "You can't—"

"Captain Burton," he said, projecting his voice so it filled the room. He looked at the boy. "Young count." He ducked his head slightly in respect. "On behalf of my colonel and my regiment, I offer our sympathies on your loss. The count was an honorable man, and a skilled opponent. We did not wish him dead, and regret your pain and loss."

The boy count looked confused. Elly Burton was still staring. She was leaned as far back in her chair as she could be. No one else in the hall spoke for almost a full minute. The only motion was the rise and fall of Burton's chest as she breathed.

Ezra simply waited. He'd said what he came to say.

Fletcher coughed. "Captain—"

Burton held up a hand. She didn't speak, but Fletcher's word had been enough to break her out of whatever mental loop she'd fallen into. She hadn't looked away from Ezra—from his uniform—since she'd spotted him.

"I can't believe you'd come here," she finally said, her voice shaking. Her face didn't hide any of the shock. "I can't believe."

"Our presence was requested," Ezra said. "If our being here offends, we will leave."

"Like hell," someone in the gallery to the side muttered. A susurrous of agreeable noise washed out in the brief silence following the statement.

"Offend . . ." Burton said. Quietly.

A hand touched Ezra's arm. It was Ortiz. She looked at him and then flicked her eyes back toward the hall entrance. He frowned and shook his head, then looked back to the front.

Elly Burton's face was flushed and her eyes were wet, but when she spoke, her voice was level. "Major Fletcher, if you'd please adjourn to a different room, I'd like to speak with my staff."

"Of course," Fletcher said, bowing his head.

"As for you . . ." Burton said, looking back at Payne. She raised an eyebrow.

"Captain Ezra Payne," he said.

"Captain Payne. I'd like to speak with you privately."

Ezra wanted to, but didn't lick his lips. "Of course, Captain," he said. He inclined his head slightly. "At your pleasure."

"Now," she said.

Then she grabbed her son and walked out through a door behind the dais. The rest of the room broke into whispers and murmurs.

Ortiz clutched Ezra's arm. "I'll go with you." It wasn't a question.

"She may not like it," he said.

"One more disappointment won't hurt her," Ortiz said. There was steel in her voice, and old pain. "Not today."

The room the steward led Ezra Payne and Captain Ortiz to was small, paneled in off-whites and tans, with a small, round conference table. Two of the walls were mirrored, carefully offset so they didn't reflect each other. That made the room feel larger. The air was fresh but with a hint of dusky oldness, as if it had been quickly swept out just for this meeting.

Perhaps it had.

His two MechWarriors had remained in the audience chamber. Hicks hadn't been happy about it, but there was no way Ezra was going to bring armed MechWarriors as escorts into Elly Burton's presence. If it came down to it, he could take care of himself.

He stiffened his back muscles as he pulled a chair out for Captain Ortiz. The scrape of his skin against the knife taped to the small of his back was refreshing, but even if Burton proved insane enough to attack him, he wouldn't need it.

He could take care of himself. He'd been doing that since he was a boy.

"That could have gone better," he said as he sat down next to Ortiz.

"I thought it went much better than I expected," she replied. She spread her hands on the table, fingers splayed, and glanced at him with a nervous smile. "I thought she'd shoot you."

Ezra grunted. "I might have given you odds."

"What do you think she'll say?"

Ezra looked up at the reflection of the ceiling in the mirror across from him. "I have no idea."

"I doubt she wants to hurt you," Ortiz said. Ezra looked at her hands, still on the tabletop. There was the slightest tremor in her wrist. When she lifted her hands, Ezra knew, she'd leave sweaty palm prints on the finished surface.

"I don't know." Ezra looked around. He really didn't. He would have said that to Ortiz, even if he had known, because Colonel Rauschenbusch had taught him—by example—that there was little to be gained in giving information away for free. His mind was going in a dozen directions, playing scenarios against each other.

He sighed. It was useless to speculate. He looked at Ortiz again. "I don't think I ever learned your first name,"

She looked at him, half-frowning and half-smiling. "Really? You're asking now?"

He shrugged. "We appear to have a minute."

She laughed. "It's Nathalie."

"Ezra."

She smiled. "I knew that."

He shrugged again. "I was raised to be polite," he told her.

Her smile widened, but the door behind them slid open before she could speak. Ezra looked back and stood as Elly Burton came in. She glared at him and stepped around the table. The door slid closed without admitting anyone else. She sat down without speaking. Her eyes slid over Ortiz long enough to take in her uniform, then glared at Ezra.

"Start talking," she said.

Ezra sat down. Ortiz did the same. "What should I say?"

"What the hell are you doing here?" Her voice was thick with anger, but she didn't show any of the hysteria he'd seen in the audience chamber. *Was than an act, I wonder?*

"I came with the Disinherited," he said. "I'm their liaison officer."

"Liaison? You're not their employer."

"Of course not," Ezra said. He didn't let the bite in her voice get at him. It was nothing less than he expected, and dealing with Kirsten Markoja had given him plenty of experience in talking with a flat tone despite being angry.

"Then what do you 'liaise' about?"

"I represent the emperor's interests," he said.

"The emperor," she hissed. "That bastard isn't emperor of his own bathroom. If it wasn't for you—" she pointed angrily at his chest, "and your damned regiment, Cliff would still be alive and we'd show you how little power your 'emperor' really has."

"Captain Burton—" Ortiz started, but stopped at the glare Burton cast on her.

"Am I talking to you?"

"I was only—"

"Then be quiet," Burton ordered. Ezra didn't have to be touching Ortiz to know she had stiffened. He saw the knuckles on her hands, again spread on the table, go white. Muscles knotted beneath the skin of her forearms.

"Whatever name I call my employer by," Ezra said, cutting into the short silence, "is inconsequential." He sat a little straighter and tipped his head back slightly. He knew that meant he was talking down his nose to the woman who controlled the fortress he sat in, but at that moment he didn't care.

"Nor does it matter what might have been," he continued, "if he had not hired my regiment." He drew a quick breath, knowing he should stop, but unable to. "He did, and here we are."

Burton glared at him. He watched the muscles in her jaw bunch, saw the way her fists clenched on the table. But, to her credit, she controlled her temper.

"Fine." She shoved herself back until she was leaning away from the table. "My original question stands: what are you doing here?" She waved at the walls. "Are you spying for an attack? You'll find the defenses at Deal quite unimpaired."

Ezra sucked at the inside of his cheeks. "I came because I was invited," he said, "and because I and my colonel felt you were owed an apology. You are a mercenary. You know people die in our business, but . . . " He stopped. He didn't want to say this with anger in his voice.

"We did not come here to kill Radcliffe McNally," he said. "We came to defeat him. It's what we were hired to do, and we did it. That he died in the doing is regrettable, to all of us. By all accounts, he was a noble man."

"He was the best man I ever met," Burton said.

"None of us wished him dead," Ezra said. It was the truth. Anyone with half a brain knew Baranov would have executed McNally about ten seconds after capturing him, had the Tigers defeated him without killing him, but that was different. That was politics.

It was probably cleaner that McNally had died on the battlefield. If Burton was smart, she'd turn the dead count into a martyr.

Not that Ezra would ever let those words pass his lips. He was, after all, on the other side. "If wishes were C-bills," Burton muttered.

Ezra pushed his chair back. "The Disinherited," he said, inclining his head toward Captain Ortiz, "intend to escort you to Brampton. Whether you accept or not is up to you, and I have no part of those discussions." He stood. "I'm sure Major Fletcher and your staff are working out the details now. If you'll excuse me, I will return to my lance outside your fortress."

Ortiz looked up at him, frowning, but Burton just glared. "You came all this way just to say that, and run away?"

Ezra looked down at her as he tugged his blouse down straight. "I follow orders," he said. He ducked his chin toward Burton. "Good day, Captain Burton." He looked at Ortiz. "Captain Ortiz."

"Just get out," Burton muttered.

Ezra stepped backward until the door slipped open, then

stepped through and let it close. Then he worked his jaw and rolled his shoulders.

"Tough meeting?" one of the door sentries sneered.

Ezra stared at him. Then he turned and walked back the way he came.

The pressure of his knife against the small of his back itched the entire way.

"We're getting unconfirmed reports from ComStar that fighting has begun on Tikonov between the forces of the Federated Suns and the Capellan Confederation. A world long held in Victor Davion's name, renewed fighting began there after the so-called prince traveled to New Avalon to threaten the archon princess.

"If these reports are true, they could signal a weakness in Victor Davion's flank even as he drives for an impossible victory on New Avalon."

–From the *Harney Morning Edition*,
Harney HV Channel Six

CHAPTER SIX

HELMAND DESERT
HALL
THE CHAOS MARCH
5 MARCH 3067

"I can't believe she came," Nathalie Ortiz said.

Ezra Payne looked at the image of her *Dervish* in his HUD and grinned. Ortiz had been marching with Ezra and his lance for most of the morning. A pair of Disinherited 'Mechs paced her, fifty or so meters behind, but that was just for show.

No one expected four Stealthy Tiger 'Mechs to attack a battalion of the Dismal Disinherited. But as Sergeant Major Halleck always said: you prepared for what *could* happen, not what *might* happen. There was most of a battalion of Dismal Ds within two kilometers of the Tiger lance. Even if they managed to kill Captain Ortiz, there was almost no chance they could escape into the desert. There wasn't nearly enough cover, nor a nice terrain feature like a river to break contact with.

And besides—with Elly Burton and her Brigade out here, a few kilometers away with the main body, no Tigers attack would go unanswered for long.

"She couldn't *not* come, really," he said.

"What do you mean?"

"Look around you," Ezra said. The wastelands of the Helmand Desert went as far as the eye—or the BattleMech sensor—could see. It was all sand and rock formations. The vegetation, what there was of it, was the ubiquitous, gnarly desert life Ezra had seen on a dozen worlds in the last decade. "There's nothing here she can use for succor. The rallying point of her rebellion, er, resistance is dead. She's a mercenary commander, not a noblewoman. Her only claim to power is her motherhood of her son."

"So?"

"So the Disinherited—and through them, the Allied Mercenary Command—are the only hope she has of getting off Hall alive."

The *Dervish* walked for a hundred meters beside the *Crusader* without either MechWarrior speaking. Finally, Ortiz broke the silence. "You think that's her plan?"

"I don't know what else it could be," he told her. "It certainly can't be defeating Baranov. Baranov won, so long as he keeps us here. She has to know her days are numbered." That the emperor hadn't already sent the mercenaries out to crush the remnants of McNally's forces was a common subject of argument back at Bravo Base. The betting pool had it on a grand final battle sometime in the spring, when the news of McNally's death started to fade from the planetary media's attention. Baranov was nothing if not a newshound. He might have been a mediocre officer, but he was a first-rate politician.

"But your contract is up next year," Ortiz said.

"Sixty-eight," Ezra muttered.

"Right—3068," Ortiz went on. Apparently her study of the Stealthy Tigers hadn't included their lingo. "All she has to do is wait it out, unless Buddy Boy can afford to hire a new regiment."

He couldn't afford us, Ezra didn't say. He heard Monet's voice in his head, urging him to confide in the Disinherited officer, but ignored it.

"She's been waiting most of a decade for victory," he said instead. "She built a life here. She had a son with the second most powerful man on the planet. And now he's dead." He looked across the sands again. His feet moved the *Crusader* around a projection of rock without conscious thought. "No. She's done waiting."

On the tactical display at his elbow, a cluster of red dots shone at the core of a circle of blue ones; the red dots were the 'Mechs of Burton's Brigade and the armored vehicles and transporters of Burton's entourage. The blue dots were the Disinherited. The display showed six kilometers in every direction around him, and there were only four friendly green dots: the one representing his *Crusader* and the three others that stood for his lance's 'Mechs.

If all those blue dots—neutral—turned red—hostile—his lance would be wiped out.

If.

"Life is a serious of ifs," the colonel always said.

"What do you think she'll tell us?" Ortiz asked after a moment. Ezra heard the hesitation in her voice, and understood it. He'd heard the same tone in Jacob Brim's voice when the spook was trying to wheedle information out of him.

"That's between you and her," Ezra said. "It's none of my business."

Ortiz said nothing. Or she might have, but his sensor console chirped at him. He looked down, then frowned. More green carets had appeared on his tactical display. Friendly units.

The only 'Mechs that keyed green on his screen were Stealthy Tigers.

Why the hell was there what looked like two companies of Stealthy Tigers coming at them in the desert?

He opened his mouth, but his comm screen flickered with transmission noise. As a courtesy the Disinherited had opened one of their general channels to the Tigers lance, which meant he could listen in on the company-level chatter. He heard one of the outrider scout platoons report the new contacts.

As Stealthy Tigers.

"Captain Payne?" Major Fletcher sent. He was back with Burton's Brigade, among the transporters. "Would you care to explain?"

"I don't know, sir," Ezra replied. He frowned and keyed a query into his battle computer, but the new contacts were still too far away for more than transponder data. "No one was supposed to come out to meet us. Wait one, sir." He changed comm channels.

"Jaguar Six to approaching Tiger force," he sent. "Identify yourself, over."

There was no reply.

"Jaguar Six to Tigers, respond."

Ezra touched a control. "Iqbal. See if you can raise the incoming."

Akhtar acknowledged. Ezra kept frowning at his tactical screen, but switched his radio back to the Disinherited channel. "I'm not getting anything from them," he sent to Major Fletcher.

Another voice broke into the channel. "If this is a trap, Payne," Elly Burton snapped, "I'll skin you alive. My *son* is in this convoy!"

"It's not a trap," Ezra said. He set his comm to transmit on all the frequencies he'd been using. It was easier than keying between channels, and besides—he didn't have any secrets.

"Jaguar Six to approaching Stealthy Tigers unit," he sent, knowing the Disinherited and Burton's Brigade were listening. "Identify yourself, over."

"No response, sir," Akhtar said a moment later.

"Hicks," Ezra said. "You try. Call Regiment. See what's going on."

"For all the good it will do," the acerbic woman muttered, and switched channels.

"Major Fletcher," Ezra said. "I'm going to meet them." He didn't ask permission. Despite Fletcher being a major and Ezra a captain, Fletcher had no authority over him. They weren't in the same chain of command. Ezra's deference to Fletcher's rank was the courtesy professionals extended one another, nothing more.

"I'm going with them," Captain Ortiz said. "My lance, let's go."

Ezra adjusted the *Crusader*'s path and pushed the throttle forward. The convoy had been traveling down one of the ancient arroyos that gave Hall its name. It took the *Crusader* a laboring few seconds to climb up the steep wall and crest the hill, 25 meters above the arroyo floor. He stopped there and tried the radio again, but still got no response.

"Any ideas?" Ortiz sent, as her *Dervish* stepped up next to him.

"No good ones," he murmured. Then he stepped his *Crusader* off the hilltop and down into the next arroyo.

The colonel would have told him if he intended to send escorts out. Hell, Rauschenbusch would have told him if he'd intended to welsh on the deal and send the regiment out to crush the Disinherited battalion and Elly Burton. There was next to no chance he'd have given that order, but there was zero chance he wouldn't have told Ezra Payne about it in advance.

But the icons were green.

"No reply from Bravo Base," Hicks reported.

"Jammed?"

"No, just no reply."

Ezra blinked. "Not even an acknowledgment?"

"Nothing. It's like they're not even there."

The *Crusader* reached the floor of the next arroyo. Ezra grimaced at the steep slope in front of him and slammed both his booted feet down on the *Crusader*'s pedals. Ports in the 'Mech's back and sides spat flame as jump jets lifted all sixty-five tons of 'Mech free of Hall's gravity and hurled it up the wall. As the 'Mech slammed down, Ezra rolled with the impact and kept moving. He was out of patience.

"Jaguar Six to Tigers, come in."

The contacts were less than four kilometers away. There was no way the communications were getting through. Ezra chewed his lip for a second and then keyed an override into his 'Mech's computer.

"Jaguar Six to incoming 'Mechs, reply. Now."

An alarm bled to life on his HUD, triggered by his transmission. The frequency and encryption he'd just used only had one purpose: last-ditch transmissions by the Tigers in emergency circumstances. They called it the guard channel, and transmitting on it, even during exercises, was strictly forbidden.

If this didn't turn out to be an emergency, Sergeant Major Halleck was going to rip Ezra a new one, Raider pin or not.

Just then Ezra didn't care. He wasn't thinking in terms of "not emergencies."

"Nathalie," he said without thinking, or even realizing he'd used her first name, "hold your 'Mechs here. Call back your scouts."

"Are you sure?" she asked.

"I don't know what the hell is going on," he said, "but the last thing we need is to have Tigers and Dismal Ds shooting at each other."

"Okay," she replied. "We'll trail by a klick."

Ezra nodded. His attention was fully on his scanners.

"Let's go," he told his lance. Then he keyed his comm to receive all channels but only broadcast on his lance's. "Anyone got any ideas?"

"An escort?" Roses asked.

"Could be."

"If it were an attack, the whole regiment would be out there," Akhtar said.

"How do you know they're not?" Hicks spat. "Those might be only the 'Mechs we can *see*."

Ezra carefully didn't say anything. He'd already been wondering that. It was right out of the colonel's playbook to distract the enemy with a showy force on one side and then hammer them on the other when they weren't expecting it. He was so used to that tactic that for a second he'd considered spinning the *Crusader* around and rushing toward the opposite flank.

The only other options were that someone else had ordered the strike—or that those weren't really Stealthy Tigers.

The someone else was easy: one of the damned Markojas. Either of them were ambitious enough to "show some initiative" and eliminate the emperor's main rival, without thinking through what it would mean if that rival was killed while being escorted by a larger, neutral-until-shot-at force of BattleMechs.

Ezra blinked. No. Not even Mason Markoja was that stupid.

All that left was fake Tigers.

Then how'd they get the transponder codes?

"Why wouldn't they warn us?" Roses asked.

"Need to know," Hicks said.

"I would have needed to know," Ezra said. "And no one told me." He halted the *Crusader* atop the next hilltop and focused his sensors. "Spread out. Someone get me visuals. I want to see who's coming."

The terrain for kilometers was the same—arroyos, Hall's famous so-called hallways. A 'Mech force moving perpendicular to the direction of flow was constantly going up and down hills. The approaching Tigers 'Mechs would be up and down. Heat rising from the baked rock distorted the air between them, but the 'Mechs' sensors could cut through that.

"None of the IDs are reading personal IDs," Akhtar said.

"Weird," Roses said.

"Contact," Hicks blurted. "Sending."

A corner of Ezra's HUD shimmered into an image window, painting the image of a desert-camouflage heavy BattleMech in motion. The image was a two-second loop, showing the birdlike 'Mech stepping awkwardly atop the hillock it was cresting and them disappearing down into the next arroyo.

"Nice picture," Roses said.

"Not really," Hicks said.

Ezra let the looped image run over and over again. When he looked away the first thing he looked at was the rangefinder. 1.8 kilometers and closing.

"Back to the Dismal Ds," he ordered.

Hicks spun her 'Mech around and dashed back down the hill. Akhtar followed, his heavier *Grand Dragon* picking its way more slowly.

Roses hesitated. "What? Why?"

Ezra turned the *Crusader* and pointed its blocky right arm back the way they'd come. "Move it, MechWarrior."

Roses' slender *Hatchetman* lurched into motion. She might

have been young and inexperienced, but there was nothing wrong with the way she took an order. She kicked her 'Mech's jump jets just as she reached the edge of the hill and angled toward the next hillock, landing just short of the incline.

Ezra grinned and followed suit. His *Crusader* came down about ninety meters from her *Hatchetman*. "What kind of 'Mech is that, Roses?"

"*Penetrator*, sir," she replied. "Seventy-five ton Davion machine. Large lasers for reach, pulse lasers in close. Jump jets. Bad news if it corners you, sir."

Ezra's grin widened, despite the situation. That was word-for-word the way Sergeant Major Halleck would have described the 'Mech: concise, all the right details, and a value judgment at the end.

"How many *Penetrator*s do we have in the regiment?"

"I—" Roses stopped. "I've never seen one."

"That's because we don't have any."

"But—" her voice changed. "Oh, shit."

Ezra chuckled, more from nervous tension than mirth. "'Oh, shit,' is right, Sergeant."

"That ain't the regiment out there, kid," Hicks said. Her *Centurion* was five tons heavier than Roses' *Hatchetman*, and faster. She passed the lighter 'Mech on the upward slope, but halted and spun at the top, covering her lancemates.

"Keep moving," Ezra ordered. "They're too far out of range."

"Not if they got artillery," Hicks said.

"No spotter."

"That you know of." Hicks said. Then, "sir."

Ezra's grin was back. "That I know of."

A minute later, they were back with Captain Ortiz's lance. Ezra adjusted his comm to send on the general frequency, and then opened a second, private line to Ortiz's *Dervish*. "Nathalie."

"You're back fast." The *Dervish*'s head tracked toward him.

"It's bad news," he said.

The *Dervish*'s body language stiffened. "What?"

"I'm going to report to your major," he said carefully. "I want you to recognize now, before I speak, that my targeting systems are off and none of my 'Mechs are painting any of yours."

"Okay," she said slowly. "What's going on?"

"Just listen. And don't shoot." He didn't wait to hear her reply. He closed the discreet channel and signaled the Disinherited commander.

"What're your people up to, Captain?" Major Fletcher asked.

"Attacking us," he said.

"You son of a bitch!" Elly Burton cried. "I'm going to see your bones before I die, I swear to all the gods—"

"You might," Ezra said, cutting her off, "because they'll be shooting at me, too." In the confused silence that followed, he quickly said, "They're not Stealthy Tigers."

"They show Tigers transponders," Burton said.

"I don't know how they got the codes," Ezra said, "but that is not a Tigers force."

Alarms blinked on the periphery of Ezra's HUD as nearby Disinherited 'Mechs locked targeting systems on him.

"Jaguar lance," he said clearly, "freeze." He could almost hear Hicks screaming profanity into her muted helmet speakers across the sixty intervening meters of desert. It couldn't be anything less than what was going through his own mind.

"This is bullshit," Elly Burton spat. Her fury turned on Fletcher. "Is this what your protection is? Attacked by mystery 'Mechs in the middle of the desert?"

"It is not," Major Fletcher said, with a quiet dignity that raised him a step or two in Ezra's estimation. "Captain Ortiz."

"Sir!"

"Deal with these people."

"Yes, sir."

Ezra smiled. Fletcher might be a fop and a braggart, but it turned out he wasn't a fool after all. Few men knew where the limits of their competence extended to, not under pressure. Fletcher knew he wasn't a MechWarrior, so he let his senior captain—Nathalie Ortiz—deal with the problem.

A light blinked on Ezra's comm panel as Ortiz opened a private channel to him. "You're sure?"

"Burn me down if I'm not," Ezra said. He sent her the video. "That's a *Penetrator*, and we don't have any of those. Not even in the salvage bays."

"We have a couple," Ortiz said.

"Painted in Tigers browns? With Tigers IDs broadcasting?"

"One hopes not," she said. A moment later. "Okay. Get back with the convoy. We'll take care of this."

"The hell," Ezra said. "They're out there in my clothes, using my name. We're going with you."

"Captain Payne—"

"Forget it," he said. "Jaguar Lance—go dark on IDs." He keyed the override that shut down his 'Mech's transponder. Around him, the other three Tigers 'Mechs did the same—on his tactical display, they became gray dots. Unknowns.

"Your 'puters tag unknowns as grays?" he asked Ortiz.

"Yeah."

"Then ask your boys and girls not to shoot the grays," he said, "and let's go find out who these bastards are."

"We interrupt your regular broadcast to report fighting in the Helmand Desert! The intruding forces of the Dismal Disinherited, here under contract to the illegally on-planet Allied Mercenary Command, have been attacked by 'Mechs reported to be the Stealthy Tigers.

"We're waiting now for comment from either the mercenaries or the emperor's press office. Viewers in the Deal, Holden, or Helmand viewing areas are urged to seek shelter immediately."

– From the *Harney Morning Edition*,
Harney HV Channel Six

CHAPTER SEVEN

**BRAMPTON
HALL
THE CHAOS MARCH
5 MARCH 3067**

Jacob Brim was frowning at a map of Harney when Carlsson slammed the flimsy door open in the Dragoons intel section. "The convoy's being attacked," he gasped out. It was clear he'd been running.

Jacob gaped at him. "By who?"

"Don't know. First reports said Stealthy Tigers, but now they're saying unknowns."

Jacob stepped past him into the corridor. Around them men and women in Disinherited grays bustled past. In the distance, an alarm spun up. Jacob recognized it—the scramble alert. In a few moments, these corridors would be jammed with MechWarriors and vehicle crewman in bulky cooling vests and combat vehicle environment suits.

He grimaced. "How long?" he asked over his shoulder.

"Be shooting any second," Carlsson said.

And I'm all the way up the hell here, Jacob thought bitterly.

A minute or two later, they were in the Disinherited's main tactical operations center. The TOC was a semi-mobile headquarters suitable for manning a combat unit the size and complexity of a Disinherited regiment. With attachments, the Dismal Ds deployed regiments that could more properly be called pocket brigades. One small corner of that HQ space was set aside for the Dragoon technicians and their leaders.

"What do we have?" Jacob asked as he walked up.

"Twenty-three 'Mechs coming at the convoy," Carillo said. He was a small, lithe man with stark white hair he kept pulled back out of his eyes. Tattoos—brilliant blue and white ink—covered both his arms to the elbow. "We're getting satellite feed now, but only one platform and it'll be out of range soon."

"Show me."

Carillo touched a control and leaned back from his console. Jacob leaned in to look.

When the Dismal Ds had first arrived, there hadn't been a single remaining orbital reconaissance platform in orbit. Neither Baranov's forces nor McNally's had much aerospace capability, but both had enough to get fighters or armed shuttles into orbit and take out the other's satellites. The Disinherited had dropped a small spy sat into place when they landed, but its ball-and-twine orbit was unpredictable. It was sheer luck that it was overhead when the balloon went up with the convoy.

A hash of red and green icons was intermixed along one axis on the screen. Jacob frowned at them for a minute, then stepped back. He didn't care about the battle. That would be decided on the field, 200 kilometers from where he stood. "How far back can we track them?"

"Sixty klicks." Carillo leaned forward and manipulated his controls. "They came from here." A circle appeared on a map display.

"What's there?"

"Holden," another technician, Gallifrey, said.

"What's in Holden?"

"Nothing, now."

Jacob resisted the urge to sigh. "Now?"

"Holden was where the Ridzik brothers had based their 'Free Army of the Republic,' before Baranov killed them a few years ago."

Jacob nodded. "Okay. What else do we know?"

"Last imagery there shows no defenses," Gallifrey said. He was big man, an orphan from the Fourth Succession War who'd been adopted into the Dragoons and become a Wolfnet analyst. "And there's only one facility big enough to hold two companies of 'Mechs."

"All right." Jacob straightened and looked around until he found who he was looking for. "Come on," he said, tapping Carlsson on the shoulder.

This could break the whole thing loose, Jacob thought. If they could get to an enemy base—and anyone attacking the AMC convoy was an enemy, sure enough—they might capture enough realtime intelligence to find the link between Baranov and the

Word of Blake. Pay records. Purchase invoices. A small, discreet wall safe locked full of incriminating holos of Buddy Boy eating caviar with Precentor Blane on Terra.

Something.

But they had to move fast. Now was the perfect time to strike, while the attack force was out striking the convoy. The base would be lightly defended, if at all. No one on Hall had had satellites for years—they wouldn't be thinking in terms of overhead observation. If the Dismal Ds moved fast enough, they could sweep the whole base up without the 'Mechs knowing anything about it.

If they were fast enough.

Jacob shouldered past an overweight Hellraisers staffer clutching an armload of hardcopy. He ignored the staffer's fading protests.

A moment later they were standing at the edge of a cluster of officers. "Colonel Marik-Johns," Jacob said.

"Not now," one of the Disinherited officers muttered, shifting his back to block Jacob's view of the colonel.

"—if we leave now, we can be there in six hours," one of the officer was saying.

"In six hours they'll have won or be dead," the colonel barked. "Don't be stupid."

"Colonel," Jacob said more loudly. No one responded to him.

"What if we airmobile?" another officer said. "If we take a DropShip . . ."

Jacob shook his head. It was a good idea—DropShips were massively armored interplanetary spacecraft. They were often used to drop 'Mechs on top of enemy positions, and it was an effective tactic. But you couldn't fire one up from a cold start in a few minutes, even if the troops were already embarked.

"Still a few hours," another officer said.

"I know where they came from!" Jacob shouted.

All of the officers turned to look at him.

"Who is that? Brim?" A path cleared between Jacob and the Disinherited colonel. "What do you mean, you know where they came from?"

"Holden, sir."

Marik-Johns frowned. "Where the hell is Holden?"

Officers scrambled toward consoles and, Jacob presumed, map screens. He stifled his grin. "A city the edge of the Helmand, sir. Sixty klicks or so from the fighting."

"How can you know that?" a captain asked. Jacob couldn't

see his nametape.

"Satellite," Jacob answered.

"How long have you known?" Marik-Johns asked.

Jacob made a show of looking at his wrist. "About a minute now."

Marik-Johns barked a laugh. "All right." He looked at the assembled officers, then at one off to the side. "Captain Sand."

"Sir," barked a short, close-coupled woman with dark hair and sandy skin. She wore a vehicle crewman's harness over her gray battledress, and a big, matte-black pistol Jacob couldn't identify in a holster across her chest.

"Your blowers are on the pad?"

"Yes, sir."

"Take Sergeant Brim and his team and a couple of squads of infantry, and get down to this—" He looked at Brim, who mouthed *Holden*. "—Holden, ASAP."

Captain Sand looked at Brim and jerked a thumb toward the door. "Let's go, Sergeant Brim."

Jacob smiled. "Yes, ma'am."

HELMAND DESERT
HALL
THE CHAOS MARCH
5 MARCH 3067

As the fake Tigers approached, Ezra Payne knew they weren't amateurs. Their missile boats halted atop hillocks just out of range and began laying down synchronized barrages to cover the advance of the lighter, faster 'Mechs toward the Disinherited lines.

"Let 'em close," Nathalie Ortiz ordered.

The Disinherited had detached two of their companies to face the marauders. The remainder were clustered around the noncombatant vehicles and the battered but bristling 'Mechs and tanks of Burton's Brigade, which were all crabbing away from the action as fast as they could. Ezra would have concentrated his forces more, but he knew it was a coin toss. Ortiz's mission wasn't necessarily to destroy the marauders—it was to protect the convoy. If she could distract the attackers long enough for the rest to escape, she accomplished her mission.

Ezra wasn't even ashamed that he didn't much care about the fate of the convoy just then. He wanted these marauders' *blood.* They'd impugned the honor of his regiment, and he would know the reason why.

Elly Burton had protested—vociferously—at being excluded, but had relented under Major Fletcher's pressure. Burton's Brigade had never fought alongside the Hellraisers, and a sudden attack was not the time to start.

Ezra hadn't pointed out that his Tigers hadn't fought with the Disinherited, either. But he had something Captain Burton lacked: a good relationship with Captain Ortiz.

"We'll be your backstop," Ezra said. "We'll snipe where we can, but—" He raised the *Crusader*'s blocky arms, brandishing the bulky MRM-30 pods built around its wrists. "—anyone who gets close will have a warm reception."

"Works," Ortiz said. Her voice was tight with tension, but her *Dervish* moved with sure-footed certainty. Ezra's eye caught the combat medal designators again. He wished he'd had a chance to look up what they meant. Maybe after the battle he'd get a chance to ask Nathalie.

He grinned. If they were both still alive, of course.

Missile fell a few hundred meters in front of them. Two lances of Disinherited medium 'Mechs broke ranks and dashed forward, hoping to blunt the marauders' attack before they got into range. That put them almost inside the missile storm, but not quite, and they were quite fast for their weight. Speed made for a difficult missile target.

"Not bad," Hicks muttered.

"Not at all," Ezra said. "Make sure your recorders are getting the full take. I want to be able to go over this all with a fine screen back at Bravo Base."

"I wonder why they're not answering," Roses said.

"Maybe they were attacked there as well," Akhtar said.

"Maybe," Ezra said. "We'll find out later. Concentrate on your zones."

The hammering sound of autocannon fire and the crackle of particle projector cannons echoed back from the next arroyo. Ezra licked his lips and flexed his hands on the *Crusader*'s controls. Fresh coolant shivered through his cooling vest, raising goosebumps on his exposed forearms.

Chatter from the Hellraisers' tactical channel blended into a miasma of background noise in the *Crusader*'s cockpit. He had his comm set to receive the Disinherited's transmissions, but send only to his Jaguar Lance. He had to manually key his throat mic to transmit on the Disinherited's channels.

"Doesn't matter what they look like," he told his MechWarriors, "they aren't Tigers. They come at you, you burn 'em down."

"Sixty-eight," Hicks replied instantly.

"Got it," Akhtar said.

"Rog—er, sixty-eight, Six," Roses said.

Ezra smiled. She was trying hard to learn from all of them—even Hicks.

The first marauder 'Mech Ezra saw was a gangly *Clint*. Up close it was instantly obvious they were not Stealthy Tigers. The colors were the same browns and tans the Tiger wore as desert camouflage, but the pattern was all wrong. The marauder 'Mechs were awash with soft angles, as if the paint had been applied by hand. The Tigers used a machine-painted cross-hatch pattern that was so different it might as well have been made from a different color palette.

The *Clint* climbed up the arroyo and, to the MechWarrior's credit, didn't pause at the sight of better than a company of enemy 'Mechs moving across the wide plain toward it. Ortiz had placed her 'Mechs on the far edge of an extra-wide series of arroyos—the "hallway" here was almost a half-kilometer wide. The *Clint* drove down the far side. Ezra knew from experience with the Tigers' own *Clint*s that the MechWarrior must have his throttle jammed to the gate.

"Contact," Akhtar said unnecessarily.

"Shoot," Ezra said.

Akhtar's *Grand Dragon* shifted position a few meters to the left, leveled its right arm, and fired. The actinic brilliance of the PPC was like lightning in the daytime—bright, sudden, and more afterimage than anything else. PPCs were heat and kinetic energy weapons: accelerators tugged a few ions loose of a packet and accelerated them nearly to light speed. The resulting plasma caused horrendous damage, even against 'Mech armor, but the cost in heat and energy was ruinous. Ezra knew Akhtar would be gasping in his cockpit after only a few shots.

Watching the *Clint* get hit, Ezra was forced to admit the cost was worth it.

The shot nailed the forty-ton 'Mech high in the left shoulder, punching through the armor there and amputating its entire left arm. The multi-ton limb fell to the ground in a cloud of sparking dust, and the *Clint* lurched to the right, off-balanced by the loss of mass. The MechWarrior kept the 'Mech upright and moving, but it curved immediately back the way it had come. The flight of long-range missiles Akhtar fired fell short. The LRMs cratered the desert floor, but that was it.

"Nice shot," Ezra said.

The *Grand Dragon* raised its PPC in acknowledgement.

More marauder 'Mechs appeared over the lip—many more. They broke to either side, as if hoping to get around the lined-up defenders. Ezra frowned as he watched them, then looked down. On his display, the marauder missile-armed 'Mechs were advancing, ignoring the sniping of the forward Hellraisers to close the range with the main body.

"What the hell?" he whispered.

Ortiz snapped out orders, and the Disinherited line came apart and split in two, each trying to blunt the advance of the marauders on the flank. Ezra held his lance where it was, in the center, the better able to support in either direction or—worst case—blunt a third attack right up the middle.

"What your enemy can *do, not what he* might *do,"* Halleck's voice said in his head.

The Disinherited 'Mechs began firing at the sprinting marauders. LRMs fell among and around them, blasting dirt or armor as they fell. Light autocannon, twenty and forty millimeter, began pecking at the enemy 'Mech's armor. Extended-range large lasers and PPCs flickered at them. Some of the 'Mechs took damage, but most of them didn't. The marauders were moving too fast, and there were too many.

"They need to concentrate their fire," Hicks said. Ezra had been thinking the same thing, and said so.

"Of course you are, Six," Hicks said. "It's the first thing the colonel taught us, wasn't it?"

Ezra grinned. It almost was. He turned the *Crusader* to the left, in the direction Nathalie Ortiz had gone, and touched his throttle, but just as he was about to push it forward, a trio of new 'Mechs appeared in front of him. He lurched the *Crusader* back around swallowed, then touched his throat mike.

"Hellraiser Six," he said, forgetting Ortiz's handle, "Jaguar Six. Three 'Mechs moving up the center."

"Deal with them," Ortiz snapped. Missile exhaust roared in

the background of her transmission; she was firing her *Dervish*'s LRMs.

"Roger" he said, and put both hands on his controls. "Jaguars, these three are ours."

"Joy," Hicks said. Her *Centurion* lurched into motion, spitting LRMs at the lead 'Mech.

Ezra worked his jaw and examined his sensors. Though there were only three, the new arrivals almost outmassed his four-'Mech lance. The leader was an eighty-ton *Salamander*, an assault-class missile boat that fired as many long-range missiles as Ezra's *Crusader* could medium-range. Beside it was a decrepit-looking *Orion*, seventy-five tons of fighting 'Mech, and on the other side a beat-up ninety-five ton *Banshee*.

Hicks' LRMs spiraled toward the *Salamander*, but the brown-painted 'Mech ignored the paltry flight and settled its feet into a stable firing platform. Twisting slightly, it disappeared in missile smoke. Ezra's experienced eye tracked the missiles and looked ahead of them—right at Jessica Roses' *Hatchetman*.

"Roses, *move!*"

Just like on the hilltop a little while earlier, Roses didn't hesitate. She kicked her jump jets and sent the *Hatchetman* leaping ninety meters to the left. It was a virtuoso display of reflexes, but it wasn't enough. A third of the *Salamander*'s incredible barrage tagged the *Hatchetman* while it was in flight, smashing armor and nearly sending the 'Mech to the ground.

Ezra dragged his crosshairs across the *Salamander*'s wide shape, but they refused to change to the solid gold of a target lock. He was too far away. His thumb smashed the *Crusader*'s throttle forward. He leaned into the run, the 'Mech's acceleration pushing him back into his padded couch.

Akhtar fired past him. Ten LRMs, nearly identical to Hicks' fire, fell out of the sky to crater the *Salamander*'s armor, but the PPC bolt spent itself on the desert floor between the *Salamander*'s legs. Had the 'Mech been a man, hot sand fused to glass and exploding off the floor with the pressure of high explosive would have flayed its legs.

Against 'Mech armor, the sand merely scraped or stuck.

Roses was staggering, but she was still on her feet. Ezra nodded quickly and looked at his rangefinder.

'Mech missiles came in three range classes: short, medium and long. LRMs traded warhead for fuel capacity—they were usually fired in thicker barrages, with more rudimentary guidance. Short-range missiles were more powerful, with better seekers, but much smaller salvos. A LRM launcher might fire as many as twenty missiles in a single push of a button. The smallest SRM launcher fired a paltry two missiles.

MRMs, like those in the large magazine buried in the *Crusader*'s left chest, were a bastardized attempt to get the best of both worlds. Their guidance was little more than stabilization; more than a rocket, but not a great deal more. Their warheads were no more powerful than an LRM's, and not as powerful as an SRM's.

But they were smaller. An LRM warhead on a missile roughly half the size. So where one of the *Salamander*'s LRM-20s fired twenty missiles, each of the gauntlet-mounted MRM-30s in the *Crusader*'s arms fired thirty.

A *Salamander* could loft sixty LRMs from its eighty tons.

Ezra's *Crusader* could loft sixty MRMs.

From only sixty-five tons.

The range fell past the arbitrary limit of the MRM's guidance systems. A beeping tone in Ezra's neurohelmet told him the missiles' warheads were seeking, and when it switched to a solid tone, he squeezed the trigger. His view was immediately blocked by smoke and flame, and the backblast shook the *Crusader* like a rag doll.

Ezra snarled through it all.

See how you like a missile storm, you prick, he thought at the *Salamander*'s pilot.

"*Salamander* is the primary target," he sent on the lance channel.

"Got it, Six," Roses said. "I owe him."

Akhtar and Hicks merely double-clicked their mics.

Moving at nearly sixty kilometers per hour, the *Crusader* ran out of its own smoke cloud in only a second or two, just in time for its sensors to drink in the missile impacts blasting across the *Salamander*'s armor.

The assault 'Mech staggered under the onslaught. It took two steps, three. Then its foot came down on a small, two-meter rock, and turned its blocky ankle. The MechWarrior at the controls threw out its left arm to break its fall, but the *Salamander* still crashed down.

"Hi there," Ezra muttered.

"Nice shooting, Six!" Roses called.

"Keep hitting it while it's down," Ezra said. "I only tripped him up."

Roses took his order to heart. The *Hatchetman* was a new BattleMech, as 'Mech models went. Introduced shortly before the Fourth Succession War, the recovery of Star League-era technology during the Clan Invasion had heralded a number of production versions. Hers carried a 100-millimeter Ultra-class autocannon, and she held down the trigger. The big cannon *slam-slam-slammed* through a double-cassette round of ammunition, hammering the struggling *Salamander*'s armor.

The scintillating brilliance of Akhtar's PPC stabbed in beneath the *Salamander*'s right armpit, scoring the thick armor there, and a flight of LRMs from Hicks' *Centurion* fell into the same spot.

If the *Salamander* had been a man, it would have just taken a near-fatal punch to the kidneys. But of course, it wasn't a man.

The *Banshee* stepped in front of the struggling 'Mech, flame belching from its waist-mounted autocannon. Ezra blinked, checked his computer, then laughed. The *Banshee* was a Third Succession War-era model, with only a paltry autocannon and a single PPC for armament. Roses' *Hatchetman* almost matched it for firepower, at half the mass.

The *Orion* reached down, hooked one of its handless arms under the *Salamander*'s arm, and helped pull it upright.

A *ker-chunk* and a chime announced the MRMs' reloading cycle complete.

Smoke obscured Ezra's vision, and a surge of heat washed over his cockpit, but he smiled a wolf's smile while centering his crosshairs and firing both launchers again.

"We break from our continuing coverage of the fighting in the Helmand to release this statement, received by our Rockfall Maze bureau just a few minutes ago. It arrived from the offices of the late Count Radcliffe McNally, and is from Captain Elly Burton, the count's mercenary lover."

"*Today, I have accepted the invitation of Colonel Marik-Johns and the Dismal Disinherited to join Burton's Brigade to the Allied Mercenary Command. Every free citizen of Hall knows Bud Baranov couldn't have gathered the army he has without help, and that help couldn't have come from anywhere except the Word of Blake. Together with Wolf's Dragoons, the Dismal Disinherited, and every other AMC member-unit, Burton's Brigade calls upon the so-called emperor to relinquish his tyrannical throne and eject the Word of Blake from the internal politics of Hall.*"

"No official comment has been made by the emperor's press office, but the unofficial reaction is one of amusement. We now return you to our ongoing coverage of the conflict in the Helmand."

– From the *Harney Morning Edition*,
Harney HV Channel Six

CHAPTER EIGHT

The second missile barrage blasted the *Salamander*'s armor again, but this time the MechWarrior was ready for it. He rolled with the explosions and stepped clear of the cloud of smoke and fire, launchers leveled. Ezra's eyes widened as the eighty-ton 'Mech disappeared beneath its own pall of missile exhaust.

He jerked his controls to the side, but was only partially successful. At least a score of missiles struck the *Crusader*, the explosions like hammers against its armor. Only the sound dampening built into the neurohelmet saved his hearing. Like the *Salamander* jock, he'd had time to brace himself, so the impacts didn't knock him over, but they did push him off-balance for several steps. Unconsciously, he spread the *Crusader*'s arms to regain its equilibrium.

The rest of his lance was still moving and firing, but the *Banshee* remained stubbornly near the *Salamander*. The *Orion* was moving away, however, trying to force the Stealthy Tiger lance to split its fire. Ezra glanced at his map display and then back at the *Salamander*. *If we could just put that bastard down, this would be easy.*

In the ordinary course of events, with heavy forces attacking and nothing of importance behind him for several kilometers, Ezra would be giving ground. He'd be using his two LRM-equipped 'Mechs—and Akhtar's PPC—to deadly effect, and relying on his own MRMs to keep the marauders from rushing them.

But the *Salamander* made that plan suicide. With its heavy LRM batteries and deep ammunition magazines, it could pound his Jaguar Lance to scrap before they got more than a kilometer back. And . . .

A flight of missiles from the *Orion* smashed into the *Crusader*'s armor. Ezra had spotted them coming from the corner of his eye, too late to evade, but they were still loud, and it was still high explosive pecking at the armor that protected him.

Staying close enough to hurt the *Salamander* meant that his lance had to stay within range of the other two marauder 'Mechs.

No, these people weren't amateurs at all.

"Back off?" Akhtar asked.

"We can't," Ezra said.

"The *Sally*?" Hicks said.

"Yeah."

"Best we do something about it, then." Hicks' *Centurion* reversed its course. It had been running flat-out, angling away from the skirmish as if it intended to do an end-run around the marauder trio's flank. Now she spun the fifty-ton 'Mech on its heel and came back, arm-mounted LB-10X autocannon leveling as missiles roared from the *Centurion*'s chest launcher.

A few steps later, her autocannon boomed.

Once.

Unlike regular autocannons, which fed shells into the breech at a variable rate and fired off "cassette" rounds of pre-counted ammunition, an LB-X cannon fired a giant, 'Mech-scale shotgun shell of discarding-sabot tungsten penetrators.

Neon-colored sparks rippled across the *Salamander*'s torso as a few of the sub-munitions ricocheted, but the scatter of armor plates that fell to the ground at the *Salamander*'s feet told of some hits. The *Salamander*'s head swiveled to follow the *Centurion*'s path.

Before it could return fire, Akhtar slammed a PPC shot dead-center into its chest, rocking the eighty-ton 'Mech backward.

Roses fired her own autocannon, this time on its regular rate of fire. The metronomic *boom-boom-boom* of the automatic loader hammered reports across the valley. Ezra watched the *Salamander* step backward. He drew his lips back from his teeth in triumph.

That's right, you run away.

"Keep hitting him!"

The MRMs chimed ready, but the range had fallen below 200 meters. The *Orion* was still edging around the side. Ezra leveled the *Crusader*'s arms and burned the heavy 'Mech with both medium lasers. The red beams did little damage, but they reminded the *Orion*'s MechWarrior that Ezra was watching him.

He was more reminded when Roses' *Hatchetman* fell out of the sky on flaming jump jets, rose out of its crouch, and buried its three-ton, depleted uranium-edged, 'Mech-sized hatchet in the *Orion*'s belly. The seventy-five ton 'Mech folded around the blow, not falling, but not quite upright either.

Roses stepped away and then dashed, opening the range.

Ezra nodded again. *Girl's got Raider potential.* She used her advantages, but didn't linger. With thirty more tons of mass, the *Orion* more than overcame the *Hatchetman*'s ax advantage. Roses would have been stupid to stay close enough for the *Orion* to cripple her 'Mech with a well-placed kick.

Across the field, a Disinherited *Battle Hawk* disappeared in the white-flash explosion of a fusion engine letting go. The explosion was notable through the *Crusader*'s canopy; Ezra didn't need the HUD's caret to find it. Two marauder 'Mechs fell at the same time, knocked down by the shockwave, but quickly regained their feet.

"We need to end this," he told his lance.

He turned the *Crusader* back toward the *Salamander*. Another missile storm erupted from its launchers, but the pilot must have been rattled. He'd aimed at Hicks' *Centurion*, but her 'Mech was moving just a hair under a hundred kilometers per hour; a few of the warheads tagged its side and arm, but most fell behind the speeding machine.

Still spreading your fire. Ezra checked his magazine status and looked at the *Salamander*. That 'Mech had the mass for deep magazines; his *Crusader* didn't. If he unloaded on the assault 'Mech again, he'd have shot off half his missiles. A flick of the eyes in either direction told him the Disinherited were still engaged on both flanks. He decided with a Gallic shrug. *I don't get paid to bring missiles back.*

This time Ezra sequenced his launches a second or two apart, first the left-arm launcher, then the right-arm. The smoke was less this time, and he was able to refine his aim in a split-second before the right-arm launcher fired.

The *Salamander* toppled. Sparks shot from its ruined knee actuator, and its left arm hung limply from the elbow. Akhtar's PPC dug into the dust cloud where the 'Mech fell, but Ezra couldn't see where the shot landed. Gasping at the heat flare in his cockpit, he looked around for the other two marauder 'Mechs.

Both were walking slowly backward, still firing.

"I want the *Orion* down," he said.

Double-clicks answered him. Ezra turned the *Crusader* that way. The 'Mech's frame rippled as the missile reloads trundled through their loading tubes toward the multi-tube launchers. He looked a little more closely at the flanks.

The marauders were falling back there, too. Several Disinherited 'Mechs were down, but more of the marauders were. Ezra looked for and found Ortiz's *Dervish*, still moving and firing. He felt better for seeing it, though he didn't have time to think about why.

The *Orion* seemed to have heard his order to take it down. The seventy-five ton 'Mech turned its LRMs on him, rocking the *Crusader* with impacts. Alarms clamored to life as the protection on his 'Mech's left arm and side dropped below fifty percent. Ezra frowned and brought the 'Mech's arms up. The range was long, but light was free . . . he triggered his medium lasers again.

Both shots missed.

Ezra rolled his eyes and kept chasing the *Orion*. His feet put random shifts into the *Crusader*'s steps without thinking about it. That might throw off his opponent's aim.

"Be interesting to learn where these boys came from," Hicks said. "And where they got our IFF codes."

"It will," Ezra agreed. The thought made him stare at the *Orion*, and impatience suddenly overtook him. He centered the crosshairs on the blocky 'Mech's chest and unloaded both MRM launchers at it, ammunition reserves be damned.

The battle was largely decided, though it would most likely continue for another hour at least. It was just a matter of how far the Hellraisers wanted to pursue the marauder 'Mechs before they gave up.

That meant the time for answers was quickly approaching.

8 KILOMETERS OUTSIDE HOLDEN
HALL
THE CHAOS MARCH
5 MARCH 3067

As the hovercraft dropped a meter off one of the low hills for the hundredth time, Jacob Brim cringed as much as his restraints would allow before the seat slammed him in the tailbone again. The armored hover APC flew over steel skirts, but the impact of those skirts slamming into the ground before the lift fans gathered enough air to fill the plenum chamber again was always painful.

He heard a chuckle in his headset, and looked up. Rudi Carlsson sat across from him, wearing a combat harness, body armor, and a vehicle crewman's headset identical to Jacob's.

"What?" Jacob asked.

"You Sevens," Carlsson said, grinning. "Always flying around in your comfy VTOLs, wearing your fitted combat armor. This is slumming for you, isn't it?"

Jacob grinned and nodded. "Where's the espresso machine?" Then he looked toward the front of the fighting compartment, where the other members of the Wolfnet team were sitting in identical gear and headsets.

Carlsson followed his gaze, then looked at him and waggled his eyebrows. "Could be worse," he yelled, covering his mic with his hand so his words wouldn't be transmitted. "You could be one of them."

"Some of us *like* sitting behind a desk, Rudi," Gallifrey shouted without opening his eyes. Jacob looked at him and laughed.

The clamor in the fighting compartment was loud and constant. The lift fans whined at different pitches, and the drive fans overhead pushed the APC at its max speed to keep up with the hovertank escorts. Dragoons infantry was no stranger to hover APCs, not even the elite of Seventh Kommando. But no one enjoyed being in the vibrating box.

You could get used to it, like Gallifrey obviously had. But no one *liked* it.

"Sergeant?" an unfamiliar voice asked in his headset. Jacob frowned and looked toward the front. It was the vehicle commander. "The captain would like a word."

"Go."

There was a brief electronic chirp and then background noise. "Brim?"

"Here."

"We're getting close."

"Thank the gods."

"How do you want to play this?"

Jacob frowned. He glanced at Carlsson and pointed to his headset. Carlsson nodded—he was hearing the conversation.

"Standard base assault," he told the Hellraiser armor officer. "Me and my boys will go in once you've made a breach."

"So you and your technicians aren't going to do this for us, running screaming at a 'Mech base with assault rifles?"

"Is that an official request?" Jacob asked.

"No," Captain Sand said dryly. "I just wanted to make sure you weren't going to say something stupid like 'Try not to shoot it up too much.'"

"You shoot all you want," Jacob said. "I don't want to get my clothes dirty with all that fighting stuff."

"Wouldn't hear of it," Sand said. The line clicked closed.

Jacob met Carlsson's eyes. "I think she likes you," the Dragoon said.

Jacob laughed. "Not my type."

"Smart?"

Jacob snorted. "Yeah." He reached into the small pack strapped onto his chest, pulled out a noteputer, and held it up. "Go over the map?" Carlsson pulled an identical 'puter out and touched the synch control. Jacob's screen lit up. Carlsson's would be showing the same image.

The map had been made from an old planetary map and up-dated with imagery captured during the sole satellite's overhead pass. It was grainy and incomplete, but it showed the layout of the base, the shape of the buildings, and the surrounding terrain. Jacob zoomed out until he could see ten kilometers in every di-rection around the base, then tapped a nav point into place on the northeast corner.

"We should be coming from here. If the good captain does her job like I think she will, she'll scream with her tanks straight across the base in a thunder run and see what she can scare up." He drew a circle around the entire base. "None of our maps show fortifica-tions, but there's nothing saying these people haven't put in mines or antipersonnel bunkers. Those wouldn't show on this map."

Carlsson nodded. He touched his own screen; the locations sprang to life as green blotches on Jacob's screen. "'Mech han-gars," he said, highlighting the buildings. "This looks like an am-munition bunker." He touched another spot. "This is either a tech shop or a commissary."

Jacob grinned. "Liao forward operating base, 2995 field man-ual, border world, one each," he said. In the last century, the Liao war machine had been woefully inadequate to defend the Capellan

Confederation worlds from its enemies in the Free Worlds League and the Federated Suns. The Capellan Confederation Armed Forces had taken a page from history and invested in infrastructure wherever they could, building empty hosting bases like this one all along their border. Each planet might not have the capacity to build and maintain BattleMechs, but concrete and steel were within the reach of almost any world worthy of being a Confederation member.

The basic blueprint of such a basis had been generated by the Capellan general staff, the Strategios, and circulated across the Confederation. Wolfnet had captured copies almost on their first mission in the Inner Sphere, all the way back in 3007. This wasn't the first time any of the Dragoons had seen a base laid out this way.

"I wish the overheads were better," Carlsson muttered. "I can't get a feel for traffic."

The pitch of the APC's drive fans changed, and inertia pushed Jacob against his restraints as the hovercraft slewed into a turn. "I think we'll find out soon enough."

An alarm light started blinking on the bulkhead over the rear egress ramp. "We just got swept by active sensors," the vehicle commander said over the intercom. "They know we're coming."

Jacob shut the noteputer off and slid it back into its pocket on his harness. Then he reached into the frame between his knees and drew the Ceres Arms Striker carbine he'd secured there when he sat down. It was the work of a few seconds to attach it to the integral recoil sling on his body armor and seat two of the big drum magazines that fed it.

Carlsson, doing the same with the Federated Long Rifle he preferred, stared at the Capellan weapon. "You shooting 'Mechs with that?"

Jacob smiled and brandished the heavy weapon. "We might be clearing buildings. I wanted the right tool for the job."

"Sixty-round mags? Glad I'm not carrying it."

Jacob smiled and looked at the egress hatch. If all went according to plan, he'd never have to fire his weapon. None of the Dragoons would. The Hellraisers would clear the base and secure any resistance, and the Dragoons would go in to sift the systems for evidence of Blakist involvement. Gallifrey and Carillo carried weapons, but their packs were full of computers preset to crack secure databases and do targeted searches.

Dooley, the accountant, had stayed behind in Brampton. Two hours in a hovercraft wouldn't have made him any more effective.

Jacob worked his hands on the Striker's grips. His thumb touched the selector switch that controlled the weapon's rate of fire. It was set on three-round burst, but his thumb ticked it back and forth between three-round and full-auto.

He shouldn't have to do any shooting.

But he was damn sure ready if he did.

HARNEY HALL
THE CHAOS MARCH
5 MARCH 3067

Adele Estwicke looked up from the screen at the chirp from Jurowicz's console.

She had been watching rebroadcast feeds of the skirmish in the desert, clicking back and forth through the pirated data feeds they were stealing from the Dismal Disinherited's own satellite. The Sixth of June's money had been well spent, but there was no chance that the marauders they'd purchased were going to accomplish the task they'd been assigned.

Still . . . the event would pay dividends. Estwicke had been investing time and, more importantly, data in this band of 'Mechs in preparation for just this sort of eventuality.

Jurowicz leaned forward, read the message, and then half-turned in her chair. "Sensors at Holden show incoming hovercraft."

Estwicke rose and walked over to the console. She leaned over Jurowicz's shoulder, one hand on the seat back and the other on the console. "Pull up the cameras?"

Jurowicz worked for a second. A holo appeared over the console a moment later. The battered bow of a Condor heavy hovertank painted in mottled gray appeared. While the two women watched, the heavy barrel of its autocannon tracked toward the camera and belched flame. The holo fell into static and disappeared.

"Dismal Ds," Estwicke murmured.

"They have armor with them," Jurowicz said. "And their 'Mechs are out in the desert, shooting."

Estwicke nodded. "Are we sterile at Holden?" The other woman nodded. "You're sure?"

"I oversaw the vacuum myself," the acolyte said. "There's a ton of evidence for the Ridziks there. It should make Baranov paranoid, if he recovers it. They've been dead for years, but they never found Nikoli's body. If the AMC gets that data, it'll send them down the rabbit hole. None of it points anywhere near Terra."

Estwicke nodded. "Perfect." She straightened up. "What have you got for me on the accounts?"

"Still digging."

Estwicke went back to her desk. "Dig faster."

She needed to understand the Sixth's presence on Hall, and why they were active now. Had they arrived with the Dismal Ds? The timing was certainly suggestive, but that seemed too obvious for the Sixth of June. But if not them, then who? One of the Tigers mercenaries? They'd been on-world for most of a year. Why wait so long to activate?

And if they weren't with the mercenaries, when had they come, and what did they want? The Sixth of June and the True Believers differed on methods, but they agreed on the ultimate goal: Hall would be brought into the Word of Blake Protectorate, another step on the path to bringing the entire Inner Sphere under the enlightenment of Jerome Blake's words. Undermining the years of work the True Believers—Estwicke—had put into achieving that did nothing for their ultimate objective.

Is this Cameron St. Jamais working against Blane, or something else?

Sitting down, Estwicke looked at the image she'd been staring at before Jurowicz had distracted her. It was one of the mercenary dossiers. Kirsten Markoja, a major in the Stealthy Tigers.

There was something about her.

Estwicke frowned.

The eyes were wrong, and the cheeks, and the skin color. The hair. But Estwicke knew how to change those as well as any intelligence agent. It was difficult to judge a stock photo against the living memory of a person.

"While you're digging," Estwicke said to Jurowicz, "get me any HV you can of Major Kirsten Markoja of the Stealthy Tigers."

"Fragmented reports from the south suggest the Stealthy Tigers might be present on both sides of the fighting. We sent a team to Fort Decker, where the emperor has allowed the Tigers to lease basing space, but haven't heard back yet. Military analysts suggest there is powerful radio jamming emanating from Fort Decker—jamming that could be hiding the first stages of a secondary attack from there.

"The emperor's office continues to refuse to comment on ongoing operations, but former Leftenant Harold Nadal, our local military analyst, believes the jamming to be the work of the Stealthy Tigers. *"It's some kind of* maskirovka," he says, *"to use the old Capellan term. When that jamming comes down, look for 'Mechs to be moving out from under it."*

– From the *Harney Morning Edition,*
Harney HV Channel Six

CHAPTER NINE

The impact when the *Crusader*'s foot struck the *Orion*'s shin was tremendous. Ezra clutched his controls and leaned, spreading the 'Mech's arms for balance, doing all he could to help his neurohelmet and the 'Mech's DI computer keep its sixty-five tons upright. He succeeded, but the resulting stagger took him a few steps away from the *Orion*.

Which was good, because Hicks' *Centurion* hit the marauder 'Mech like a giant linebacker—shoulder down and moving over ninety kph—a few seconds later. Ezra heard the impact through his cockpit sound dampening, and even his helmet protection. The booming *clang* shook the desert floor.

The *Orion* staggered backward and flopped down. The *Centurion* caromed off the larger 'Mech and skidded to a stop on its right side. Hicks was immediately working the battered 'Mech to its feet, though.

The *Orion* didn't move.

Ezra steadied up and looked around. The *Banshee* was already half-over the arroyo wall where it had come from, and when he looked left he saw a lance of medium Disinherited 'Mechs charging toward it. The rest of the Dismal D force from that direction was headed back toward the Stealthy Tiger lance, except for a few 'Mechs standing with the characteristic look of machines on standby while their MechWarriors dismounted.

A beat-up *Dervish* was in the lead.

"Captain Payne, you all right?" Nathalie Ortiz sent.

Ezra looked around. All four of his 'Mechs were still moving, though they'd all need significant time in the repair bays. Roses' *Hatchetman* and his own *Crusader* had taken scores, if not hundreds of missile hits. Hicks' *Centurion* was limping, and its left arm hung off-center. Akhtar's *Grand Dragon* looked the best, but it had taken several hits from the *Banshee*'s PPC before it broke off.

"Yeah," he replied. "You?"

"Some people down," she said. "A lot more of them down."

"Any idea who they are?"

"Not yet. We have some prisoners." The *Dervish* reached his *Crusader* and stopped. Together, the two 'Mechs looked around the field. The *Salamander* lay smoking a hundred or so meters away, the *Orion* a little nearer. "Looks like you had some fun here."

"A little."

"Better than Caph?"

Ezra swallowed. His hands were suddenly icy. "Easier, for sure." He stared at the *Orion*. "I want to know where they came from, and how they got our IFF."

"We might know soon," Ortiz said.

"Prisoners?"

"No, we've got a hovertank company going into their base about now," she replied.

"How the hell do you know where they came from already?"

"Our pet Dragoons found them in satellite footage. While we've been out here, they sent a flying column toward their base. A little place called Holden, I think they said. An old Capellan facility."

Ezra looked around. The sounds of combat still echoed out of the arroyos in front of them. An errant missile shot almost straight up and disappeared into the distant sky. A blinding column of white and gray told of another fusion engine cutting loose.

"Any of them surrender?" he asked.

"None of them."

"Strange."

"Makes me think they're not mercenaries," Ortiz said. "We don't usually fight past the point of good sense. Probably find they're locals, pissed at Burton for some reason. Or maybe some of the count's old people, trying to get to you."

Ezra grunted. Ortiz might be right. There were a lot of factions on Hall, and while two companies was a big gathering of 'Mechs, it wasn't impossible that someone could have put it together for a big mission.

A *big* mission, though. What in this convoy would have rated that level of firepower? If McNally had been able to gather that much force during the lean years before the Stealthy Tigers arrived on Hall, he might have been the one to offer them a contract to destroy Baranov. Most of the noblemen across Hall could only claim a 'Mech or two, and the larger, more prosperous countries could muster a lance or, at best, a company.

Hell, he thought. *Burton's Brigade has survived here for a decade, and they're only a company.*

So where the hell had two companies of 'Mechs come from?

"Are you headed back with the convoy," he asked after a minute, "or going to this Holden place?"

The *Dervish* pointed toward the fighting. "I'm going to see to running these people down. If they're not giving up, they can't be allowed to break contact and catch our people in Holden in the back." The 'Mech lowered its arm and turned. "You can come with us, or you can try and catch up with the convoy. I'm sending my cripples in that direction once I get my prisoners secure."

Ezra looked off into the desert in the direction they'd been heading. The convoy was too far away to see, of course, but he could see who was there. Fletcher. Burton. "We'll go with you."

The *Dervish* stepped off. "Let's go, then."

Ezra followed. After a few steps he frowned. "Wait—you're in commo with Brampton?"

"Of course."

"Then—" he stopped. "That's good. I may ask you to relay a report in a few minutes."

"You can't raise your people?"

"Not so far. I'm going to give it another try."

"Okay."

Ezra touched his mic and closed the Disinherited channel. "Everyone try to contact Bravo Base," he said. He keyed the *Crusader*'s transmitter back onto the emergency frequency. "Jaguar Six to Bravo, come in."

Nothing.

He kept trying, with the same result. The others reported the same results a few minutes later.

"Keep trying," he told them.

His hands were cold, despite the heat. He couldn't think of

any situation that would keep the duty officer at Bravo Base from answering emergency calls. If there was anyone at the desk, standing orders *required* it.

So either they weren't getting through—or there was no one at the desk.

The sounds of fighting got louder as the *Crusader* crested the first hillock. He caught a glimpse of a Hellraisers *Wolfhound* dropping down the other side of the next one, lasers flashing, and he tried to put thoughts of Bravo Base out of his mind.

Whatever was wrong there would keep.

He needed to concentrate on here, just now.

HOLDEN
HALL
THE CHAOS MARCH
5 MARCH 3067

"This doesn't make any sense," Jacob Brim muttered.

He stood in the center of the main 'Mech hangar in the Holden facility, hands on his hips, and looked around. All of the twenty-four bays in the cavernous building showed signs of recent use. Some had fresh scrapes on the ferrocrete floors, or stank with the stench of fresh lubricant. Ammunition crates were empty and discarded. The place had every indication of a bustling, active service base.

Except no one was here.

Oh, they'd taken some prisoners. Technicians and vehicle mechanics, all very old or very young. Sons and daughters, fathers and mothers. All claiming to be a part of the Free Army of the Republic. Which was stupid, because that army had been destroyed years ago. It was one of the first things Baranov had done after putting down the rebellion inside his own ranks, before he turned his full attention to McNally's coalition.

"Jake," Rudi Carlsson called, making him look up. Carlsson trotted up and held out a scrap of paper. It was the bottom of an authorization form, some kind of purchase order. Jacob couldn't tell what because the top half was missing. "The signature."

Jacob looked. There was a scrawl with several prominent letters, an N at the beginning of the first name and an R to begin the second. The full name was printed beneath: *Nikoli Ridzik*.

"There's no way," Jacob said.

"They all swear it's him."

Jacob slipped the paper into a pocket and stared at his second-in-command. "Think about it, Rudi. There's no way."

Carlsson shrugged. "I'm just showing you the paper."

"What're Gallifrey and Carillo saying?"

"Nothing, yet. They're still getting hooked up." Carlsson nodded and trotted back toward the office where the techs were connecting their gear.

Jacob looked around. His mind worked, trying to fit the puzzle pieces together, but it just wasn't happening. Holden was too close to Harney, to Deal. Two companies of 'Mechs was too powerful a force. There was just no way.

Pavel Ridzik had been a brilliant military commander in the Capellan Confederation a generation earlier. He had risen to the post of strategic military director—the overall commander of the Confederation military—before being enticed away from the Confederation during the Fourth Succession War by House Davion intelligence agents. His defection and the subsequent creation of the short-lived Tikonov Free Republic cut the heart out of the Liao defenses in the Terran Corridor. His assassination had taken the wind out of the Free Republic's sails, though, and the Republic's citizens voted to join the Federated Commonwealth's Sarna March shortly after the war's end.

That same Sarna March had become the Chaos March twenty years later, and Yuri and Nikoli Ridzik, Pavel's twin sons, had been determined to resurrect their dead father's dream. The collapse of the Sarna March had given them and their loyalists the perfect opportunity to bring the old Free Republic back to life, and they'd led their burgeoning military to Hall, hoping to use it as the capital of their new republic.

It had been as laudable a goal as any the other independent worlds had had during the bad years of 3057 and 3058, but it had been doomed to fail. Baranov's spies had discovered the Ridzik brothers before the end of 3058, and he had crushed them beneath a tidal wave of 'Mechs and combat vehicles early in 3059. It had been one of Baranov's earliest victories. He'd parlayed it into a public relations coup on Hall, claiming he'd "maintained Hall's freedom in the face of dictators and tyrants."

Jacob looked around again. There was just no way that Nikoli Ridzik, even if he had survived the intervening years, could have built a force of the size and sophistication of the one that had attacked the Dismal D convoy without someone noticing.

It just wasn't possible.

But that's what the evidence said.

Captain Sand, the Disinherited armor officer, walked up to where Jacob was standing. "What's the story here, spook?"

Jacob looked at her. She had asked with a smile, so he swallowed the frustrated rebuttal and came to mind and smiled back. "I know it will surprise you to hear a spook admit this," he said, "but I have no clue."

"Only been here an hour," she said, looking around.

"The evidence says—that this was the last of the Free Army of the Tikonov Free Republic."

She looked at him. "The what of the who?"

"Exactly."

"Well," she told him, "my scouts have confirmed your data. This is where those 'Mechs came from. The regiment is busy running the rest of them to ground, and they're saying they got a couple of prisoners."

"Ridzik?" Jacob asked.

"No names, but it's possible. He was a MechWarrior?" Jacob nodded. "Then if he was still alive, and these were his 'Mechs, he could be one of the ones out there."

Jacob rubbed his hands together. "I just don't see it."

Captain Sand gestured toward the floor. "I've seen a lot of strange things on a lot of strange worlds," she told him. "You get used to it. If the evidence says it's true . . ."

"I know," he told her. "And I'm death on anyone trying to make claims based on preconceptions instead of data, but there's preconceptions, and then there's just plain logic." He shook his head. "We secure here, Captain? Are we holding this, or do we need to clear out before the bad guys get back?"

Sand shrugged. "I know Nathalie Ortiz," she said. "She'll run them to death in those canyons if anyone can. I think we can hold this place against anything that might slip past her. If you want to get back to Brampton and get interrogations going, though . . ." She raised an eyebrow.

"No," Jacob said, shaking his head. "I want to stay here, get into the data."

"Find out if it's fake?"

"Something like that."

"Well, keep your cannon there handy." Sand pointed at the Striker carbine resting against his chest. "I think we cleared it pretty good, but half the people here were dismounted tank crewmen who maybe know the small end of the gun is the dangerous one." Jacob tapped the Striker's receiver. "Oh, I will," he told her.

He looked around again as she walked away. Nothing she'd said had changed his mind. It just didn't make sense. But . . . he smiled. When something didn't make sense, that just meant there was something more to be found.

Inventing a cover with fabricated Ridzik evidence was just the sort of shell game the Word of Blake had already played on a half-dozen worlds. If that was what had happened here, he would find that evidence. And when he did, the AMC mission to Hall would be vindicated.

Across the hangar, a string of prisoners climbed aboard a Disinherited hover APC not unlike the one that had carried him here.

BRAVO BASE
HALL
THE CHAOS MARCH
5 MARCH 3067

The communications room at Bravo Base was small, well lit, and fit only a handful of people. It wasn't a meeting room; it was a working room. There were only two chairs, one for the officer manning the console and another for an assistant.

Kirsten Markoja sat in the assistant's chair with a noteputer in her lap. The officer on duty was Lieutenant Evan Ryan, one of her lance commanders.

Every screen on the wall console was blank or covered in static. Ryan held a handheld chrono. It beeped, he nodded, and looked at Markoja. "Duration testing complete, ma'am."

Kirsten looked up from her 'puter. "All good?"

"Within parameters, ma'am."

"Then let's shut it down," she told him. "I'm sure people want to use their radios again." She had been sitting with her feet up, but now she dropped them and keyed her noteputer off. Then she carefully held down a series of controls that activated a hidden wipe program, and disconnected the cord she'd plugged the noteputer in with to charge it. That cord she coiled and put in her pocket.

Ryan keyed the active jammers offline.

Alarms screamed to life.

Ryan flinched and lurched forward, touching controls and quieting alarms. Several lit back up as quickly as he turned them off. "I don't—" he stopped, squinting. "Loki's balls, ma'am," he said, "there's an alert call!"

Kirsten reached across the console and touched the general alarm before Ryan could. It was important she be the one—that she be *seen* to be the one, and *recorded* doing it—to trigger the alarm. A Klaxon screamed to life, and the emergency lighting began to flash all across Bravo Base. It was only a few seconds before the priority channel lit with an incoming call.

"Tiger Six," rasped Colonel Rauschenbusch. "Report."

"Leopard Six," Kirsten said, taking the call before Ryan could. "Sir, we're getting emergency calls from Captain Payne's lance in the Helmand. They started coming in as soon as we concluded the jamming test."

"Jamming test?"

"It was on the schedule, sir."

"You're telling me we've been *jamming* the whole time we had a lance out in the cold?"

"Colonel, the call—"

"What's it saying?"

Kirsten looked at Ryan. "Sir," the lieutenant said, "I've only got the last minute or so. It seems like there was a fight of some sort, and Captain Payne's lance won. They're still with the Dismal Ds, and they're moving toward some place called Holden."

There was silence on the line. When Rauschenbusch spoke again, it was clear he was controlling his temper. "We're going to get into this later. But for now, try and get Payne on the radio. I'll be there in two minutes." The line clicked closed.

Ryan looked at Kirsten, who shrugged and pointed toward the comm console. "Try and raise him."

"On it," he said. He slipped a headset on and began speaking quietly. He looked up when Kirsten stood up.

"I'm going to roust the battalion," she told him. "I'll send relief for you as soon as I can." Ryan nodded, but didn't stop talking.

Out in the corridor Tigers bustled past, some pulling on cooling vests, others dashing for duty stations. Kirsten had barely taken four steps before her burly brother appeared in front of her, waited until she caught up, and then turned to fall into step beside her.

"Did they get him?" Mason asked.

"No," Kirsten said.

"Damn."

"It's enough," she said. "For now."

"Are we good?"

"As good as we can be," Kirsten said. She reached the end of the corridor and stopped. Traffic continued moving around her and her brother, but that wasn't out of character. There was only one person in Bravo Base who could interrupt them, and he was busy worrying about Ezra bloody Payne.

"Right now, let's just play along," she told Mason. "We need to be out in front, making sure we're doing everything a Tigers officer would be doing when one of our lances is fighting in the desert 200 kilometers away."

Mason looked at her, then nodded. "Put on the show."

Kirsten restrained her sigh. "Yes. Put on the show." She didn't say that it didn't have to be entirely a show. It had been part of the plan all along to put Mason in command of the Tigers once Rauschenbusch retired or died. Being seen to care about the men and women under his command during a moment of crisis worked toward that goal.

Even if she *had* created the crisis in the first place.

"Go," she told him. "Get the Panthers up and into their 'Mechs. Make some noise about protecting our own. And wait for orders."

"Got it," Mason said, and turned toward Panther Battalion's 'Mech hangars. Kirsten turned the other way, toward the Leopard hangar.

No one saw her roll her eyes.

"The following address was given by General Tolliver, one of the emperor's senior military commanders, today:"

"The rumor mill claims that the forces destroyed in the desert last week by the Stealthy Tigers were a unit of the Army of the Free Tikonov Republic. That is false. The Tikonov Republic is relic of Hall's past, just like the Star League. Republican intelligence has determined that the force was a mercenary unit hired to disrupt the peaceful talks between the Allied Mercenary Command and the emperor's government. It was only the bravery and courage of the Stealthy Tigers, mercenaries whom the emperor brought to Hall to protect the people from the tyrant Mc-Nally, that prevented them from doing more damage."

"Already news outlets loyal to the late Count McNally are disputing the official record of events, but that is only to be expected."

– From the *Harney Morning Edition*,
Harney HV Channel Six

CHAPTER TEN

The man in the chair beneath the light was a MechWarrior, or at least he had been one. He was in his mid-thirties, with dirty brown hair and bad teeth. His skin was pasty white, almost green. His eyes were brown and bloodshot. From the stains, he'd been wearing those clothes for days. He'd been the pilot of the *Orion* Ezra and his lance had put down in the Helmand the previous week, in fact. Then he had been a competent, if not showy soldier.

Now he was just a man, looking scared, in a room by himself.

"None of this makes any sense," Jacob Brim said.

Ezra looked at him. He, Brim and Nathalie Ortiz were the only people in the small room that shared a wall—and a piece of mirrored transpex—with the room the prisoner was sitting in.

"You keep saying that," Ortiz said, "people are going to forget you know any other words."

"Well, it doesn't." Brim sat at the small table with a recording console. He was half-sprawled back, with one arm thrown over the back of the chair. His other hand tapped the desktop as he stared at the man in the chair. Ezra could tell he wasn't really looking at him.

"This is Arthur Soren." Brim pointed at the man in the chair. "Mr. Soren was a MechWarrior in the service of Sir Edward Aylmer, former captain in the AFFC, lately sworn to the service of Nikoli Ridzik."

"Lately," Ezra said.

"Sir Edward swore that oath in 3057, when the Lyran Alliance was born," Brim continued. "Since the apparent death of the Ridzik brothers in 3059, Aylmer's 'Mechs have been here and there in the Chaos March. Mr. Soren isn't much of a navigator. He couldn't tell me all the worlds they've been on. Apparently Sir Edward would lead them wherever he felt the Ridziks' legacy needed upholding."

"Aylmer?" Ortiz asked.

"Drove a *Salamander*," Brim said, looking at Ezra.

"Ah," Ezra said.

"'Ah' is right," Brim muttered. "Anyway, a few months ago, Aylmer gets a message that he tells his people came from Nikoli Ridzik, who it turns out isn't dead and has been rebuilding his forces for the last decade in secret."

"Rebuilding where?" Ezra asked.

"Here on Hall."

"Bullshit," Ezra said.

Brim looked at Ortiz. "Can I say it?"

"That it doesn't make any sense?"

"Yes."

"Consider it said. Move on."

Brim glared at her. She smiled sweetly back. Ezra watched the byplay with satisfaction, but saw Ortiz's grin and something twitched inside him. She had a lovely smile—white teeth, full lips, and the way her cheek pulled into lines . . . He inhaled and looked away.

"So. 'Ridzik'—" Brim did air quotes with his hands around the word. "—is returned and rebuilding on Hall. Aylmer follows his orders—Soren tells me—to come to Holden on Hall all quiet-like, to sneak in under the noses of Buddy Boy and Count McNally."

"So this is before December," Ezra said. "McNally died then."

"It could be. Soren isn't solid on dates, and we have to account for communication lag. We don't actually know when the message was sent, or from where, or by whom. All I have is the story Mr. Soren told me."

Ezra nodded. "Got it. Keep going."

"So Aylmer comes here. And finds Nikoli Ridzik—or at least, an imposter good enough to impress Soren and his fellows."

"They actually *saw* him?" Ortiz said. "Seriously?"

"They say they did?"

"And where is Ridzik now?"

Brim looked up at her. "He drove a *Cataphract*."

"Oh."

Ezra looked at her. "'Oh?'"

Ortiz looked at him out of the corner of her eye. "PPC to the cockpit." She looked a little embarrassed, but Ezra didn't know why. It's not like her MechWarrior had known who he was killing. People died in combat.

As he'd tried to explain to Elly Burton what felt like a lifetime ago.

"Oh."

Brim looked back and forth between them. "So that's as far as I've gotten."

Ezra pulled an extruded-plastic chair away from the wall and sat down. The legs bowed beneath his weight, but he ignored it. Cupping his chin, he stared at a point across the room where the wall met the floor, going over the details.

"If we accept—even for a second—that they are who they say they are, why did they attack today?"

Brim opened his mouth, then closed it. "That's the funny part." He stared at Soren. "To rescue Elly Burton."

"Huh?"

"From *us*," Brim said. "Aylmer told them we—the Disinherited—had come to arrest Elly Burton and take her back to Outreach. Ridzik—or Aylmer, or whoever was giving the orders—told them if they could free her, she could rally enough forces that they could sweep Baranov off-planet and the Free Republic would be reborn."

Ezra sat back and crossed his arms. "That doesn't make any sense."

Brim looked at Ortiz and pointed an accusing finger at Ezra. "See? It's not just me."

Ortiz pulled a chair out and sat beside Ezra. He pretended he didn't notice. She wore a perfume with vanilla in it; it was faint, and if you weren't right next to her it couldn't be smelled, but he smelled it. It was heady.

"And there's evidence at Holden putting Ridzik there?" she asked.

Brim spread his hands. "There's evidence there *implicating* him. There's nothing definitive—no holos, no DNA, no smoking gun."

"And the 'Mechs?"

"That's a tech question. I don't do forensics on 'Mechs, but if you can get me lot numbers and parts references, I can put my team on it. You know 'Mechs, though. It's unlikely that'll tell us anything."

Ezra and Ortiz both nodded.

Before the coming of the Clans in 3050, the Inner Sphere had suffered an almost 300-year decline in advanced technology as the Successor States—those interstellar nations who'd been members of the Star League—fought and bombed each other into near-destruction. BattleMechs, as the only real interstellar resource left, were kept in service far longer than anyone had ever dreamed they would be. Repaired, salvaged, modified, stolen, captured . . . a 'Mech's original genesis was sometimes almost impossible to determine. New construction since the recovery of Star League technology and the rapid rebuilding since the Clan Invasion sometimes increased that possibility, but only if the machine had been built in the last decade or so.

Ezra's *Crusader*, for instance, was only a few years old. It had been one of the 'Mechs captured by the Stealthy Tigers during their many skirmishes with Lindon's Battalion on Caph. He knew exactly when it had been manufactured. The 'Mech's purchase information had been recovered with it. But the *Grasshopper* he'd trained on as a cadet was more than 150 years old, so far as the Tigers technicians could make out. How many hands it had passed through in that time was impossible to determine.

"So, we don't have anything," Ortiz said.

"No," Brim said. He was smiling. "We have the best news: confirmation."

"Confirmation of what?"

"Ill intent."

Ortiz looked at Ezra. He looked back at her. Then they both looked at Brim.

"I'm serious."

"You're going to have to explain that."

Brim sighed. "Look. All of us are here because we're on a contract. Payne is here because his employer wants him to keep an eye on us. We're here because we're keeping an eye on Payne's employer, and looking for his sugar daddies." He stopped and held out his hands, palms up, as if asking for permission.

"Go on," Ortiz said carefully.

"But now, people we can't tie to anyone are shooting at us."

"Technically they're shooting at *us*," Ortiz said. She looked at Ezra. "No offense, but they pretended to *be* you."

"They did," Ezra said. He looked at Brim. "Any idea why?"

"Ill intent," Brim said. When Ezra just glared, he held up his hands again. "I mean it. They were trying to frame you. What does it say to the Dismal Ds—" He pointed to Ortiz. "—if the Stealthy Tigers come and 'abscond' with Elly Burton when they've placed her under their protection?"

"It says Baranov has something to hide that he doesn't want the Disinherited knowing," Erza replied, drawing a nod from Brim. "And when they come to Bravo Base, demanding we produce the secret strike force and Elly Burton, the colonel would say he doesn't know what the hell they're talking about."

Ortiz was nodding. "Which is what he *would* say if he'd arranged a secret mission to kill me and take my protectee."

Ezra looked back and forth at each of them. "Son of a bitch. That's it."

Brim just smiled, crossed his arms, and leaned back.

"Someone wants us fighting each other," Ortiz said.

"Yes," Brim said.

"Who?" Ezra asked.

"No idea," Brim said, still smiling.

"Have you slept in the last week?" Ortiz asked Brim.

"Not really," Brim said, waving the question away, "but let me explain. The easiest way is to do the list." He held up one finger. "First option: Baranov."

"No," Ezra said. "What's his angle? He's our employer. He looks bad if we go rogue, and he gets a hell of a lot of better press out of us beating your asses off-world."

Ortiz stared at him. "Theoretically beating your asses," he corrected. She nodded.

"Right. No angle." Brim held up a second finger. "Next would be, I guess, us. The AMC."

"Stupid," Ortiz said. "If the commander wanted us fighting Baranov or the Tigers, that's what he'd have contracted us for. Not wasting our time looking for hidden agendas."

"Also right," Brim said. He held up a third finger. "McNally—or, I guess now, Burton?"

Both Ortiz and Ezra shook their heads, but he gestured for her to speak. "No cash. No reason for the subterfuge. If she could afford a regiment to drive Baranov off-world, she'd have hired one.

Paying two companies to pretend to be Ridzik loyalists does nothing for her, especially when she's the target."

Ezra nodded. "What she said."

"Right." Brim held up a fourth finger, his pinky. "That leaves a mystery guest to be named later."

Ezra frowned. "This is where you're going to say the Word of Blake, aren't you?"

Brim put his hand down. "Who else is left?" He pointed to Soren. "We know they use patsies all the time. We know they have the commo expertise to fake messages from Ridzik to Aylmer. We know they have the funds to pay for it. And we know their ROM is more than smart enough to stage all of this."

Ortiz clasped her hands in front of her. "So we've found them."

Ezra kept his face blank. He knew they were right, but he couldn't tell them. As far as they knew, he was only here to determine who had attacked them. And Brim's logic was sound. Which meant that the Word of Blake had tried to lure the Stealthy Tigers and the Dismal Disinherited into conflict.

They'd put his lance in danger of being killed. That should have been enough reason right there.

He should tell them right now, lay out all of Monet's research, but he couldn't. It wasn't his place to make that decision. Only the colonel could do that.

"No," Brim said, breaking Ezra's concentration. "Because there's no proof."

"Then what was all of that?"

"Conjecture."

"Isn't that enough?"

Brim looked away. "No. Maybe for some people. For the media, certainly. But not enough to base a military campaign on."

Ortiz looked down her nose at him. "Come on. You know and I know people hire mercenaries to do missions with a lot less basis in fact than that." "People do," Brim said, *carefully*, Ezra thought, "but the AMC doesn't."

"So what do we do?"

"We keep gathering data. We keep chasing leads." He looked at Ezra. "And we stay in touch so we don't end up accidentally shooting at each other."

Ezra nodded. Then he looked through the window at Soren. "We took more prisoners than him. What do the others say? Anything different?"

Brim shrugged. "Not really. All but two of the MechWarriors are from Aylmer's bunch, and the other two are freelance mercenaries he hired along the way. Most of the technicians are Aylmer's, though a couple are local hires."

"That doesn't seem strange? That this mystery Ridzik should be 'rebuilding his army,' but the only army nearby was Aylmer's? Didn't he wonder where the rest of Nikoli's army was?"

"Don't know. Someone killed him, remember?"

Ortiz inhaled, held it, and exhaled. "So we still don't really know anything."

Brim shook his head. "No, we know someone is here and wants us fighting among ourselves. That's important. It's much easier to find something you *know* exists than it is to wonder about mysteries. We have an enemy on Hall. That's for certain. And they want us fighting. That's for certain. Whether that's the Word of Blake or the Federated Suns or the ilKhan of all the Clans, we don't know. But they're *real*."

Ezra and Ortiz left Brim in the interrogation room and stepped into the corridor. He held the door for her, and she smiled at it. He saw that and his insides clenched. *This is so stupid*, he told himself, but he couldn't stop. "I wanted to eat before starting back to Bravo," he said. "Care to join me?"

Ortiz—*Nathalie*—smiled. "Yeah." She led him through the maze of corridors to the officer's mess. A few minutes later they were sitting at a small table against the wall, poking at food and smiling.

"So," she said. "I think Jake needs some sleep, don't you?"

"Oh, yes," Ezra said. He was trying to remember all the lessons his mother had given him—so many years ago—about table manners. He knew the napkin went in his lap, and there was only one fork, so that helped, but . . . *but it's been years since you sat down with a woman and worried about what she thought of you.*

"Do you think he's right?"

"About it being the Word?" *I know he is.* "I don't know. His logic certainly holds up, but we both know with a little thought we could build plausible—" He smiled. "—*conjectural* arguments for almost anyone."

"I guess." She took a bite of her salad. She was eating with one hand, slightly leaned forward. Her other hand was in her lap. Ezra mimicked her.

"I guess I like the idea because it would validate our mission. It would give the last couple months some point, other than being here, glaring at you." She wasn't looking at him, but he was looking at her.

Suddenly Ezra realized he hadn't spoken. "My sergeant major would tell you, if he were here, that you're trying to make the pieces fit together into the shape you want." He frowned. "Not that they couldn't come together in that shape, but it's too early to tell."

She looked at him. "True." Then she smiled. "Do you usually take your sergeant major on dates?"

Ezra coughed. "He's a hell of a cook," he said, smiling.

"Good," she said, her cheeks dimpling. "Then this *is* a date."

He smiled. "I certainly hope so."

She smiled and went back to eating. "What if Jake turns out to be right?" she asked a moment later.

"What do you mean?"

"If it is the Word pushing us at each other," she said. "If their plan had worked last week—and it might've, if you hadn't been there—we'd be fighting right now. Our regiments, I mean."

Ezra sipped his water and leaned back, considering. "I probably wouldn't be sitting here," he said jokingly.

"Probably not," she agreed. "But still?"

Ezra set his water down. "Then we'd do our duty." It was kind of a fake answer, and it wasn't. He knew Nathalie well enough to know she was as much a professional he was. If it came to blows between their regiments, they'd each do what they had to. "But I don't think it'll come to that."

"No?"

"No. We know what's going on now. No matter who it turns out to be, we know someone is trying to get us fighting. You'll brief your CO, and I'll brief mine. We won't let it get out of hand."

"Good." Nathalie smiled. "I'd hate to think our first date might be our last."

Ezra smiled back. "I think that depends on dessert, don't you?"

She laughed, and Ezra put the serious thoughts out of his mind. He knew he had a long and serious conversation coming with the colonel. Monet's data needed to be shared, especially if the Word really was the one trying to get Tigers killed. Rauschenbusch would put up with a lot in the name of a contract, but not betrayal.

If Monet was right, and the Word had financed Baranov's hiring of the Stealthy Tigers, then they were putatively in the employ of the Word of Blake. If the Word had then tried to frame the Tigers for a sneak attack, then their employers had just turned on them.

Not even Kirsten Markoja could talk that away.

"Units in the employ of the Capellan March have successfully driven the final Taurian invaders from the worlds along the Federated Suns' border with the Taurian Concordat. The only Taurian military units remaining in Suns space are in the Pleiades Cluster, and Duke George Hasek, commander of the Capellan March, has already promised swift action to eject them.

"The campaign against the Taurians has been largely ignored by New Avalon, wracked as it is right now with fighting between Katherine Steiner-Davion, who calls herself Katrina, and her brother, former Precentor Martial Victor Steiner-Davion. Along with the fighting on Tharkad, most INN military analysts expect the endgame of the Federated Commonwealth Civil War to begin presently."

–From the *Daily INN Download,*
ComStar Hall Hyperpulse Station Harney

CHAPTER ELEVEN

BRAVO BASE
HALL
THE CHAOS MARCH
13 MARCH 3067

Ezra may have overestimated his powers of persuasion.

"That's ludicrous," Kirsten Markoja said as soon as he finished recounting the conversation with Brim and Nathalie from the day before.

"Ludicrous," Mason Markoja repeated.

The two majors and Colonel Rauschenbusch stood in the Panther Battalion 'Mech hangar, watching one of the Tigers repair teams putting a salvaged 'Mech through its early test phases. Between the fighting on Caph, Carver V, and now Hall, the regiment possessed quite a haul of damaged but repairable 'Mechs. The technical staff, however, had only limited time devoted to putting those 'Mechs back together, and the cost wasn't cheap.

Ezra looked at the new 'Mech. It was a sixty-ton *Quickdraw*, taken from the defunct Critchley's Cavaliers during the last push against Count McNally. It had lost a leg and been taken mostly intact, but none of the right parts to get it quickly back into service were available on Hall. It had taken the tech teams this many months to machine the requisite parts from bar stock.

And from the way the *Quickdraw* moved, they had done a good job.

"There's no evidence for it," Ezra said, not looking away from the 'Mech. "For it being the Word of Blake, I mean." He glanced at the colonel, but Rauschenbusch was still looking at the 'Mech. "But it makes sense."

"You've been talking to Monet again," Mason Markoja said. *What if I have?* Ezra wanted to say. But the Markojas weren't privy to the data Monet had pulled. They weren't Raiders. He resisted the urge to touch the enameled pin on his lapel. He glanced again at the colonel. Monet didn't make any bones about his hatred of the Word, but his data—the damning contract data—was a Raiders-only secret. It's possible Calhoune had taken the information to the colonel before he died. The dead XO and the colonel were old cronies. But Ezra didn't know. Rauschenbusch had never said anything, and Ezra had never brought it up.

"This didn't come from Monet," he said instead. "It came from the AMC."

"What possible motive could the Word have for maneuvering us and the Dismal Ds into a shooting conflict?" Kirsten asked. She stood a meter or so away from the colonel, arms crossed. She wasn't making any pretense of watching the techs at work. She was glaring at Ezra.

"I can think of several," Ezra said, glaring back. "None of them have any evidence."

"So you're guessing."

"Of course I'm guessing," he spat. "But my guesses fit the facts."

"I doubt we're even on the Word's radar," Kirsten said.

"Probably not," Ezra said. *I hope not.* "But we don't have to be the target. Think about the politics."

"Politics?" Mason asked.

I'll have to use small words. "The Disinherited is here to look for the Word. Not to get involved in the skirmishes between Baranov and McNally or anyone else. So they leave us alone. We leave them alone. They want to go talk to our employer's mortal enemy, we let them. We even send observers." Ezra looked at the colonel, but there was still no reaction.

"Now. Burton and the Dismal Ds hit it off. Burton intends to return to Brampton with them. That puts her within a commute of Harney. Where she can raise all kinds of hell if she gets on the HV, says the wrong thing. You know how Baranov has the HV locked down. The whole planet's broadcasts come out of Harney."

"The Word doesn't want the AMC here. It doesn't matter why the Word is here, only that the AMC is here at the same time. They're public enemies. Hell, hating the Word is the entire reason the AMC exists."

He pointed to the *Quickdraw*. "So they get some 'Mechs and steal our transponder codes. They send *them* into the desert with orders to kill Elly Burton and make it look like *we* did it."

Ezra stopped. The colonel was still watching the *Quickdraw*, but he didn't miss much. Kirsten was watching Ezra with her lips pursed. Mason was frowning.

"It's all in the story, don't you see? If the marauders—if *we*, so far as anyone knows—kill Elly Burton while she's with the Dismal Ds, Baranov can play it as his loyal mercenaries halting the interference of the AMC in Hall's affairs. He looks good on the HV for standing up to the Allied Mercenary Command—to Wolf's Dragoons, really—and the AMC is smeared."

"And now? Since 'we' didn't actually kill her?" Kirsten asked.

"If we hadn't figured it out, we'd be rogue mercenaries. The Disinherited would be camped right out there—" Ezra pointed at the wall. "—demanding we surrender. Depending on the situation, Baranov would either support us against 'outside aggression' or hang us out to dry. Despite the news stranglehold, there's a lot of sympathy for Burton out in the sticks. Baranov could throw us under the bus to curry favor with them."

"You keep talking about Baranov," Mason said. "What does the Word of Blake get out of any of this?"

"Unrest," Rauschenbusch said, turning to face them.

"Yes, sir," Ezra said. He tried not to show the relief he felt flowing through him.

"Colonel?"

"The Word," the colonel said, "or whoever it is, clearly wants there to be fighting on Hall. They want us fighting the Dismal Ds, the emperor fighting everyone else, probably Elly Burton fighting with her kid, if it suited them."

He pointed toward the hangar entrance. All of them started walking. Behind them, the *Quickdraw* took a ponderous step. The rumble of sixty tons of mass coming down on a single footpad shook the ferrocrete floor. Ezra felt it in his boot soles.

"Then, assuming it's not someone here," Rauschenbusch said, "the Word can sweep in with peacekeepers, or wait to be invited, and in six or eight months Baranov, or whoever replaces him, petitions for entry into their new Protectorate."

"That's reaching," Kirsten Markova said.

Rauschenbusch shrugged. "Could be. Makes as much sense as anything else right now."

"So what do we do?" Mason asked.

"Nothing." The colonel stopped, so the other three did. Ezra said nothing. "We don't get involved."

"Sir, if someone's gunning for us—" Kirsten began, but the colonel held up a hand. "I didn't say put our heads in the sand. Keep on this. Let's figure out who it is. But I'm not letting this regiment get pulled into someone else's fight without knowing who's behind it and why." He looked at Ezra. "They've already shot at us once. They don't get a second chance." He looked at the Markojas with an expression that said *dismissed*. Both of them nodded—Tigers didn't salute—and walked away, back into the hangar.

Rauschenbusch turned and met Ezra's eyes. "I want to see you and Charles Monet in your office in ten minutes."

"Colonel?"

Rauschenbusch reached up and tapped his own Raider pin. He was a member, of course—had been since before Ezra learned to pilot a 'Mech. But by custom, the regiment's colonel wasn't an active Raider member. He wasn't in the meetings. He stood apart, for the good of the regiment.

Sometimes Raiders had to say things that couldn't be said with the commanding officer standing there.

"I want to see his data for myself," Colonel Rauschenbusch said. When Ezra just stood there, gaping, the colonel chuckled and slapped him on the shoulder. "Well go, son." Then he stepped past him, still laughing.

"He knows," Mason said, as soon as they were inside the hangar and out of observation.

Kirsten frowned at him, but didn't say anything. She kept walking toward his office. She would have preferred her own, but they were in the Panther hangar, and Panther was his battalion.

"Kirsten—" he started, but she just held up a hand and walked faster.

"Not here."

A few minutes later, they were in Mason's office with the door closed. Kirsten walked around her brother's desk and keyed a specific code into his console; when the lights came back green, she stepped back and gestured for him to sit.

"He doesn't *know* anything," she told her brother.

"But—"

"He *suspects*. He and that damned Dragoon and that Disinherited bitch. They suspect. That's all."

Mason looked confused as he sat down. "But the way he described it . . ."

"I didn't say he was *wrong*. I said he doesn't *know*."

Kirsten sat down in the single uncomfortable chair her brother kept in front of his desk. She went back over the conversation in her head, examining what Payne had said from all the angles she could come up with. It was disturbing how well the AMC was guessing her—the Word's—intentions, but there wasn't any truth. And besides . . .

"Even if they guess," she said out loud, "the evidence—*any* evidence, and there *isn't* any that I know of—points back to that twat Estwicke, not us."

"You're sure?"

Kirsten glared at him.

"Of course you're sure," he said. He settled back in his chair and regarded her, hands clasped across his belly. "What's our next move, then?"

"What the colonel said," she told him. "Lay low for a while. The AMC will be weeks, if not months, sifting the data and poking at Aylmer's people who survived." She frowned at that; it was sloppy. Estwicke had created the Ridzik persona years ago against just such an eventuality, but not putting suicide charges in the 'Mechs' cockpits was sloppy.

So what if the captured MechWarriors didn't know anything? What they could guess—or worse, make up—said enough.

She wondered about arranging for at least a couple of Aylmer's MechWarriors to suffer "accidents" in the AMC's custody, but dismissed that thought almost immediately. Now that direct action had warned them, the Disinherited would be alert for such intrusions.

"We're on schedule?" Mason asked.

Kirsten blinked her thoughts away and looked at him. "Schedule?"

"The Third Transfer—"

She hissed at him, chopping a knife-hand down in a *no!* gesture. There were things they weren't supposed to talk about, not even in supposedly secure rooms. So many of the things they'd learned on Jardine were so secret she was afraid to even *think* them. Her right hand itched. She scratched at the skin there, not really noticing she was doing it.

"Sorry," Mason said.

"We're on schedule," she said. "If Estwicke's on her own schedule, she should be able to take advantage of this with Baranov in the next month or so."

"Good." Mason looked past her, out the one-way window into the 'Mech bay. She twisted around to look. The technicians were putting the *Quickdraw* back into its repair gantry. There must have been faults discovered in the testing.

"Are you getting that one, or me?" she asked. She had a couple of MechWarriors due for an upgraded 'Mech, but so did Mason. There were a lot of wanting MechWarriors in the Stealthy Tigers.

"Neither," Mason said. "Payne."

"Payne." Kirsten's lips sneered the word. "It would have been so damn convenient if Aylmer's people had gotten him in the desert."

"Yeah," Mason said. "If we're not careful, the colonel will build a Third Battalion around him."

Kirsten sucked air through her teeth. "Over my dead body."

Her right hand itched even more.

Ezra and Charles Monet sat very still as the colonel read Monet's report.

They were in Ezra's office in the Jaguar Company bays. Behind him, out the window, technicians worked two shifts repairing the damage his lance had taken in the Helmand the previous week.

Colonel Rauschenbusch preferred paper to noteputer screens. Monet had printed his reports up just for this meeting, but Ezra knew the MechWarrior would burn the documents immediately after the meeting. He hated paper. It led to paper trails.

The colonel exhaled and closed the folder. He handed it back to Monet. "It's not enough."

Incredibly, Ezra felt relief. Even as Monet began to argue, Ezra realized how worried he'd been that he'd made the wrong decision months ago, in not telling the AMC about the Blakist connection.

"Sir," Monet was saying, "if I could just show you the connections—"

"No, Lieutenant," Rauschenbusch said, holding up a hand, "I read them. I don't doubt them—I think you're right, in fact—but they're not enough to break our contract." He looked at the two men sitting across from him, holding each one's gaze until he was sure he had their full attention. "And that's what this would be. We'd be going rogue."

"Sir—"

"*No*, Charlie," the colonel said, more softly.

"I don't doubt that the Word of Blake gave the emperor the money to hire us." He pointed to the folder clutched in Monet's hands. "You've convinced me, even if we can't take any of that to anyone as evidence."

"Sir—"

"And I don't doubt Ezra's logic here," he said, looking at Ezra, "that they might have been behind the fight in the desert last week." He licked his lips and looked away for a second. "You can imagine how I feel about that."

"I was there, Colonel," Ezra said. He hadn't realized he was going to speak until he did. "I don't have to imagine."

"No, you don't," Rauschenbusch said. He ran a hand over his forehead and up into his hair, then scrubbed it back and forth on top of his head, as if trying to get something out. "You surely don't."

No one spoke for a long moment.

"What do we do?" Ezra asked.

"Nothing," Rauschenbusch said.

Monet gulped so hard he almost choked. Ezra put a restraining hand on his arm, keeping the lieutenant from leaping to his feet, but only because he knew he had to control him in the colonel's presence. The man was a Raider. It was Ezra's job to look out for him.

If it had been just Ezra and the colonel alone in the office, Ezra would have leaped to his feet on his own.

The colonel looked like he was chewing on something sour. He held up a hand to quiet Monet. "I know, Charlie. I know. But there is nothing we can do."

Then he looked at Ezra. "You're good at this—what are our options?"

Ezra thought for a moment. "Two choices: something, or nothing."

"Maybe a little more than that," the colonel said with a chuckle.

"Well, nothing is nothing. There are a lot of somethings." Ezra licked his lips.

"We could take our evidence to the Dismal Ds." He looked at Monet and the colonel, but neither spoke. "Jake Brim and his team would confirm Charlie's data. Then they'd tell us good work, but its all conjecture. We can't tie a Blakist directly to any part of it."

"Right," Rauschenbusch said.

"We could hand it all over to ComStar," Ezra said next. "Despite Baranov's trying, they still control the HPG in Harney. We could ask them to look into it. They hate the Word of Blake worse than the AMC does."

"And?"

"And the same result—except we poison the relationship with Baranov, and get a black mark from the bonding commission because we breached our contract."

Rauschenbusch nodded. "And there it is. We could fight it out, but it would kill us." He frowned. "You know how it is for mercenaries. Our reputation is all we have. We can't afford a note on our jacket saying this one time, on a no-name contract on a backwater in the Chaos March, we decided our contract didn't mean anything. We'd end up in the Periphery, protecting water-haulers from dust storms."

Monet looked between them. "I don't think the damage would be that bad, once we shared the evidence—" He stopped when the colonel held up a hand.

"It would. Trust me."

Monet sighed. "So we do nothing."

"Yes."

Ezra cleared his throat. "What do we tell the AMC?"

"Nothing."

He frowned. "We'll have to give them something. If we don't, they'll know we're hiding something. If nothing else, we have to at least appear to be looking into Aylmer's bunch from last week."

Rauschenbusch rubbed his head again. "We'll do that. But none of that—" He pointed at Monet's folder. "—goes to them. Not one word." He looked at both of them. "I shouldn't have to say this to Raiders, but that's an order."

"Sir," Monet said. Ezra just nodded.

"Okay." He stood up from behind Ezra's desk. "Charlie, I want you to keep looking. Report only to Ezra or me. No one else, got it?" Monet nodded.

The colonel looked at Ezra again. "I want you to keep on with the AMC. Stay close. Keep your ear to the ground. They may uncover something that will help us."

Ezra nodded. "I will."

"Good." Rauschenbusch stepped around the desk, toward the door. He moved stiffly, as if he'd been sitting too long. There was a slight limp when he took a step. Ezra frowned and stood up as well. The colonel patted him on the shoulder.

"You did good out there, Ezra," he said. He looked past him. "You too, here, Charlie. Both of you. Acted in the best traditions of those pins you wear." He seemed to deflate. "Be glad you're not the colonel."

Then he walked out. Monet frowned after him, then glanced at Ezra and followed, clutching the paper folder to his desk like it was a child.

Ezra went around and sat down behind his desk. He didn't want to think about the Word of Blake or Kirsten Markoja any more.

Instead, he thought about Nathalie Ortiz's smile.

It only felt a little like shirking work.

"The Federated Commonwealth Civil War is over, but the cost has been staggering. Hundreds of thousands, possibly millions, are dead. Trillions, if not quadrillions of C-bills of damage have been done. The infrastructure of entire worlds has been ruined, and at the end of it, the winning side has stepped away from power.

"On Tharkad, Archon Peter Steiner-Davion rules the Lyran Alliance. On New Avalon, Princess-Regent Yvonne Steiner-Davion rules the Federated Suns. Victor Steiner-Davion, eldest child of Hanse Davion and Melissa Steiner, former archon prince of the combined Federated Commonwealth, defeated his sister in a stunning military victory and then . . . went away.

"As the two nations begin the long process of recovery, Victor Davion had announced his intention to return to ComStar as its precentor martial. To the hundreds of thousands of soldiers, spacers, and airmen who fought to remove Katherine Steiner-Davion from her usurped thrones, he offers his thanks, and his hopes that they will find peace.

"After years of fighting, peace has returned to the worlds of the Suns and the Alliance. Many expect the upcoming Star League conference on Tharkad this year to be overtaken with war reparations and negotiated settlements as the peace hammered out of combat is shaped into a working model of the future."

– From the *Daily INN Download*,
ComStar Hall Hyperpulse Station Harney

CHAPTER TWELVE

HARNEY
HALL
THE CHAOS MARCH
1 JUNE 3067

Adele Estwicke did not like Emperor William Baranov. He was fat, coarse, and uneducated. He'd become emperor of Hall because he commanded a 'Mech regiment, because he could sense the winds of politics, and because he was as ruthless as a pit viper. Those were all qualities she could admire in another person, but in Bud Baranov, she found the combination repulsive.

If only McNally had won, she thought as she bowed politely to the rotund man seated on the park bench. "Your Grace."

The emperor wore a simple suit, brown fabric that showed a vertical pattern when the light caught it just right. It was three-piece: jacket, vest, and pants. His shirt underneath was white. He wore gaudy gold rings on three of his fingers, and the skin bunched at his neck where his collar was too tight. He sat on a stone bench, beneath the overhang of an imported Terran willow tree. When he looked up at her, his eyes were bloodshot.

"Adept Estwicke," Baranov said. His voice was deep, and in its rumble she could hear the man he must have been twenty years ago. It was a voice weakened by age and excess, but still used to being obeyed.

"I had this garden built soon after I came to power," he said, looking past her. She knew what he saw: green fronds and multicolored blooms from a dozen worlds around Hall. The gardens in the emperor's palace were known all across the planet. Baranov made sure of that. He hosted almost all of his public events on this grass.

"It's beautiful," she commented.

Baranov laughed. "It better be—it costs me a fortune."

Thereby demonstrating that you're an uncultured cow, Estwicke thought. *Of course it costs a fortune; fine things always come with a cost.* "What can the Word of Blake offer to the emperor on this fine day?" she asked instead.

Baranov stood. Behind him, two bodyguards stepped clear of the tree. They were both large men, with the look of former infantrymen. They wore identical suits. Both their jackets were cut too wide—to make room for weapons carried beneath, Estwicke assumed—and both wore wraparound headsets.

In other words, they were stereotypical comic-opera bodyguards.

Everything about Bud Baranov was comic-opera.

"Did you know," the emperor said as he began strolling along a line of bushes, one hand held out to brush his fingertips against the stems, "that the sum total of the Word of Blake's material assistance to me has been money?"

"Money has no provenance," Estwicke quoted. "You declined to enter the Protectorate when we offered last year, and you have declined our offer of direct military support again and again."

"Those things have costs I wasn't willing to bear," Baranov told her. "I can read a map. I know what you're building here, in the worlds around Terra. I know what you sold to the people of Caph and Keid."

Estwicke said nothing.

"Do you remember 3057?" he asked.

"I was on Terra in 3057," she said. "But I recall the year."

"It was one of those moments you read about," Baranov said. His face had that faraway look of someone recalling a favored memory. "Overnight, the Federated Commonwealth came apart."

Estwicke said nothing, but inside she was sneering. It had only seemed like overnight to idiots who didn't pay attention to history. To anyone with an ounce of foresight, the alliance was doomed from the start.

The marriage of Hanse Davion of the Federated Suns to Melissa Steiner of the Lyran Commonwealth had created the largest superstate the Inner Sphere had ever seen. The industrial juggernaut of the Commonwealth married to the martial excellence of the Federated Suns had allowed them to conquer half the Capellan Confederation in only two years. It was only through the craftiness of Theodore Kurita of the Draconis Combine, and the inevitable internal dissent that kept cropping up in the Federated Commonwealth, that kept the Steiner-Davions from rolling across the rest of the Inner Sphere.

Well, Estwicke reminded herself, *all of that, and the Clans.*

Regardless, the collapse of the mighty Federated Commonwealth into the Federated Suns and the Lyran Alliance, the successor to the Commonwealth, was anything but a surprise to the Word of Blake.

If anything, Estwicke and the others had been surprised it lasted as long as it did.

"In one sweep, the central authority and threat of the Armed Forces of the Federated Commonwealth was gone," Baranov said. "Worlds were declaring independence or reforming old nations left and right." He stopped next to a black-leafed bush. The fronds were slender, like evergreens on Terra, but night-black. The stems looked flimsy. They were pasty white. The emperor caressed the black fronds, and they flickered with bioluminesence. "I still remember when the HPG messages came—conflicting orders from the Lyran State Command and the Suns State Command."

"It was a propitious time," she ventured. It felt vague enough, and she could say it softly enough to hide the disgust.

Heady, you called it. When you turned your back on your oaths and carved out your own domain.

"It was," Baranov said. "It was a time for men of courage to grab opportunity when it presented itself." He crushed the glowing leaves in his hand. "And I *did.* I didn't hesitate." He looked down at his palm. The sap provided the glow—it was visible even in the sunlight, smeared against his palm. He squatted down and wiped his hands on the grass to clear them.

"It wasn't easy," he said, still squatting. "It was hard. It cost me a lot of good men and a good bit of my stomach to bring this day to fruition." He rose and faced her.

Estwicke hadn't missed the cue. *This day,* the emperor had said. She schooled her features and waited for his next words.

"I rejected your offer of membership in your Protectorate because it's obvious that it's not membership," he said. "If I gave you Hall, it wouldn't be as a free world joining its peers. It would be an acquisition for you." He grinned, showing yellowed teeth and pale gums. "I doubt I'd live out the year."

Estwicke said nothing. There was no question in his tone, and she wasn't going to waste time denying his statements. Baranov's reach didn't extend too far beyond Hall, but he controlled a Jump-Ship, and he had sources of information that didn't come through either the Word of Blake or ComStar.

"You offered help," he went on. "I took it. I knew there'd be a price, eventually, but I was willing to deal with that when it came if it meant being able to deal with McNally and his people."

Baranov rubbed his hands together. The glowing sap dried quickly to an off-brown, now that it was dead and the proteins that fueled the glowing reaction were exhausted. It must have been sticky; he kept his hands constantly moving against each other.

"McNally is dead," Estwicke said. It was nothing to state a fact.

Baranov nodded. "He is. And without the mercenaries you provided, it might have taken me years to accomplish that."

Estwicke incline her head. "When the Word of Blake promises assistance," she said, "it carries that promise out." She took a chance and met his stare. "Our word is good, Your Grace."

Baranov smiled at her. It was not a pleasant smile. "So I've been told." He looked behind her and nodded. Frowning, Estwicke turned and saw two more bodyguards stepping out of the bushes behind her. She looked back at Baranov.

"Your Grace?"

"I sent a message through ComStar this morning," he said. "To the office of the captain-general of the Free Worlds League."

Acid burned in Estwicke's stomach. Her fingertips went icy cold, and a shiver shook her shoulders, despite her best efforts as adrenalin surged through her.

"Now that we can reasonably say that Hall has a unified planetary government, thanks to your help," the emperor said with a nod, "I have petitioned for membership in the Free Worlds. From the negotiations undertaken on Zion in my name over the last few months, I expect to hear back immediately." He smiled. Like a snake.

"You—" Estwicke coughed. Her mouth was dry. She kept her fingers clutched together, and worked her tongue until she could speak. Then she realized she didn't know what to say.

"I'm not going to be your puppet," he said, his smile vanishing. "I know what happened on Keid and Caph. I've corresponded with the leaders there, or—" He huffed. "—the survivors there. I'm not going to be an accident." He held a dirty fist up to her. "I control Hall. Not you, not the AMC, not McNally. *I* do."

"Only because we helped you," she rasped.

"I had my lawyers check the contract," Baranov said. "With the Stealthy Tigers? It was publicly registered on Outreach. They're contracted to *me*. Not to you, not to Hall. To *me*." He lowered his fist. "That contract will last long enough for the League to get troops in here to keep you out."

"We *helped* you—"

"You tried to *buy* me," Baranov interrupted. "There's a difference. Trust me. I've used the same tactic often enough. I know what it looks like from both sides." He took a step past her, exposing his back.

For a moment, Estwicke wished she was a Light of Mankind operative, that she'd been trained in close combat. She knew there were soldiers of Blake who could have killed the emperor in that opportunity.

She wasn't one of them, but for that moment, she wished she was.

"And it's not like you have to call all of this a failure," he said, continuing to walk. He spoke over his shoulder. "The Word of Blake administers the hyperpulse generators on League worlds; I'll be able to get ComStar and their self-righteousness out of the way, too. Your people will get that contract. You'll get all the other benefits your bunch gets from Thomas Marik." He stopped and turned. "You just don't get everything."

"You think the Mariks have your best interests at heart?" she spat.

Baranov laughed, a full belly laugh. He laughed for at least fifteen seconds, bending over and resting his weight on his knees while he guffawed. When he straightened up his face was red, his eyes were wet, and his skin sweaty. He looked at her with an expression of incredulity.

"Woman," he said, "of course they don't. They'll fleece me as much as anyone would, but at least I'll be the man at the top." He chuckled again, and gestured to the bodyguards behind Estwicke.

One of them gripped her elbow from behind. She tried to flinch out of his grip, but his fingers clamped down. When she changed direction, trying to elbow him, he twisted and took the blow in the hard muscles of his side.

"You're making a mistake," Estwicke said.

"Possibly," the emperor said. "If so, it won't be the first I've survived."

You won't survive this one, she didn't say. Antagonizing Baranov wouldn't do anything for her chances of getting out of this audience alive. She made herself calm down and straighten up as much as the bodyguard holding her would allow.

"The Peace of Blake be with you, then," she said. "If I may take my leave?"

Baranov's face hardened. "This is politics, Adele," he said. "Don't take it personally. It would be a shame, after our time together, if I had to . . ." He worked his mouth. "You played a good game. Your masters should be proud of you. It's not your fault the game was rigged all along."

Estwicke said nothing.

"You are free to remain on Hall," Baranov said. "But there's nothing you can do to stop this. Annexation is coming."

Estwicke said nothing. After a moment's silence, Baranov nodded at the guard. He released her, and Estwicke turned and stalked back the way she'd come through the garden. She felt her comm banging against her thigh, inside her pocket, but she didn't take it out.

She'd either make it out of the building, or she wouldn't.

She did.

And that, frankly, surprised her.

Stepping to the curb, she hailed a taxi. The first one passed her by, so she pulled a 100 C-bill note from her pocket and waved it. The second cab skidded to a halt in front of her. She climbed into the back, slid the C-bill through the slot in the scratched transpex barrier between the driver and the passenger compartment. "Drive."

"Where to?"

"Until you need more cash," she said. "I don't want to know where. Just away form here."

The cab driver looked at her, looked at the hundred, and shrugged and accelerated back into traffic.

Estwicke touched the control that engaged the privacy screen in the back of the cab, then connected the cab's communication system to her phone. The handshake went quickly. She pressed a preset ID and held the phone to her ear.

"Jurowicz."

"I'm going to say a code word in a moment," Estwicke said, "and it's for real. Got it?"

"Of course."

"Before I say it, though, I need you to do one thing. You've cracked the secure comms at the Stealthy Tigers base?"

"I have."

"I need to meet Kirsten Markoja," Estwicke said.

"When?"

"ASAP."

"Where?"

"You pick it. Don't tell me now."

There was silence.

"Mir Jafar," Estwicke said, speaking the code. She didn't wait for an acknowledgment. She disconnected her phone from the cab's system, slid the window down, and tossed the phone out the window. Then she disengaged the privacy screen.

"Everything okay back there?" the driver asked.

"How long left on the meter?"

"'Bout half an hour."

Estwicke slid another hundred through the slot. "Take me past Fort Decker," she told him. "Just before that runs out."

**BRAVO BASE
HALL
THE CHAOS MARCH
2 JUNE 3067**

The beep of her comm was the last thing Kirsten Markoja expected to hear while hanging upside down.

She looked up—down—at the screen, but she couldn't see the caller. Reaching up, she grabbed the bar and unhooked her knees, then swung down. Sweat reversed course down her back, chilling her bare skin beneath her sports bra. When she picked up her phone, she didn't recognize the code. It was an internal call, though, so she answered it.

"Markoja."

"There is a small deli four kilometers south of Fort Decker," a woman's voice said. "Where the access road meets the highway. It's called Marko's."

"Who is this?"

"Be there in two hours," the voice said. "Someone wants to meet you."

"How did you get this number?"

"Aleph three four seven yod nine," the woman said.

"Tet two two six," Kirsten said without thinking. Then she blinked.

"Peace be with you," the woman said, and disconnected.

Kirsten lowered her comm and stared at the blank screen. Her mind was awash with half-remembered recognition codes. Most of them had been implanted through posthypnotic suggestion, and she couldn't recall them without hearing them. But Aleph codes had been an exception.

Aleph codes meant something serious. Depending on the circumstances, an aleph code could mean "run for your life," or "kill everyone in sight." It was the yod modifier at the end that provided the context: the mission.

The mission was in danger. And since it was a Word of Blake recognition code, that meant that the Word of Blake's mission on Hall was in danger. The only people on Hall who had access to those codes were herself, Mason, and . . .

"Son a bitch . . ." she whispered.

Adele Estwicke.

The bitch had penetrated Kirsten's identity.

Kirsten peeled the earbud for her comm out of its slot and slid the phone into her waistband. She grabbed her towel and started out of the gym at Bravo Base. "Dial Mason," she said. The comm chirped, then scratched with a connected signal.

"Sis?"

"I'm hungry," she said, putting a false cheer into her voice.

"Okay," Mason said.

"I was thinking of going off-post. You interested?"

"I—"

"It's not far. A deli called Marko's, just down the road toward the highway." Kirsten smiled at the Tigers she passed, playing the cheerful battalion commander coming back from her workout. When a particularly fit technician on the bench press machine sat up to watch her go by, she half-twisted and winked at him. *Look at my ass*, she thought. *Don't notice that I'm talking to someone.*

"Look, I have to get this done," Mason said.

"We can take the aleph," she said. She felt the little mental twitch in her head just saying the word. She knew Mason would feel the same thing.

"I could eat," he said in a different tone of voice.

"Ninety minutes," she told him, and hung up.

"Of course the emperor selected the Free Worlds League, Max. What other realm can we trust to really safeguard the people of Hall? The Federated Suns? We, as a planet, once voted to join the Federated Suns when it was the Federated Commonwealth. And here we are, thirty years later, independent and hurting. The Capellan Confederation? I think you know the answer to that–no Hall citizen is going to ally his or herself with a nation that's been using state-sponsored terrorism against our neighbors for years.

"No, the only real option to secure the future of Hall is the Free Worlds League. The Free Worlds League. *Where other factions might seek to conquer us, the Parliament of the Free Worlds has waited until we decided–on our own–to join them."*

"Those were the remarks last evening after the stunning announcement of the emperor's negotiations with the Free Worlds League. In a moment, we'll go out in the streets of Harney to get the average citizen's opinion."

–From the *Harney Morning Edition,*
Harney HV Channel Six

CHAPTER THIRTEEN

BRAMPTON
HALL
THE CHAOS MARCH
2 JUNE 3067

It happened during dessert.

Ezra Payne was sitting in the Disinherited officers' mess, finishing dinner with Nathalie Ortiz, when a lieutenant ran into the room. He skidded to a stop just inside, looking around. Ezra saw him come in out of the corner of his eye and looked over, a forkful of cheesecake halfway to his mouth. The lieutenant—he couldn't have been more than twenty years old—found who he was looking for and walked—just short of ran—toward the table where Colonel Marik-Johns sat with Major Fletcher and Captain Elly Burton.

"You off cheesecake all of a sudden?" Nathalie asked.

Ezra set his fork down. "Something's up," he said, nodding at the colonel's table. It was behind Nathalie, so she half-twisted in her chair to look.

The lieutenant reached the colonel, who looked up with a frown. The lieutenant leaned down to whisper in the colonel's ear, while Major Fletcher and Captain Burton looked on. Marik-Johns listened, then jerked his head back and looked up at the lieutenant. He asked a question. The lieutenant nodded.

Marik-Johns sat back in his chair and pushed his plate away.

"Uh-oh," Nathalie said.

"Yeah," Ezra said. He looked around the room. At least half the officers present had noticed the commotion, and those who had were nudging their companions who hadn't. No one had stood yet, but soldiers—especially mercenary soldiers—were past masters at anticipating alerts. Plates were pushed away. Mouths were dabbed with napkins. The sense of chairs on the edge of being pushed back was tangible in the air.

The Disinherited colonel waved the lieutenant back to his duties and leaned across the table toward Fletcher and Burton. Both leaned in to hear the news. Whatever it was, it was quick. Major Fletcher flinched as if he'd been struck.

Elly Burton stood up so fast her chair flipped over. "That *bastard!*" she yelled.

Nathalie turned back around in her chair. "Baranov," she said.

"Seems likely." Ezra looked down at his cheesecake. There were only a few bites left. He frowned. "It seems wrong to waste it . . ."

"But?"

"But I've never liked eating good food while I got bad news."

Nathalie looked over her shoulder, then back. She smiled. "Eat it fast. The colonel is heading for the HV."

Ezra picked up his fork and shoveled in his cheesecake, chewing as fast as he could. While he did that, he watched the Disinherited colonel stride across the room to the low dais in the front. There was a full-size holovid projector built into the dais. Marik-Johns stepped up, activated the standby field, and stepped into the pickup.

"Listen up, Hellraisers," he said.

"And you, too," Nathalie whispered, *sotto voce.*

"This'll be through the regiment in no time," the colonel said, "so we'll just watch it together." He turned toward the HV controls as whispers erupted in the room. Ezra looked at Nathalie, swallowed, and set his fork down.

The lights in the mess dimmed automatically as the HV came up. It projected the local Harney news desk. The anchor, a fit woman with lustrous brown hair and a false smile, was already speaking.

"—don't know exactly how else to say it, Brent," she was saying to her co-anchor, "so we'll just play it again. If you're just joining us, the message we're about to show you was recorded less than ten minutes ago at the emperor's impromptu press conference."

The holo shimmered and reformed to an image of Bud Baranov, dressed in a brown suit. His hair was slicked back, his beard trimmed, and even at this distance, Ezra could see the fierce gleam of satisfaction in his eyes.

"Citizens of Hall," he started, "this is a momentous occasion."

"This is new," Nathalie said. "Usually he calls people 'my subjects.'"

Ezra grunted, but didn't say anything else.

"Ten years ago, we embarked on a great adventure," Baranov said. "When we were abandoned by House Steiner, we found ourselves alone. The wars that we've all fought continued. Pirates sought us out, thinking us weak. Rebels rose to challenge the rights every citizen of Hall is granted."

Nathalie wasn't the only person who snorted at that.

"When Hall and the rest of the Tikonov Free Republic voted to join the Federated Commonwealth, our parents and grandparents chose their own destiny. They knew that no world, no matter how special, how independent, could still exist in the bosom of the Inner Sphere. Not with the Capellans still lashing out. They chose the power of the time: the Steiner-Davions.

"But the Steiner-Davions rose, like the Star League, and eventually fell. In 3057, we found ourselves alone, and took steps to protect ourselves. Our erstwhile protectors, the Steiner-Davions, ignored us. They ignored our pleas for help. They ignored our requests for aid."

"They couldn't spare a regiment to put Baranov down, is more like," Nathalie said.

"None of us have missed the last few years of civil war, as Katrina Steiner fought Victor Davion to see who would rule the Federated Commonwealth. Now that the war is over, and Victor has won, we might expect some attention once more. Ten years after we needed them, we might expect the Federated Suns to come back." Baranov frowned convincingly into the HV lens. "As if we would let them."

Scuffling sounds filled the mess as people shifted. Ezra looked around. "We should get Jake in here."

"I'm sure he's watching." Nathalie didn't look away from the HV. Her earlier joking was gone. Ezra looked at her, saw the set of her jaw and the tension in her shoulders. She saw where this was going, too.

"For ten years, Hall has had to fend for itself," Baranov continued. "I've done—we've all done—the best we can to prove to everyone, be they Steiners, or Davions, or anyone else—that we're a free people who won't be bullied." He lowered his chin a little, as if challenging anyone to argue with him.

"We've done a damn good job," he said. Then he straightened

up and nodded at the camera.

"This morning I signed an agreement," he said. "One that will bring Hall the security it deserves without sacrificing any of its independence."

He's going to say the Word of Blake, Ezra realized. He looked around at the Disinherited, each of whom was there at the behest of the Allied Mercenary Command to stop this very thing from happening. He looked at Nathalie.

She looked at him, and he knew she was thinking the same thing.

"There's only one interstellar nation that guarantees the rights of its citizens without qualification," Baranov said. "One nation that *asks* worlds to join it, not forces them. Over the last few months I've been in negotiation with that nation, and I'm pleased to say they've agreed to my proposal."

He beamed. "In a few months," he said, "units of the Free Worlds League military will arrive to guarantee Hall's security. They will keep us safe, and provide an immediate example of the benefits of membership in the League."

Ezra blinked. Conversation, some of it heated, overrode the next several sentences of the emperor's speech. On the holo, his lips kept moving, but the only sound Ezra heard was the roaring of the Disinherited.

Nathalie looked at him, then back at the holo, then back at him. Ezra shrugged.

The Free Worlds League.

That wasn't what he expected.

The breast pocket of his utilities buzzed. He pulled out his comm and read the message: RTB ASAP. The code was from Colonel Rauschenbusch.

A captain in Disinherited grays stood up. "Siddown and shuddup!" he yelled. The conversation ceased almost immediately. The captain nodded to his colonel, then sat back down. During the yelling, Marik-Johns had switched the HV back to standby. The lights came back up.

"I want everybody at their action stations in ten minutes," he said. He looked around the room. "Captain Ortiz?"

Nathalie shot to her feet. "Sir!"

"My office. Now."

"Yes, sir!" She turned and pushed her chair back in. Which put her face to face with Ezra, who'd already stood and stepped around the table. She licked her lips and stepped close to him. "Are you coming?"

Ezra held up his comm. "Called home," he said. He reached out and touched her elbow. It wasn't much, but it was something, and he felt the same electric shock he always did when he touched her.

He smiled. "Not what I expected to hear him say."

"I was expecting the Word, for sure," she said.

"What's Marik-Johns going to do?"

Nathalie shrugged. "I guess I'll go find out." She looked down at his comm, then back up at his face. "See you soon?"

Ezra squeezed her elbow. "As soon as I know when."

She nodded. For a second, he thought she was going to lean in for a kiss, but instead she just nodded again and pulled away.

He let her go, then stepped into the line of people exiting the mess hall. Most were turning left in the corridor, toward the 'Mech bays and the staff offices.

Ezra hesitated, then turned right.

Toward the exit.

It didn't feel right.

MARKO'S DELI
HALL
THE CHAOS MARCH
2 JUNE 3067

Kirsten let the announcement play on the small table holo one more time, then leaned across and turned it off. Beside her, Mason squirmed. He sat stiffly, holding a white porcelain coffee mug with no handle in both hands. He hadn't said a word since they sat down.

On the other side of the booth sat Adele Estwicke, who stared at the now-dark holotank with a fierce expression. Her hands were bending and straightening a cheap, pressed-metal butter knife.

Every other patron in the diner—all four of them—were clustered around the full size HV in the corner, watching reruns and media commentary on the emperor's speech. None of them—not even the waitress—had looked at the table in ten minutes.

"Well," Kirsten said.

Mason sucked air through his teeth. "Yeah."

"Three years," Estwicke muttered. "Three years I've been here, simpering at that asshole. All for this." She set the knife down and clenched her hands together. "I have to go back to Terra and tell Precentor Blane that I let Hall slip into the Free Worlds League."

Kirsten frowned at her. "It's not quite as bad as all that."

"Isn't it?" Estwicke glared at her, a touch of mania in her eyes. Her pupils were more dilated than the light suggested they should be. "Unless you can bring your regiment around, I don't see how we can stop it."

"We have time," Kirsten said. "He made a mistake announcing the annexation before he had this 'military presence' on-world."

"It doesn't matter," Estwicke said. "Blane will never allow military action against the League. *I* wouldn't allow it. The League is the only reason we're here today."

Kirsten said nothing. She had been to Jardine. She had read the chronicles of the Hidden Worlds. She had sat at the hand of the Master, and become one of his servants. The Free Worlds League was far from the only reason the Word of Blake existed.

She looked at Estwicke. The True Believers knew next to none of that.

"What is your contingency?" she asked instead.

Estwicke snorted. "Contingency? This is a diplomatic mission. There is no contingency."

I am the contingency, you mopey twat. "So you're saying the True Believer mission to Hall is over," Kirsten said.

Estwicke just held up and dropped her hands.

"Then we move to the Sixth of June mission," Kirsten said. "I'll need a full accounting of your resources, your personnel, and all the local intelligence you've gathered in your time here."

"What?"

"You may have failed," Kirsten said, "but I haven't even begun."

"What are you talking about?"

"You heard Baranov's speech," Kirsten said. "He could only pull this off because we finally killed McNally for him. Either because he needed a 'world government' to take to the League, or because he just needed the thorn out of his side. It's only now, that he's relatively at peace, that he can make this happen."

She hoped she sounded more certain than she felt. The "Sixth of June mission" to Hall was about forty minutes old. She'd worked most of it out on the drive down to the diner. Baranov's speech had played while they were driving, and she'd listened on her comm, watching on the small flatscreen.

"If we can show the League—or more importantly, the people of Hall—that Baranov's façade of peace is just that, a façade, then maybe we can make the League reconsider. Maybe we can get him back to the bargaining table." *Or maybe we get can to a place where we can kill him and be done with it,* Kirsten didn't say. She knew the True Believers didn't always agree with the Sixth of June's methods.

She was a mercenary. She agreed with the Sixth of June's methods.

"How will we do that?" Estwicke asked, and Kirsten knew she had her. She heard the nascent hope in the other woman's voice. She heard the desperation, too. The need to not return to Terra in failure.

"Think about how Baranov opened his speech," Kirsten said. "He mentioned the plebiscite that brought the Free Republic into the Sarna March. We'll use that. You've already laid the groundwork with Aylmer."

"Aylmer's dead."

"Yes, he is. But his idea isn't." Kirsten sat back. "We'll make Hall think Nikoli Ridzik is back, and opposing Baranov." She waited to see how Estwicke would take it.

"Ridzik is dead," she said. "And the mercenary I was paying to pretend to be him is dead, too, out in the Helmand with Aylmer's bunch."

"You know that," Kirsten said. She gestured toward herself and Mason. "We know that." She waved out the diner window at the rest of Hall. "They don't know that." She looked at Mason, but he said nothing.

"We'll use the Ridzik name to rile up what's left of McNally's people. We'll use it to create entirely new groups to fight Baranov. And we'll use it to make Elly Burton so mad at being marginalized that she'll have to do something to stay relevant. All that woman knows how to do is fight Baranov. It won't be difficult."

"What about your regiment?" Estwicke said. "Except for the AMC, you're the most powerful force on the planet, and you're contracted to Baranov. He made a point to tell me that this afternoon, when he was rubbing my face in it."

Kirsten grinned. She indicated Mason. "It just so happens that my brother and I are the second- and third-most ranking officers in the Stealthy Tigers. There's not a lot that can happen without us saying so."

Estwicke frowned and looked down at her empty plate. None of them had ordered anything more than coffee. Which was good, because if they had, it would be burning on the stove in the back of the deli; the staff was still crowded around the HV.

She pushed her napkin around on the table. Kirsten waited. She felt Mason tense to say something, but knocked her knee against his to keep him quiet. He took the hint.

"I'll need to call for help," Estwicke said. "I need a new Ridzik."

Kirsten smiled. "Between us, I think we can get a Light of Mankind squad out here."

Estwicke nodded.

"You'll have the data by morning," she said, sliding out of her side of the booth. A moment later she was gone.

Kirsten looked at Mason and smiled again. He smiled back.

"We can make this work," she told him. "Let's go."

It wasn't easy, but Jacob Brim managed to crouch in such a way that he could see the HV out of the corner of one eye and the trio at the table near the door at the other. When the Blakist woman, Estwicke, stood up to leave, Jacob was careful to make sure he was looking at the HV. He was actually watching the reflection in the window behind the HV, but it'd take a careful observer to notice that.

The two Stealthy Tigers she'd spoken with waited a minute or so longer, than stood up and left, too.

Jacob leaned back and sat down in the chair he'd been half-crouched on. "Isn't that something," he said to himself.

One of his Wolfnet trainers had always said it was better to be lucky than good. And the best way to be lucky, the old man had maintained, was preparation and planning.

Jacob had IDed Adele Estwicke as the local Blakist within a month of landing on Hall, but had all but dismissed her. He hadn't even been following her at the moment. He'd been headed to Bravo Base at Fort Decker, hoping to get a word with Ezra Payne. He'd just stopped at Marko's for a quick bite.

He'd recognized Adele Estwicke the moment she walked into the deli.

And the Stealthy Tiger uniforms were unmistakable.

Majors Kirsten and Mason Markoja.

And Adele Estwicke of the Word of Blake.

At a table.

Talking.

On the same night that Buddy Boy announces his big agenda. The same big agenda that doesn't *take Hall into the Word of Blake Protectorate.*

No wonder Estwicke looked pissed.

This would bear thinking on.

"Across the Inner Sphere, leaders and bureaucrats are already taking ships for Tharkad, to be present at the next Star League Conference. This will be an interesting one, to say the least, and already political pundits are lining up to predict, examine, and dissect the conference's events.

"The first point of contention will certainly be the election of the new First Lord of the Star League. Most experts agree Thomas Marik is the likely choice; the leader of the Free Worlds League enjoys a strong reputation, and after the administration of Christian Mansdottir of Free Rasalhague, many are looking for strength.

"The aftermath of the FedCom Civil War, voting on the status of the Word of Blake and the Taurian Concordat to move from provisional to full voting members of the Star League, and issues of rising tension in the Clan occupation zones are also expected to be dominent topics of conversation."

–From the *Daily INN Download*,
ComStar Hall Hyperpulse Station Harney

CHAPTER FOURTEEN

HARNEY
HALL
THE CHAOS MARCH
22 JULY 3067

"If you're sleeping in there, Talb," Sergeant Major Halleck growled, "I'm going to get a can opener, come in there, and put my boot so far up your—"

"I wasn't sleeping, Sergeant Major!" MechWarrior Nichole Talb shouted.

Ezra Payne looked at the image of her *Apollo* in his HUD and tried not to smile. He heard the drowsiness in her voice, and he couldn't quite bring himself to completely blame her.

Jaguar Company's 'Mechs had been standing in the full Hall sun for almost ten straight hours. The pilots were baking in their cockpits. This wasn't the instant sauna of combat. This was much worse.

This was the gentle warmth of sunlight.

Ezra had been yawning for two hours. He stifled another one as he glanced at the sergeant major's *Jinggau*. There was no way Halleck could see him, not through the *Crusader*'s polarized cockpit port. But Ezra looked at the sixty-five ton, bullet-nosed 'Mech and felt guilty nonetheless. He looked at the chrono display in his HUD.

"Look alive, Jaguars," he said. "We can expect Burton and her escort in about half an hour."

"Sixty-eight, sir," Sergeant Major Halleck said immediately.

"Sixty-eight, Captain," chimed in Lieutenant Nico Reynard. Reynard was the only other officer in Jaguar Company, a slight man of twenty-eight who'd won a commission after the fighting on Carver V, just before the regiment came to Hall. He piloted a fifty-ton *Enforcer* that had been upgraded with advanced technology, and didn't say much.

"Sixty-eight," Ezra replied.

The *Crusader*'s sensors were on watch, but Ezra kept his eyes moving, too. His company was deployed around the government center in Harney. It was a squat, thick-walled building only a few years old. Baranov had ordered it built after the destruction of Cater's Cohorts—the breakaway faction of his own Fourth Republican. The fighting between the halves of the Republicans had spilled into Harney with painful regularity, which had created a series of firebreaks. In the intervening years, Baranov had spent lavishly to rebuild those destroyed districts, creating a staggered order of gentrification that still caused problems for the Harney constabulary.

The government center—the locals smirkingly called it the Hall—was almost as much fortress as it was seat of power, and today that might be needed. In the month since Baranov had made his announcement, much had changed.

First to go was Ezra's liaison assignment. It hadn't taken Colonel Marik-Johns more than a few hours to declare the League annexation a ploy by the Word of Blake to claim control of Hall. Baranov's denunciation had been speedy and obviously preplanned. Most of the Fourth Republican was out on the edge of the city now, "patrolling" to keep the Dismal Ds away from the city. The Disinherited had distributed itself across much of the south of the city in dispersed packets. "The better to keep an eye out for the inevitable Word of Blake presence," was Marik-Johns' official position.

To be ready to respond in any direction, was the unofficial word he got from Nathalie Ortiz.

Thinking of Nathalie made Ezra frown. It hadn't been easy for them to communicate once his access was revoked. Neither of them was unprofessional enough to push it—if it came to shooting, they'd get enough side-eye from their comrades as it was. But they'd kept in touch nonetheless. Messages and comm conversations. He hadn't seen her in the flesh since the announcement.

Maybe he would today.

With the new tension, Baranov had called on the Stealthy Tigers to provide security, which was what Jaguar Company was doing in Harney today. Baranov had agreed to meet with Colonel Marik-Johns and Elly Burton. The rest of the regiment was either on alert at Bravo Base or on maneuvers in the Helmand. Kirsten Markoja had taken her battalion into the desert to train; a Raider lieutenant in her battalion told Ezra they had gone armed.

"Have you heard from the Rep security yet, sir?" Halleck asked on a private channel.

"Not yet," Ezra said.

"Typical."

"Yep," Ezra replied.

The Stealthy Tiger 'Mechs had arrived before dawn. Ezra had reported into the Hall's security center and drawn his company's positions, then climbed back into his cockpit. He'd been assured that one of the Republican security teams would come out presently and get in touch, so they'd be able to set zones of control and all the other little things that made BattleMechs working with infantrymen safe.

He hadn't heard a word since.

"I should climb down and rip someone a new asshole," Halleck said. "This bush league crap is going to get someone killed."

"If they were in my chain of command," Ezra told him, "I'd *order* you to."

Halleck grunted and clicked the line closed.

Ezra smiled, but it was half-ironic. Halleck was right. None of the regiment had a very high opinion of the Fourth Republican— the Reps, as they were called—but they were the primary force of the Tigers' employer. It wouldn't look good if the mercenaries couldn't work with the Hall military.

But what if the Hall military isn't trying to work with us? What then?

The timer in the corner of his HUD counted down beneath twenty-five minutes. Ezra squeezed and let go of his controls, and considered climbing down to try and get someone's attention inside the Hall, but he didn't have time. It'd take him five minutes to get down, and then five to get back up. That gave him fifteen minutes to get inside, find an officer or at least someone who could make a decision, and get that decision made.

Not a chance. He keyed his radio.

"Jaguar Six—" His callsign. "—to Castle Six—" The Hall's headquarters. "—over."

No response.

Just as there hadn't been a response all day. If he hadn't seen people coming and going, he'd have worried the building had

been taken over. He set the transmission repeat every ten seconds and warn him if there was a reply, then switched his channel.
An alert chimed on his console—his sensors had picked up a new
contact.

A BattleMech. Its pennon code was for the Dismal Disinherited.

"Head's up," Ezra said. "They're early."

"I still can't believe they're letting us in there," Jacob Brim said. He
looked out the window of the groundcar he was sharing with Nathalie Ortiz and Geno Carillo. It was the fourth car behind the APC
carrying the colonel and Captain Burton. A pair of Disinherited
'Mechs from Ortiz's company kept pace in front of and behind
the convoy.

"Why not?" Ortiz asked. "From Buddy Boy's position, he's already won."

"By calling in the League, you mean?" Carillo asked. Ortiz
nodded. "You're probably right. The invitation is sent and accepted. It's a done deal. Unless we can find the link between Baranov
and the Word before they get here."

"Which is why I can't believe he's letting us into his headquarters," Jacob said. "It doesn't—"

"Don't," Ortiz said, holding up a hand. "I can't take you saying
it doesn't make sense any more."

"It doesn't," Jacob said.

"Of course it does," Carillo said.

Ortiz and Jacob stared at each other, then looked at the analyst. He blinked back at both of them, then cleared his throat. "It
looks good on HV," he said.

"What?"

"Think about it. Hall is about to become a member of the Free
Worlds League, a Successor State built around the idea of free
membership. Unity, it has *free* in the name of the nation. So if Baranov can fill the airwaves between now and the time whenever
the League gets a regiment here with stories of him reaching out,
trying to find accommodation with his former foes . . ." he trailed
off. Jacob and Ortiz were staring at him. "What?"

Jacob shook his head. "Nothing. Keep going."

"He can't just sit in his fort and wait for the League to rescue him. He can't just hide behind the Stealthy Tigers. When the League gets here, it'd look like they were rescuing him from some kind of bunker." Carillo looked out the window. Jacob followed his eyes, watching the parked cars on either side of the street flash by as they headed down Alexander Avenue.

"He *has* to get in front of it. He has to make every appearance he can, make sure everyone who has an HV sees him extending olive branches, trying to make peace, to make the lives of the everyday citizen of Hall a little quieter, a little more secure."

Ortiz frowned. "So we're *helping* him, is what you're saying?"

Carillo shrugged. "Maybe a little. But we can't not take this opportunity. We have to get inside his headquarters. We have to find the evidence that will undo all of this."

Jacob nodded. He sat back in his seat and stared out the window.

"I wonder if the colonel's figured that out," Ortiz said quietly.

"If not, we can explain it to him," Jacob told her. He looked past her out the window.

And because he was looking, he saw a man step out of the alley between two buildings with a light anti-vehicle weapon on his shoulder. He triggered it as the groundcar passed the alley—the rocket's backblast blew trash into the air for a dozen meters.

Jacob didn't see where the rocket went. He knew it was behind them, because shrapnel didn't explode into the car and kill all three of them. He dove for the floorboard, pulling Ortiz down next to him. The explosion shoved the rear of the civilian car like a 'Mech had kicked it.

Carillo's head hit the window next to him with a sound like a hammer hitting a melon. The tough glass starred, but didn't shatter.

More explosions rocked the car.

"Jesus!" one of the Jaguars shouted. Ezra didn't know which one. He only knew he agreed with the sentiment, if not the deity, and the shout broke him free of the instant's pause the explosion gave him. The *Crusader*'s sensors careted the alley where the shot had come from. He thumbed the *Crusader*'s throttle forward.

"Freeze!" Sergeant Major Halleck cried.

Ezra's thumb dialed the throttle back before his conscious mind caught up to the fact that the regiment's seniormost enlisted man didn't have the authority to give him orders. But his mind caught up almost as fast.

The two Disinherited 'Mechs in the lead had half-spun toward the explosion. The nearer one, a seventy-ton *Caesar*, immediately turned back around. The *Crusader*'s alarms blared as the *Caesar*'s targeting sensors swung across it. Ezra flinched, but kept his systems on standby.

"If he shoots me, no one return fire," Ezra said quickly.

"Six—" Hicks began, but Halleck cut her off.

"You heard the captain!"

The beeping of the *Caesar*'s targeting settled into the keening whine of a target lock, but Ezra didn't move. He hadn't taken more than one step, and his *Crusader*'s arms were still down at its sides. His sensors were on standby, collecting data passively only.

It would be the worst possible outcome if the Tigers and the Dismal Ds started shooting at each other right now. It didn't matter who had fired from the alley. If the two 'Mech contingents started shooting, they'd destroy most of the neighborhood and probably the Hall as well. That would be worse than letting them escape, worse than taking a few rounds in the armor, maybe even worse than Ezra getting killed.

Worse even than whatever had happened to those poor bastards in the groundcar, Ezra knew.

Two blocks behind the ambush, Adele Estwicke half-hid beneath the table in the Café Denise along with all the other patrons. She'd been sitting, nursing a coffee and reading on her noteputer; the very image of someone waiting for someone else to show up. She'd taken a seat by the window, one that looked all the way down Alexander Avenue toward the government center. If anyone had asked, she'd have said it was so she could watch for her friend.

No one had asked.

The ambush had triggered exactly when she'd been told it would. Even knowing it was coming, the explosion of the rocket warhead against the last car in line had shocked her. The windows had rattled in their frames, silverware danced on tables. Most citizens of Harney remembered the fighting in the city when Baranov had put down former major Dick Cater. It was second nature to duck under a table at an explosion.

But Estwicke had to watch. She had a role to play. She squinted over the edge of the table, wishing the smoke would dissipate faster. The 'Mechs in the rear had stopped; one was bent over, trying to right the car that had been flipped up on its side. The other was leaning into the alley, one arm poked inside. Red laser light reflected as it fired.

The 'Mechs in front . . . weren't moving. And past them, the Stealthy Tiger 'Mechs at the government center . . . they weren't moving either. No one was firing. Down the street a few dazed civilians stepped outside onto the sidewalks, clutching heads and looking around.

Estwicke swallowed and touched her comm. The signals were simple: either no signal, for no further action needed. Or a signal, a text message, if further action was needed.

More people appeared on the street. A man climbed out of one of the groundcars in the convoy and looked back the way they'd come. He shouted something at the 'Mech, but Estwicke didn't hear him.

She sent the signal.

Then she ducked fully under the table.

She didn't want to see what came next.

Jacob's ears rang. He blinked tears out of his eyes and shook his head. He felt dizzy. He looked around at a wash of light and fresh air—Carillo had opened his door and climbed out. Jacob frowned and tried to say something, to tell him to come back, but his throat was dry with dust.

Next to him, Ortiz pushed herself up. From her frown, she felt like he did. Jacob swallowed and tried to call to Carillo again. The technician's head was covered in blood from where he'd struck his head. He was looking back the way they'd come. Jacob saw his mouth moving, but he couldn't hear anything but the ringing in his ears.

"Geno—" Jacob croaked.

Then light flashed everywhere, the car door slammed shut, and more explosions drove Jacob and Ortiz back down to the floorboard.

"It wasn't us," Ezra was saying, slowly and clearly, over and over again.

The Disinherited *Caesar* hadn't let up on its target lock. The keening alarm was still cutting at Ezra's ears. He hadn't moved the *Crusader* a millimeter, and he was broadcasting in the clear, on an unencrypted channel. Civilians with handheld radios could pick up this transmission. He didn't want there to be any doubt that he was being sincere.

"You move," the *Caesar*'s pilot said, "and—"

And what, Ezra didn't know. At the MechWarrior's first syllable of the next word, one entire row of parked vehicles exploded along the side of the street parallel to where the convoy had stopped. Windows shattered for an entire kilometer up and down the avenue. The force of the blast flung the convoy's vehicles up onto their sides. Flames and smoke from fuel tank explosions from the other cars parked along the street added to the conflagration.

The avenue was easily a hundred meters wide; fire and flame filled the entirety of it. The fireball swallowed the *Caesar* and the other 'Mechs from view.

"Oh shi—" was all Ezra had time to say before the shockwave hit his 'Mech. Though attenuated by distance, the impact still struck with powerful force. The *Crusader* was shoved back a step.

A PPC fired from inside the fireball—the *Caesar*. It didn't come anywhere near any of the Stealthy Tiger 'Mechs. It might not have even been aimed, for all Ezra knew.

"Jesus," someone whispered again on the lance channel. It was Sergeant Roses.

"Anybody hurt?" Halleck asked. There was a chorus of *no's*. "Captain?"

"I'm fine," Ezra said. He stared into the wall of smoke and debris. Dust, papers, and other debris fluttered down from the buildings around them. At the *Crusader*'s feet, from inside the government center, a steady stream of people ran out into the street. Some of them carried weapons.

"I'm fine," he said again. Then he keyed the *Crusader*'s loudspeakers. "Everyone keep back! There might be more explosives."

One or two of the running people pulled up and looked around. Most of them just kept running.

There was movement in the smoke. The *Caesar* emerged, flame-blackened. It sensors acquired Ezra's *Crusader* again. Ezra raised the *Crusader's* arms over its head, about as far out of firing position as he could. "Two Lance, Three Lance, hold your position unless attacked," he said calmly. "One Lance, he's going to shoot at me in a second. Do not fire back."

"Six—" Hicks grumbled.

"That's an order."

The *Caesar* lurched to the side. It was moving almost drunkenly. Ezra was sympathetic. He couldn't imagine what it must've been like to be inside that conflagration, but he didn't think it would do good things to his balance. "It's not me," he told the *Caesar's* pilot.

"*You* say," the *Caesar* said. Its PPC fell into line with the *Crusader.*

"Six—" Hicks said again.

"Hicks, you disobey the captain again and I'll have you cleaning Mason Markoja's latrine until you're sixty," Sergeant Major Halleck said. "Shut your mouth."

"We're not attacking," Ezra told the *Caesar.* "Stand down and we'll *help* you."

"Help this," the *Caesar* said.

The PPC fired.

*"An explosion has been reported on Alexander Avenue, near the govern-
ment center. It's unclear if this was an isolated incident, or the opening
shot of a series of attacks. Eyewitnesses have confirmed BattleMechs in
Allied Mercenary Command colors approaching through downtown.
It's possible the AMC has finally decided to make a move against the
emperor, but that seems unlike–wait.*

*"We're getting uncomfirmed reports now of additional explosions
in the same area, and of weapons fire."*

–From the *Harney Morning Edition*,
Harney HV Channel Six

CHAPTER FIFTEEN

A PPC shot moved too fast for the eye to follow. Ezra saw the blue-white flash and felt the impact at the same time. He clutched his controls, bringing the *Crusader*'s balance under control. He had to shift the 'Mech's feet, but it didn't take more than that, because his attention right then wasn't on the *Caesar* or even his footing. It was on the other three Jaguar Company 'Mechs standing nearby.

"One Lance," he called, "*hold*. I'm okay. Do not fire."

"He shoots at you again, Six, and you and the sergeant major can do what you want," Hicks growled.

"He shoots at me again, and you won't be shooting alone," Ezra promised. He lowered the *Crusader*'s arms. "*Caesar*: I'm not returning your fire. My lance is not returning your fire. We didn't do this. Now stand the hell down so we can help your people."

The *Caesar* didn't move. Smoke or steam rose from the muzzle of its PPC.

Ezra squeezed his controls, then put his finger near the switch for his active sensors. If the *Caesar* fired again, he and his lance would put the Hellraiser down. It'd be hell to explain later, but he wasn't going to take more than one shot in the name of peace.

He hadn't taken more than that from the Always Faithful on Caph. He sure as hell wasn't going to here, not when rockets were flying and cars were exploding.

The *Caesar*'s tracking sensors shut off. The sudden absence of the keening alarm was more jarring in Ezra's cockpit than the alarm noise had been. The 'Mech turned away without another word, plunging back into the thinning smoke.

Ezra exhaled more tension than air.

"Okay," he said. He blinked and looked around his cockpit, mind working.

"Three Lance, put your 'Mechs on standby and dismount. You're with me and One Lance—we're going to offer what aid we can."

Sergeant Major Halleck, who led Three Lance, double-clicked his mic in affirmative.

"Nico, get a report to Bravo Base. Then keep your lance mounted on security. Hold the government center." Ezra scanned his HUD, but the only contacts were his company and the remnants of the Dismal Disinherited convoy. "It were me, this is when I'd push in a general attack. Be ready for that."

"Roger, Six," Nico Reynard said.

"I don't know if you'll get anyone from the Hall to listen now that it's a war zone out here, but you've got the 'Mechs. You retain command of the security situation. Let aid crews in and civilians out, but we're going to have to figure out what happened. Try and preserve the scene as much as you can."

"Got it."

"You're going to see more Disinherited people show up pretty fast," Ezra predicted. "It's their people in there. They get what they want, got it?"

"Sir."

"One Lance," Ezra went on, "put 'em in standby, get your ground mount on, and let's see who survived." He clicked the channel closed, leaned back, and let go of his controls. It was a toggle and some security codes to put the 'Mech into standby.

Only then did he let himself think about Nathalie Ortiz. She was supposed to have been with that convoy, and none of the escort 'Mechs had been a *Dervish*.

Ezra slapped his harness release and pulled his neurohelmet off. Through the *Crusader*'s canopy he saw the roiling smoke cloud that had been Alexander Avenue.

His hand shook as he reached for the hatch release.

Jacob Brim's tongue tasted like smoke and dirt, and it hurt when he tried to swallow. Something was digging painfully into his side, and his left shoulder hurt like he'd been stabbed. He opened his eyes and immediately wished he hadn't; dust and dirt and God only knew what else fell into them as soon as he did. He tried to swear, and only succeeded in starting a coughing fit.

He couldn't hear very well.

Using his right hand, he wiped at his eyes until he could see. The light was dim and diffuse. The air was thick. He saw motes floating in the still air inside the groundcar. A sheet of office paper fell across his face. He pulled it away and looked at it. *Osman Accounting Services.* He frowned and threw it away. He blinked and tried to remember.

Something moved against his left foot.

Jacob flinched, and that motion was enough to spring his mind back to reality and out of the fugue he'd awakened in. He was in the car with Nathalie Ortiz. There'd been an ambush. Carillo . . . he looked around. There was no sign of the analyst. Then he looked around again, and realized why he was so off-kilter.

The groundcar was lying on its side. The pain in his side was the handrail on the door. And the movement on his foot—he looked. It was Nathalie Ortiz. She was lying half on top of his legs, half against the now-vertical bench seat. She looked up at him and blinked grit out of her eyes.

"Are you okay?" he asked, or tried to. His throat felt like he'd been gargling broken glass. His tongue was swollen—had he bitten it? He was in too much pain to tell.

Ortiz frowned at him. Her mouth moved, but Jacob didn't hear her.

"What?" he asked.

She grimaced, freed one arm, and pointed at her ear, then made a questioning gesture. Then she pointed at him.

Jacob tried to shrug, but his shoulder screamed pain at him. He looked down at it. "Oh, shit," he tried to say. There was a jagged piece of glass sticking out of his arm, a few centimeters above his armpit. He could tell from the angle that it was likely jammed between his pectoral muscle and his sternum, but that was small comfort. He looked up at Ortiz and raised an eyebrow.

She nodded and tried to move. She only made a small movement, and then grimaced. She might have yelled, but Jacob couldn't tell. All he could hear was the solid ringing in his ears. He hoped it was temporary.

A moment later, Ortiz knelt next to him. Her face was covered in brown-white dust. There were wet rims around her eyes, mouth and nose, and a muddy streak across her cheek where she'd wiped at her face with her sleeve. She frowned down at him and poked at the glass in his shoulder.

He screamed. He would have writhed away from her involuntarily, but he could barely move.

She grimaced and moved her hand. He looked up at her. She made a pulling-out gesture. Jacob shook his head no.

Ortiz made the gesture again.

Jacob shook his head again.

Ortiz frowned.

Then she grabbed the shard and yanked it out in a single motion. There was more screaming. Jacob didn't bother holding back on the profanity. He knew she couldn't hear him any more than he could hear himself, and just then he didn't care.

Ortiz jammed her hand over the exposed wound in his shoulder and pressed down, hard. Her other hand scrabbled around Jacob's ribs. He felt her pull and felt something slither along his side: the jacket Carillo had taken off in the car. She balled it up and pressed it against his shoulder.

The jacket reminded Jacob. He caught her eye and mouthed *"Carillo?"*

Ortiz shook her head.

Jacob tried to swallow. It still hurt. He did his best to ignore the pain in his shoulder and looked around. The light was getting brighter, but still diffuse. His trained mind told him he was seeing illumination through a smoke cloud, but until he got outside he couldn't tell how big the explosion had been. It had for sure been larger than a LAW rocket would create.

The car body trembled against his side. He looked around, but nothing changed in the light. The car trembled again. He looked at Ortiz to see if she'd felt it, too. She was looking at him. He raised his eyebrows in question.

"'Mechs," she mouthed at him.

By the time Ezra had climbed down from his *Crusader*'s cockpit, the other three members of his lance were waiting. Roses and Akhtar looked worried, and Aurel Hicks just looked furious. All three carried their cockpit aid kits, though, and Akhtar had found a pry bar somewhere. He looked at them, and then up the smoke-filled street.

"Right now we're not Tigers," he told his lance. "And they're not Dismal Ds. We're not on Baranov's side, and they're not on the AMC's. They're people that need help, and we're people who can help." He looked each of his MechWarriors in the eye until he was sure they understood.

Halleck and his lance jogged up just as Ezra finished speaking. The sergeant major nodded to the captain and then looked at the assembled group. "You give them the speech?" he asked Ezra.

Ezra nodded. "Then what he said," Halleck told them.

"What if they attack us?" Sergeant Quinn asked. He drove a *Charger* in Three Lance.

"Defend yourself," Halleck said before Ezra could speak. "The captain already took all the free shots we're going to take."

"That's right," Ezra said, "but hopefully it won't come to that." He gestured. "Let's go."

The MechWarriors started walking that way. Even this far away the air was already thick with smoke and dust, making Ezra's sinuses burn.

Halleck fell into step with him at the rear of the ersatz column. "You did good."

"Sergeant Major?"

"Taking that shot. Not shooting back. That will make it look a lot more convincing that we didn't do this, after."

Ezra looked at him. "We *didn't* do this, Bob."

Halleck grinned at him. "I know that, and you know that," he said, "but we both know it'll only matter how it plays on the HV later."

Ezra grimaced. "I wasn't thinking about that."

"Didn't think you were," Halleck said. "But it's good that your instincts led you to the right places."

A gust of wind blew smoke and dust across the Stealthy Tigers group. Both Halleck and Ezra raised an arm to half-block their faces, but it did little good. It was only reflex; the dust and other crap in the air was already in their lungs and throats. Roses started coughing. Ezra tried blinking the grit out of his eyes, and only succeeded in driving it deeper.

The first person Ezra saw up close was a civilian woman. She appeared suddenly out of the deep smoke and almost collided with him. Her face, skin and clothes were all coated with brown-white dust and grime. Tear tracks glistened muddily on her cheeks. Her eyes were dazed. Her clothes were torn.

"Are you all right?" Ezra asked, and immediately castigated himself. He couldn't imagine a more stupid thing to say in this situation.

"Here, miss, why don't you sit down?" Sergeant Major Halleck said. He took the woman by the arm and led her toward the edge of the street so she could sit on the curb. He nodded for Ezra to keep going.

More people appeared. A man was staggering, holding a clearly broken arm. Sergeant Roses went to him and urged him to the curb next to the woman with Halleck. Two teenagers were walking, leaning on each other, both with drying blood on either side of their heads. It came from their ears.

"Are you the police?" one of them shouted. Iqbal Akhtar shook his head and gestured them toward the curb. He opened his aid kit as soon as they sat down and began trying to clean the blood off them. The wipe he was using was black with soot and dust almost immediately.

Ezra coughed. Throngs of people were appearing as the smoke and the dust settled. Dozens, scores, hundreds. Some of them were helping each other, and some of them were clearly dazed. A number of them were sobbing.

Some were lying dead in the street.

As the smoke cleared, Ezra saw the Disinherited *Caesar* moving about forty meters down the avenue. It was hunched over, one arm outstretched while the other rolled an armored personnel carrier back onto its wheels.

"Sergeant Major," Ezra said, "get someone else to help that woman, and come with me." He didn't wait for Halleck to acknowledge the order—he wanted to be there when that APC was opened.

There was glass in Adele Estwicke's hair, and grit in her eyes. Her ears were ringing, but she could hear, and as she stumbled along behind the other café patrons on the sidewalk, she tried not to look like she was paying too much attention. She squinted and wiped at her eyes again. She'd need to be able to report. Report more than the groans of stressed buildings shifting and the sobs of the wounded, that is.

The Light of Mankind operative who'd briefed her had understated the power of the explosives they'd planted in the parked cars. Light of Mankind was the special operations branch of ROM, the Word's intelligence service. Its agents were expert at nearly any mission of warfare or intelligence, and that agent had obviously thought Adele was trained in explosives as well.

Every window in sight was broken. Each footstep Estwicke took crunched on broken glass. She'd already passed a dozen bodies, and more injured people than she could count. As foot traffic bunched up in front of her, she struggled to see through the smoke. Something was blocking half the sidewalk. When she got close enough to see what it was, she stiffened.

It was a 'Mech's foot.

One of the AMC 'Mechs with the convoy had fallen against the building. Against, and then into. It lay like a comatose, twelve-meter-tall man in the wreckage of four floors of the build. Glass and broken ferrocrete half-covered the torso. As she passed, Estwicke touched the 'Mech's foot—it was vibrating. The 'Mech was still active, but the MechWarrior inside was unconscious or worse.

Estwicke carefully hid the smile that knowledge gave her.

Then she followed the throngs of civilians into the smoke.

By the time Ezra and Halleck reached the APC, a pair of men—indistinguishable from each other, they were so covered in soot and dust—were heaving against an improvised pry bar, trying to force the hatch open. Ezra reached to help, but just before he could grab it, the bar shrieked and bent at the join; it was useless. One of the men swore and slammed a fist against the unyielding metal.

Ezra looked around, but Halleck was already stepping past him. He'd brought Akhtar's pry bar. "Look out," he said to the men in front of the hatch. "Let me try." The two men turned, saw him coming, and stepped aside.

Halleck leaned in, eying the hatch. He looked up, then down. Then he raised a heavy boot and kicked the hatch. Ezra thought he watched where the dust fell from. Then he nodded, set the bar's tip, and leaned against it.

There was a *pop*, a *sprong*, and the hatch creaked open a half-meter or so. The pry bar fell out of the now-open gap, and Halleck let it fall. His thick hands grasped the edge of the hatch and he leaned back. The heavy metal hatch groaned open another couple of centimeters.

"Come on," Ezra said to the two men. He stepped close, got a grip, and pulled. Halleck fell into Ezra's rhythm immediately; the two men realized what they were doing and suited their own motion to the Tigers'. After a few yanks, the hatch was open a meter and a half. One of the dust-covered men immediately climbed into the dark interior.

Ezra and Halleck stepped back. There was motion inside, but not enough light to see any details.

"Get out of my way!" yelled a voice Ezra recognized. He didn't frown, but only because he didn't want that to be the first expression Elly Burton saw on his face when she came into the light and recognized him.

Because, as sure as gravity was holding him against Hall's surface, she would recognize him.

Burton climbed out of the APC and lurched onto the street. She immediately coughed and sneezed and wiped at her eyes. Because the interior had been modestly airtight, she wasn't yet covered with the ubiquitous dust.

Behind Ezra, the *Caesar* shifted its feet and carefully stepped past the fallen APC. It was moving deeper into the ambush zone, probably to investigate the next vehicle in line. Ezra wanted to go with it to check, but he couldn't be sure who else was inside the APC. If Burton had been in this one . . .

"Colonel?" someone inside the APC asked. Then, louder, "Colonel!" If there was a reply, it was too faint for Ezra to hear.

"He's unconscious, but his pulse is strong," Burton shouted. She frowned and pressed her hand against both of her ears, as if equalizing pressure. She let go, listened for a moment, then did it again. Listened again. "Damn it," she muttered.

Ezra stepped into her line of sight. "Captain Burton?"

She looked at him, drawn by his movement, if not his voice. "What?" Ezra could tell by the tone that she meant *what did you say*, not *what are you asking*.

Ezra leaned closer. "Can you hear me?" he asked more loudly.

She focused on his face. She frowned, then her face worked into an expression of disbelief. "Payne?" She looked around. "Did you attack the convoy?" None of the people in sight could be identified by uniform. She shrank back. "Are you insane?"

"No," Ezra said loudly, holding out his hands, "No—we were at the government center. We saw the ambush and came to help."

She didn't hear him. She kept looking around, wiping at her

eyes. She looked up past the wreck of the APC at the shape of the *Caesar* moving in the middle distance. She spun back to look at Ezra. "You son of a bitch!" she screamed, and slapped him.

Ezra saw it coming, and took it. It was open-palmed, thankfully, and stung like hell. His right eye started watering immediately. Otherwise he didn't move, though he felt Halleck step closer.

"Captain—" he started, but she swung again.

This time, he caught her wrist in the air. She frowned at the strength in his grip. Burton opened her mouth, but something snapped inside of Ezra. He shoved backward, still holding her wrist. Burton had to step backward to keep from falling over. Her hip and then her back hit the hull of the APC, but Ezra didn't stop. He shoved until her wrist and his fist rang painfully against the APC's hull.

"Listen," he growled. He knew others were watching, and he felt Halleck's hand on his shoulder, but shrugged it off. "You get the one shot, because you just got blown up and you can't be expected to have your head on straight. I sure as shit wouldn't."

Burton jerked her hand, trying to get free. Ezra held tight.

"But that's *all you get.* I've done nothing since we met but bend over backward trying to keep from pissing you off. Because of the count. But that's over." He let go of her wrist, but he didn't step back. "I didn't blow you up. I'm here, out of my 'Mech, with most of my company out of their 'Mechs, trying to help people— *including you*—in what might be a war zone any second."

He took a deep breath. "If you can move, head back toward the government center. The smoke clears after about forty meters. You can wait for help there." He stepped back. "If you can help, help." His tone made it clear what his opinion of her was. "But make no mistake—I'm done being nice to you. Don't ever try and touch me again."

Then he turned his back on her, nodded at Halleck, and stepped around the APC to go to the next vehicle in line.

As he did, he saw Nathalie Ortiz helping Jacob Brim climb out of an overturned groundcar. He was bent over and favoring a shoulder, and she walked with a limp, but she saw him almost immediately. She waved.

It was all Ezra could do not to fall down in the street.

The recent attack on the Allied Mercenary Command unit was our work. We will not allow outsiders to determine the fate of the people of Hall. None of us voted to join the Free Worlds League. None of us asked for this. And none of us swore allegiance to Bud Baranov except at the point of a gun.

The people of Hall deserve better. The people of Hall deserve a government they choose. The people of Hall deserve to be part of something chosen by all of its people, not just the ones with BattleMechs. And so we offer the last model government that offered Hall such freedom: the Tikonov Free Republic.

Join us. Help us eject the outsiders and the unfit. Help us rebuild the nation my father died to build. Help us find security in shared defense, hope in renewed effort.

Eight years ago, Bud Baranov killed my brother and tried to kill me. He cannot be allowed to rule Hall. No one who was not chosen by her people can.

My name is Nikoli Ridzik, and I stand for the people of Hall.

—Transcript of a message blasted
through Hall+3.3s' media networks

CHAPTER SIXTEEN

**BRAVO BASE
HALL
THE CHAOS MARCH
23 JULY 3067**

"The *Harney Morning Edition* received a letter claiming credit for the attack last night," the hologram of Jacob Brim said.

Ezra frowned at the image, though not at the message. He wasn't processing that, not yet. He was looking at the heavily bruised and obviously in pain image of his friend. The others at the conference table didn't share his priorities.

"Who was it?" Colonel Rauschenbusch asked.

"Nikoli Ridzik and the Army of the Free Republic," Brim said.

"That's impossible," Mason Markoja said. He sat across the table from Ezra, at the colonel's left hand. Next to him was one of his company commanders, Captain Wesley Eberhardt. Eberhardt was a small man, wiry, with a balding head and an irritating smile. Ezra didn't like Eberhardt any more than he liked Markoja. Eberhardt wasn't a Raider, either. "Ridzik is dead."

"He was dead a couple months ago when he attacked me in the desert, too," Ezra snapped without thinking. He realized what he'd said almost as soon as he'd said it, but by then it was too late, of course.

Mason was staring at him. Eberhardt was looking at him like he'd just tried to set the tabletop on fire. The colonel . . . Ezra relaxed. Rauschenbusch was looking at the holo of Brim as if Ezra hadn't spoken.

"Any proof?" he asked.

The image of Brim shook its head. "No. Just the letter. Similar letters were delivered the same day to every major news bureau on the planet, according to my information."

"That suggests a level of sophistication," said the disembodied voice of Kirsten Markoja. She was still in the Helmand with her battalion. The attack in Harney the previous day had urged caution, so the colonel had decided to keep the regiment a little spread out. Kirsten was away from a holoprojector, so she was voice only.

"It does," Brim confirmed.

"How are your people, Sergeant?" Rauschenbuch glanced at Ezra, then back to the holo Brim. "Captain Payne told us one of your men was killed. You have our sympathies."

"Thank you, Colonel," Brim said. "Four of the Dismal Ds were killed, and more than thirty injured." He tried to raise his arm and grimaced. "We're all healing."

"So if it's not Ridzik," Kirsten Markoja asked, "then who is it?"

"I can't say with any certainty," Brim said.

"Guess."

"It could be you guys," Brim said. Ezra heard the edge in his voice, his anger at being pressed. "I'm just throwing out all the options, of course. Your regiment has the sophistication." He looked at Rauschenbusch, and then at Ezra, and grimaced. "You wouldn't, of course. You'd come right at us."

"We would," Rauschenbusch said. "Go on."

"It could be Baranov, independent of you," Brim said. "There's some hope for that theory over here."

"For obvious reasons," Captain Eberhardt said. Ezra frowned at him, but no one else said anything. They might share the same rank, but not all captains were created equal. Ezra was here because he'd been the liaison between the regiment and the Allied Mercenary Command. He was expected to participate on that basis. And because he led the independent Jaguar Company.

Eberhardt was a line officer—he led one of Mason Markoja's companies—but he didn't routinely operate at the level of meetings like this. He was trying to curry favor.

From the look on the colonel's face, Eberhardt was failing.

"It could be one of McNally's loyalists, trying for a last-gasp attack, even though his cause is dead." Brim glanced at Ezra. "Captain Burton's presence in the convoy mitigates that possibility, though. Most of McNally's people are behind her because of her son."

"Of course, her being there is the perfect cover for that," Mason said. "She survived, after all."

"That's true," Brim said, after a moment. *You boor*, Ezra heard unsaid.

"Or it could be the Word of Blake," Brim said.

"So you're saying it could be anyone," Kirsten said. "You don't have any idea."

"I have plenty of ideas. I just can't say which one is right with any certainty."

The colonel cleared his throat. "Thank you for sharing this data with us, Sergeant," the said. "I was surprised to get this call."

Ezra had been surprised, too. When he and the Jaguars had returned to Bravo Base early that morning, having worked most of the night at the recovery operations on Alexander Avenue, he'd found the invitation to a briefing call waiting for him. He'd thought the sharing of information was over with the end of his liaison role.

Brim looked to the side. "About that . . . " he touched a control, and a second holo shimmered to life on the dais.

Colonel John Marik-Johns.

"Colonel," he said, inclining his head toward Rauschenbusch.

"Colonel Marik-Johns," Rauschenbusch replied. "Are you well, sir?"

The Disinherited colonel grinned. He was sitting down, where Brim was standing, and from the background of the holo they were in different rooms. "I'm healing, sir, thank you." He arranged his features. "I wanted to get on this call for two reasons, Colonel. First, to thank you and your troops for your assistance yesterday." He looked at Ezra. "Despite some overreactions on our part, your company on the scene rendered immediate aid to my wounded. We—none of us—won't forget that."

Rauschenbusch smiled and looked at Ezra. "It's no more than you would have done for us, were our positions reversed, Colonel," Ezra said. "And more, it was the right thing to do."

"I'm told one of my 'Mechs fired on you, Captain," Marik-Johns said.

Ezra waved the comment away. "It's nothing. I took it in the armor."

"Still . . . "

"Colonel, if I'd just seen my commander blown up with someone else's 'Mechs in sight, I might have done the same thing." *I might not have*, Ezra didn't say, but that wouldn't have been politic.

"As I said, Captain, Colonel—we won't forget."

"You said two things, Colonel," Kirsten Markoja put in. "The second?"

Marik-John's face took on a more serious expression. "I approved everything Brim just told you," he said. "And I'll continue to authorize the sharing of information on this matter, as a courtesy, because I don't believe your regiment was involved, and I don't want anyone else—whoever it might be—blowing up any more city streets."

"Thank you, Colonel," Colonel Rauschenbusch said.

"That being said, I no longer believe I can keep my people safe this close to Harney. Not without moving to a more, ah, aggressive stance." He looked through the holo and met Colonel Rauschenbusch's steady gaze. "I think we can agree that would be a mistake?"

Rauschenbusch nodded.

"Because of that, I'm pulling my headquarters back to Rockfall Maze. I'll be maintaining a presence in Brampton, and most of my dispersed stations will remain, but we're taking the noncombatants south.

Ezra kept his face impassive, but that was startling news. Rockfall Maze was almost two thousand kilometers away from Harney. It would completely cut the AMC off from direct access to the city. From a certain point of view, it was an admission that they'd failed their mission.

"We'll be using the DropShips for most of it, and our movement will begin in less than ten hours."

"I'll communicate your plans to the emperor's staff," Rauschenbusch said. "Thank you for letting us know."

Marik-Johns frowned at Baranov's title, but nodded nonetheless. "Whatever else goes on, we're professionals, Colonel." He manipulated a control out of the holo's pickup and vanished. Only Brim remained.

"Anything else, Sergeant?" Rauschenbusch asked.

"No, Colonel," Brim said. "Except to add my thanks, and the Dragoons', to the colonel's for your company's actions yesterday." He looked at Ezra, nodded, and clicked off.

Ezra glanced at Mason, ignored Eberhardt, and stopped at the colonel. "They didn't have to do that."

"No, they didn't." Rauschenbusch glanced between his officers. "But I'm glad they did."

"We need to find out who did this," Mason said. At his side, Eberhardt nodded. Ezra held in his sigh. That statement had been on par with *we need to chew our food* and *light comes from the sun*. No wonder Eberhardt agreed.

"We don't have investigators on the scene," Kirstin chimed in. "Which means we need to wait for them to *tell us* who did it."

"That's a good point, Kirsten," the colonel said. He looked at Ezra. "Do you think they'd take you as an observer?"

"They might," Ezra said. "But I'm less concerned with the investigation than I am with their move." He manipulated the controls on the tabletop in front of him, and brought up a map of the Farnorth continent. A glowing button appeared over Harney, and a second over Rockfall Maze, deep in the south.

"Someone blew up one of my convoys, I might think about getting the kids and technicians out of harm's way," Rauschenbusch allowed. "Makes a little sense."

"It makes perfect sense," Ezra said, "except that they've just put themselves out in the cold. Their mission is Harney. It's Baranov. With the Free Worlds annexation breathing down their necks, they can't be putting more space between their primary forces and their target. They don't have time."

"Maybe they're realizing there really isn't a Word of Blake presence on Hall," Kirsten said. "Maybe they just want to get to the end of their contract without getting blown up?"

"Maybe," Ezra said, carefully not looking at the colonel. Of everyone in the room or on the comm, only Rauschenbusch and he knew of Charles Monet's research. "Or maybe it's a ploy."

"A ploy for what?" Mason asked. "So they're moving their HQ to the ass end of nowhere. They've still got most of two battalions scattered around the Helmand and the smaller communities around Harney. They've still got Burton and her lot bunched up at Deal. It's not like they're really that far away."

Ezra shrugged. "I don't know the answer, Major. It just feels odd."

Rauschenbusch audibly breathed in, and then out. "We'll figure it out later." He looked at the holo map. "Kirsten, anything else?"

"No, sir."

"Mason?" Mason shook his head. Ezra watched Eberhardt open his mouth to speak, but the colonel didn't even look at him. Ezra knew better than to speak.

The colonel slapped the table with both hands. "Okay. Ezra, get some rest. Good work yesterday." He looked at Mason. "Mason, let's go look over some deployments. With the Dismal Ds pulling back, I think we can draw down the number of troops were have out in the cold . . ."

**BRAMPTON
HALL
THE CHAOS MARCH
23 JULY 3067**

Jacob Brim looked up as Colonel Marik-Johns walked into his office. He was seated, half-leaning, at his desk. The bandage on his shoulder limited his movement, and made it impossible for him to use his keyboard, but he could read hardcopy. He pushed the stack away and indicated the office chair with his chin. "Have a seat, Colonel."

Marik-Johns sat. "Do you think they bought it?"

"I think they'll buy part of it," Brim replied. "But Payne is smart. He'll figure it out."

"Will they listen to him?"

Brim forgot himself, tried to shrug, and yelped in pain. He sucked air through his teeth. "Sorry. I don't know."

The colonel fidgeted. "You haven't told Payne about the diner?"

"No."

"Don't." Marik-Johns rubbed his hands together, looking down at them. "I don't think he's one of them, but we can't be sure."

Brim didn't laugh. *"One of them."* Is this a spy holo? Instead, he said, "I trust him, Colonel. The Markojas are dirty. I know it, even if I can't prove it. It's the same way I know the Estwicke woman is the Word's agent here."

"I still think that's a little obvious," Marik-Johns said. "She's the accredited envoy. She'd be the first person anyone would look at if they were looking at Blakists."

"Where's the best place to hide something, Colonel?"

"I know—in plain sight. But still . . ."

"We need evidence, sir." Brim rarely called Marik-Johns sir, and the colonel knew it. "We have to make them feel complacent. We have to make them believe we've given up, so they'll get sloppy."

"I know." He stood up. "Burton says we should attack." He looked at Brim. "What do you think about that?"

"I think Elly Burton says attack when she wakes up each morning," Brim said. "She's been here too long, got too many attachments."

"A son isn't an attachment."

Brim laughed. "Of course it is."

"It would be simpler."

"It would," Brim agreed, "but we'd get eaten alive in the media." He didn't have to say what would happen to the Disinherited and the AMC if the Word of Blake's media picked up the Hall-based story; the PR hit would be deadly to the AMC, and none of its other members would stand for that.

Nor would the Wolf. And Jacob knew John Marik-Johns looked up to Jaime Wolf.

"Yeah." Marik-Johns sighed. "Okay. We need to make something happen."

Brim tapped his bandaged shoulder. "Something *else* happen, sir. Something else."

HELMAND DESERT
HALL
THE CHAOS MARCH
23 JULY 3067

Kirsten Markoja looked up as a man in a Tigers technician uniform stepped into her field tent. With her battalion in bivouac, the support detachment had brought up tents, and she'd been working at her small field desk. The radio with which she'd participated in the meeting was stacked in a corner; it was a short-range re-transmitter that tied into the more powerful comms in her *Nightsky*.

The technician secured the tent flap behind him and then faced her. He was a nondescript man: brown hair, brown eyes, not especially remarkable physically. He closed his eyes for a moment, sighed, and then subtly changed his stance. When he opened his eyes again, his manner was completely different.

"Peace," he said. His voice was deep without being remarkable.

Kirsten smiled. "And with you," she replied. "We're secure here." She indicated the small camp stool opposite her, and the "technician" sat down.

"Developments?" he asked.

Kirsten regarded him. She had met very, very few Light of Mankind operatives during her time on Jardine. She had met far worse—she had *become* far worse—but they still fascinated her. They were as fanatical as those not blessed with knowledge of the Hidden. Looking at this man, she could almost see their strength.

"The Ridzik persona is working as well as it can," she said. "No one believes it, but that's the point."

The operative inclined his head. "What's next?" he asked.

"We proceed," she told him. "In a few weeks, you will strike again, this time at Elly Burton directly. That will direct attention away from Harney." Kirsten rubbed her right wrist with her left hand absently as she spoke. "After that, we'll stage something that will finally get the Tigers and the Dismal Ds fighting. That will draw in everyone else, and when the League arrives, they'll find Hall covered in blood and anything but unified and waiting to greet them with open arms."

The operative didn't speak for a moment. He was obviously thinking. Kirsten watched him think. These men and women were not simply tools; they couldn't be. If St. Jamais had sent her just a special operations soldier from the Word of Blake Militia, that would have been simpler. She held rank—secret rank, but rank nonetheless—in that organization. She could have just given him or her orders.

An operative was different. An operative had to be flexible. He had to use his judgment.

"I'll need a 'Mech soon," he said. "It would be best if we could get 'Ridzik' seen by the people in the outskirts."

"Robin Hood?" she asked.

The operative nodded. "Once the rumors are coming from all sides, it will be more and more difficult for our enemies to concentrate their attention against us."

"Estwicke will have some mercenary contacts left," Kirsten said. "Contact her. Get them. A man bent on rebuilding the Tikonov Free Republic—" she smirked as she said it, "—should have an entourage."

He nodded. He stood, but paused. "You've arranged your extraction, I take it?"

Kirsten clenched her right hand into a fist. "I won't be extracting," she said. "I'll be staying here."

The operative inclined his head. Then he breathed in, held it, and closed his eyes. When he opened them again, he was the nobody technician. The fire that Kirsten had seen in his eyes was gone. Fatigue slumped his shoulders.

And then he was gone.

Kirsten turned back to her console. She'd meant what she said; she wouldn't be extracting. Part of her long-term assignment had been to suborn the Stealthy Tigers, and put her brother in command. So far that plan had proceeded accordingly, but events on Hall were speeding things up. She wasn't sure they could rely on Rauschenbusch retiring before they needed—*needed*—control of the regiment.

So more direct action might be needed. And if so . . .

Kirsten called up the private boards where enlisted Tigers hung out. She had a number of dummy accounts, and hacks that would let her post as any Stealthy Tiger she wanted. Removing Rauschenbusch would be easy, if it came to that . . . but first she had to erode his power base.

First she had to undermine the one thing that held the Tigers together: their sense of professionalism, of loyalty. She had to destroy their current exemplars, and replace them with her own.

She pulled up a small, private board that had very little traffic. Seeds planted in darkness often grew into the strongest trees.

First, she had to destroy the Raiders.

Who are these Raiders? They all wear those little pins, and walk around so high and mighty, but really—what have they done that we haven't?

We were on Caph and Carver V. We fought Lindon's Battalion and the Faithful. We walked and ran and bled the same blood they did. We kept our contracts and did our jobs.

What did they do that we didn't?

Why do they get little pins and smiles from the colonel, when we don't?

I'll tell you why. Because they think they're better than us, that they're more Tiger than us. Because they think there's some kind of honor in being a sycophant, in not thinking for yourself.

This is the regiment. We're all professionals. And its time we stopped tolerating some kind of old-timer's club in our midst. Especially one run by a guy who can't keep it in his pants when the enemy is around.

—Message posted on the
internal Stealthy Tiger message boards

CHAPTER SEVENTEEN

BRAVO BASE
HALL
THE CHAOS MARCH
6 AUGUST 3067

Ezra stood in the Jaguar Company 'Mech bay, staring at the brown-and-red paint of his *Crusader*, when he heard footsteps behind him. He was, as far as he knew, alone in the center of the bay. He liked to come out here sometimes and think, away from the stifling confines of his office. Gods knew he had plenty to think about.

He turned and saw Heather Hargood walking up to him. "Captain," he greeted her.

"Captain," she replied. They shared a grin. She stepped up next to him and aped his stance: legs slightly spread, hands clasped behind his back. She looked at the *Crusader*, then at him, then back at the 'Mech. Then she chuckled.

"You're doing your colonel thing again."

"My what?"

"Your colonel thing." When he scoffed, she laughed again. "Come on, Ezra. You know you've seen the colonel out here, except in one of the battalion bays, doing the exact same thing. Standing here, looking all official, making sure the people see him."

Ezra raised his eyebrows. "And that's what you think I'm doing?"

"I'm not thinking it—you're *doing* it."

Ezra shook his head, then stood a little straighter and put his hands in his pockets. "Better?"

"I don't know," she said, turning to face him. "Now you kind of look like a used car salesman."

Ezra blinked. Hargood burst into laughter, and he laughed with her. "Now that you've shattered all my illusions, did you have a reason for coming out here?"

She sobered up and nodded. "In point of fact, I did," she said. "Raider business."

"Let's hear it."

"It's not good news," she said.

"Is it ever?" He crossed his arms and gave her his full attention.

"Roth brought me something the other day," she said. "I don't know if it's true, and honestly I don't care if it is because I don't think it's important." She paused. When he raised his eyebrows, Hargood frowned and glanced away and then back. "Are you sleeping with a Dismal D?"

Ezra blinked. "What?"

"There's a feed on the enlisted forums—"

"Wait—*this* is your Raider business?"

"There's a lot of people—"

Ezra scoffed. "You're kidding. The boards are pissed off because I'm getting laid?"

"So you are?"

"I was."

"Oh."

Ezra grimaced. "No—it's not like that. I was seeing a Dismal D officer, yeah. Nathalie Ortiz. She commanded the company out in the Helmand when we got hit. But I haven't seen her since I got put off the liaison mission."

Hargood looked uncomfortable. "So it's over?"

"I don't understand what the big deal is."

"They're saying you're sleeping with the enemy."

"The *enemy*?" Ezra sputtered for a second. "Are you kidding me?"

"That's what they're saying."

"And you *believe* them?"

"Of course not," she said, and the steel in her voice snapped Ezra out of the outrage that had overtaken him. He saw the concern in her face, and remembered who he was talking to. He glanced at the Raider pin on her lapel. "I'm sorry." He reached out and touched her shoulder. "I mean it—Heather. I'm sorry."

She shook her head. "It's stupid, I know. But that doesn't mean they're not saying it. And if they're saying it on the boards, you know they're saying it in person and in the mess halls and at the poker games." She looked around the cavernous bays. "It'll be to the techs by now, too."

Ezra looked around, too. "I must be a little dense. Explain this to me."

Hargood shook her head. "Come back to your office. Roth and Monet are there, and Monet has some scary news."

"You're just *full* of good news today, aren't you?"

Charles Monet looked, for the first time since Ezra had known him, disheveled. It was jarring enough that he said something.

"Are you all right, Charlie?" He nodded to Lieutenant Roth as he sat down behind his desk, but his eyes were on Monet. There were dark circles under his eyes, and his clothes were rumpled. He didn't look like he'd shaved since the day before.

"I'm fine," Monet snapped.

"Are you sure?" Roth asked. The big man sat next to Monet, and for once he looked a lot fresher, but that wasn't a comment on how much Roth had improved. Monet had fallen that far. "Because usually I'm the smelly asshole in these meetings, and right now you're making me look good."

"I haven't slept," Monet admitted. "I've been working all night."

"On?" Ezra prompted.

"We have a mole," Monet said.

"What?"

"There are rumors appearing on the enlisted boards," Monet said. "Rumors about you, about the Raiders, about our contract with Baranov, about the AMC. One of my tracking bots picked up the increased traffic. I've spent most of the night parsing it out, and it points to only conclusion: someone is planting these rumors."

Ezra sat back. "Could we have been hacked?"

"It's possible," Monet said.

"But you don't think so."

"The trail would be different if this had come from outside." Monet shrugged. "It feels like someone inside the regiment."

Ezra sat back. "Have you reported this?"

"Not yet."

It wasn't outside the realm of possibility that someone in the Stealthy Tigers had entered the pay of one of the factions on Hall.

To be honest, Ezra would be surprised if several people weren't already making a little extra cash on the side letting certain people know what was going on in Bravo Base. Certainly the colonel—or rather, Kirsten Markoja, who oversaw such things—spread money around on every contract looking for information they couldn't get any other way.

But there was an order of magnitude between passing the weekend duty roster to a planetary constable looking for a mercenary who'd torn up a bar the weekend previous and someone inside the base actively planting malicious data.

"You'd have said if you knew who it was," Ezra said.

Monet nodded.

"What are they saying—exactly?"

Hargood cleared her throat. "The rumors about you, I already told you about." She looked at Roth. "Charlie asked Roth and I to help him skim."

"There's a lot of the usual crap about the Raiders being an elitist club," Roth said.

Ezra nodded. That undercurrent of bitterness among those who believed they should be Raiders but weren't was always present. And it wasn't wrong—the Raiders *were* an elitist club. Any invitation-only organization was.

"A couple fools are trying to get a story started, claiming the reason the emperor called in the Free Worlds League is because we used to work for them," Hargood added. He looked at her and she rolled her eyes. "I didn't make it up."

"One idiot even thinks the AMC is here to recruit us," Roth said.

"As if," Ezra said. He looked at each of the three in turn. "What do we think?"

"Someone is undermining confidence in our command staff," Monet said.

"In the colonel, you mean," Ezra said.

"Partly," Monet allowed. "The rumors about you, though, are very specific. And they tie to the anti-Raider people. It generalizes to 'the people in charge are bad at it,' but it could be just the colonel."

"Right." Ezra thought for a few seconds. "And it could be anyone. The AMC, the Word, even Baranov's people. All of them would stand to gain something from us getting into trouble."

"I think it's a lot worse than trouble," Hargood said, frowning. "Someone is undermining our authority. This is a military unit. That's called mutiny."

"Mm," Ezra grunted, still thinking. "Who else knows?"

"That we know?" Roth asked. "You're looking at everyone. But the rumors have already been picked up. People are talking. I overhead two of my sergeants making smartass remarks about the Raiders this morning."

"What'd you do?" Hargood asked.

"Nothing." Roth tapped the pin on his lapel. "I know why I got this. It wasn't for smacking people around for being idiots."

"None of us did," Ezra said. He thought for a moment longer. "Do we take it to the colonel?" He looked at Monet. Only the two of them knew that the colonel knew about the Word of Blake connection.

"I think we have to," Roth said. "None of us can stop this crap." He looked at Monet. "Well, I mean, Charlie can fight them on the boards. But none of us has the authority to affect anything real."

"The Markojas?" Ezra asked.

Hargood hissed. She was one of Mason Markoja's company commanders, and it was an open secret that she despised him. In Raider meetings, she didn't bother to hide her contempt.

"Mostly clean," Monet said. "I mean, a lot of people have added them to the general griping, but none of the original posts I've been able to identify mention them."

"That's telling," Hargood mused. "You don't think—"

"I don't think Mason is smart enough," Ezra said. "And I don't think Kirsten is stupid enough." He sucked in a deep breath. "No, I think it's the Word. Or whoever is bankrolling this Ridzik nonsense."

"But why?" Roth asked. "Ridzik is fighting for Hall. What do we have to do with that?"

"We're in the emperor's employ," Monet reminded him.

"I know that," Roth said, "but we're out in a few months. What does making the sergeants unhappy about their leaders do for Ridzik when we'll be gone? The worst that happens is that the colonel has to sack someone on the next contract."

Ezra could think of several far worse scenarios, but he didn't see any benefit in saying them out loud. Instead, he rubbed his hands together. "Okay. What do we do?"

"Shut the boards down," Roth said.

"No," Hargood and Monet said at the same time.

"Charlie first," Ezra said.

"That would warn whoever it is that we're on to them," Monet said.

"Heather?"

"That would piss the enlisted off even more than they are now," she said. "It would look like we're afraid of the criticism. And the only reason we would be afraid of the criticism is because it's true."

"That's nonsense," Roth said.

"It's how people think," Ezra told him. "We all do it. We take in information and shape it toward the conclusion we want. They're right."

Roth frowned, but didn't say anything else.

"Heather," Ezra said, "I want you to go find the sergeant major. Tell him about all of this."

"Okay."

"And then tell him I want him to get himself assigned back to the colonel's command lance."

All three of the Raiders frowned. He grinned at them. "I know—I just got rid of my best MechWarrior. But if there's something brewing, I want him close to the colonel."

"You're worried," Hargood said.

"Aren't you?"

She didn't say anything.

There wasn't anything to say.

**HARNEY
HALL
THE CHAOS MARCH
6 AUGUST 3067**

Adele Estwicke sat on the loveseat in her safehouse apartment and stared at the small black pistol sitting on the coffee table. It was a slug-thrower, a nine-millimeter. Two extra magazines sat next to the pistol. She'd been sitting there long enough that her left foot had gone to sleep. She was aware of that fact, but she still didn't move.

When she closed her eyes, she saw the bodies on Alexander Avenue she'd had to step over to escape.

Every time. When she blinked. When she slept. When she squinted too tightly while facing the sun.

Every time.

For three years, she had been the Word of Blake's agent on Hall, and that mission had failed. Precentor Blane had given her all the diplomatic and hidden assets he could, and she had failed him. Baranov had made a different decision, because she had miscalculated.

Because she had gotten complacent.

It had seemed impossible that she should fail. Baranov was a boor from the backwater, and she was the representative of the true Word of Blake.

She sighed.

Her comm chirped, breaking her concentration. The only person had the code for that comm was Jurowicz.

"We have a problem," Jurowicz said when Estwicke answered.

"Okay."

"I'm outside. Let me in." The line clicked closed.

Estwicke looked at the phone, then the door, then the gun on the table. With a shrug, she stood up and went to open the door.

Jurowicz looked her up and down before she stepped inside. Estwicke closed the door behind her and locked it, then turned and leaned against it.

"Problems," she said.

Jurowicz stood opposite the couch, looking down at the pistol. She looked at Estwicke, who still stood by the door, half-shrugged, and sat down in the armchair opposite the couch.

"Markoja is going to get caught," Jurowicz said.

Estwicke lurched up off the door and walked to the couch. "Caught doing what?" She sat down. She reached for the gun, then stopped and pulled her hand back.

"The AMC intelligence section is getting good," she said. "They've been trying to penetrate the Stealthy Tigers' networks, and they're just about inside."

"So?"

"So she's been using the Tigers' internal networks to weaken her colonel's position. Someone built her that access—someone good—but good access needs regular updating." Jurowicz sighed. "I could have done it. If I'd been asked."

"So they'll catch a mercenary trying to get ahead in her own regiment," Estwicke said. "So what?"

"Her tools are our tools, Adele." Jurowicz leaned forward, putting her weight on her elbows. "Once they crack her in the Tigers system, they'll have the tools they need to get into our files here." She spread her hands. "It's like an autopsy. Once the AMC spooks get through her models, they'll have our templates."

"So what do we do?"

"Can you stop Markoja?"

Estwicke looked down at the gun. "I don't think so." She thought about the sound of the explosions on Alexander Avenue. It was the loudest sound she'd ever heard; she'd felt it, slamming into her like a wall of pressure. She'd felt her insides ripple. For an instant, she'd thought she was dying.

Then the instant had passed. And she'd had to step over people who would never have another instant, ever again.

"Then maybe we need to pack up," Jurowicz said. "Leave, now."

"No," Estwicke said.

"Why?"

Estwicke looked at the gun. "I don't know."

"You don't know." Jurowicz looked at her, then at the gun, then around at the apartment. Estwicke followed her eyes, as if seeing the room for the first time. She saw the dirty dishes, the half-eaten food, the clothes crumpled on the floor.

Jurowicz looked back at her. "You want to talk about it?"

"I—" Estwicke sighed. "We—*I*—failed here. As soon as Baranov told me he called in the Free Worlds League, I knew it. I knew I'd have to go back to Terra. To Blane. And tell him I let him down."

"Missions fail," Jurowicz said. "It's part of the job."

"I know that." She pressed her hands together and looked down at them. "But I wanted this one to win. I *needed* this to win." She glanced at the gun, then back at her hands. "Kirsten Markoja offered me a way to a win." She looked up.

Jurowicz was staring at her. "I get that."

"I can't—I can't walk away, not while there's a chance. I've worked too hard. I've done too much." *I've* literally *stepped over too many bodies*, she didn't say. She frowned. "Do you understand?"

"Yes."

Estwicke gasped. "I-I didn't expect you to."

Jurowicz stood up to leave. "I understand. I didn't say I agree, but you're in charge."

"Thank you."

"Try and get her under control. It's a race to see if the AMC finds her before the League gets here."

Estwicke looked up. "Or until her plan works."

Jurowicz looked back from the door. "Or until that."

Then she left.

"It's been three months since the emperor announced the Free Worlds annexation, and so far, not much has changed. The Com Guard has begun removing its garrison troops from the hyper-pulse generator station in preparation to hand the facility over to the Word of Blake, who administer the HPGs in the Free Worlds.

"The AMC regiment remains, as does Burton's Brigade, the mercenary company that previously fought for the late Count Radcliffe McNally. They continue to occupy strategic places across Farnorth, claiming they're searching for Word of Blake involvement in the emperor's government.

"Many expected the AMC to lift ship once the League annexation was confirmed, but Colonel Marik-Johns of the Dismal Disinherited has refused to leave. *"It's a travesty of justice,"* he told us, *"the way Baranov has colluded with the Word of Blake to manipulate Hall into giving up its freedom."*

–From the *Harney Morning Edition*,
Harney HV Channel Six

CHAPTER EIGHTEEN

CAMDEN HOLE
HALL
THE CHAOS MARCH
19 AUGUST 3067

Ezra smiled when he saw the *Dervish* appear on his scanners. He couldn't see it yet, not in the evening twilight. Three more blue icons appeared along with it, a full lance of Disinherited 'Mechs. He looked around the area he'd chosen for his lance to wait, but none of his 'Mechs reacted to their presence.

"Here they come," he transmitted.

"We have scanners," Hicks muttered.

Ezra smiled. He didn't expect any other answer from her.

Camden Hole was a hole in the desert; an oasis where the steep-walled hallways of the desert broke beneath millions of years of water erosion. It was a common stopover point on the road between Rockfall Maze and the north, and that made it a natural place for a contingent of Tigers and Dismal Disinherited to meet clandestinely.

It had been Jacob Brim's idea, one he'd pitched privately to Ezra over coffee at Marko's. If there was really a Ridzik—or whoever was pretending to be him—he almost had to strike at Deal, at McNally's base. He'd already struck at the AMC and Baranov with his ambush on Alexander Avenue. Now he had to show the rest of the planet that he wasn't in McNally's camp. A free Hall, as the centerpiece of a resurgent Tikonov Free Republic, needed a leader free of the tensions of the last ten years.

"It's the only thing that make sense," Brim had told him.

New icons appeared behind the Dismal Ds, and Ezra's smile disappeared. They showed gray instead of blue, because they weren't Disinherited machines.

They were the bait.

The only thing of interest to the mystery Ridzik at Deal would be Elly Burton and her son. So Brim had let the AMC put out a notice warning Baranov that Elly Burton would be visiting Rockfall Maze with her son, and that her travel would be protected by the Allied Mercenary Command. The notice hadn't been public, but Brim was certain that whoever was behind the ambush had penetrated Baranov's communications, at the minimum.

It had been easy to convince Colonel Marik-Johns. He was certain "whoever" was the Word of Blake, and it wasn't a stretch for him to believe that they were reading his own mail, much less the emperor's.

The leading elements of the arriving force appeared in the flesh; it was Nathalie Ortiz's *Dervish* and a Hellraiser *Stealth*. A moment later two more machines appeared; a sixty-ton *Merlin* and all eighty tons of an assault-class *Victor*.

Behind them came Elly Burton's *Cyclops*, escorted by a *Guillotine* and a hulking *Charger*.

"What's a guy like you doing in a place like this?" Nathalie sent. Ezra smiled to hear her voice and checked: she was using a discreet channel with its own encryption, and her radio power was dialed down enough that it wouldn't propagate very far.

"Looking for a girl," he told her. "Hi there."

"Hi back."

"Any trouble on the way down?"

"Nothing."

"Jake will be sorry to hear that," he told her.

"The night is young."

Ezra opened his mouth to reply, but a new signal blinked for his attention. "Hang on," he said. Then he switched channels. "Jaguar Six."

"Status?" Elly Burton asked.

Hello to you, too. "All quiet."

"So either this little plan isn't going to work," she said, scorn evident in her voice, "or else it just hasn't worked *yet.*"

"My money's on yet," he told her. "Bring your 'Mechs into the bivouac, Captain, and shut down if you like. My Jaguars will take the first watch." Instead of a reply, the channel clicked closed.

He switched back to Nathalie "I hate that woman."

"I heard," Nathalie told him. While she spoke, her 'Mechs and Burton's entered the circle of Tiger 'Mechs. Two of her MechWarriors spun their machines to face outward and kept upright, but two of them lurched into the telltale slump of standby. Her *Dervish* was one of the upright ones. "I think she feels the same way about you."

"I don't blame her," Ezra said. "But that doesn't make her any more pleasant to deal with."

"I'm sure." There was a lingering silence, then a squelch as if she'd started to talk and stopped. Then she spoke. "Ezra . . ."

Ezra knew that tone. "We don't have to do this now," he told her.

"I think we do."

He swallowed. "Okay. Do you want to climb down and do it in person?" It would be safe enough—there were at least six 'Mechs still on watch, and no one would get within kilometers of the Hole without being detected far enough away for their to be time to get back into his cockpit.

"No, I think that would be worse."

Oh. That bad. "Go ahead, then."

"I'm hearing rumors," Nathalie said. "From Bravo Base."

"Rumors?" *Who the hell is she talking to at Bravo Base?* So far as Ezra knew, he was the only Stealthy Tiger she was on a first-name basis with.

"That you're taking some hits about us. About me."

Ezra didn't speak for a moment. "How did you hear about that?"

"Jake monitors everyone, you know."

Ah. "Right."

"Is it true? Are you getting in trouble with your people about me?"

"Trouble is a strong word," he said. He should have known Brim would be getting into the Tiger networks. At some level he must have known that, but he thought of Brim and Nathalie as friends, not rivals. It hadn't entered his mind that they might be keeping tabs on him. He was both comforted and disturbed by it. Comforted, because everyone liked to know he was important to people he respected. Disturbed, because he'd hoped the Tigers' electronic security was better than that.

And, a little, because a small, quiet voice in his mind wondered if it was Jacob Brim or one of his people Charlie Monet had caught planting rumors. But that made even less sense than any of the other ideas they'd discussed.

"Something, then."

"It's nothing I can't handle," he told her.

"You shouldn't have to handle it," she said. There was a hint of surrender in her voice. It made his fingers cold and his mouth dry.

"I—" he started, but a contact alarm chirped on his HUD.

"Unknowns at three klicks," Sergeant Hicks said. She transmitted on an open, but weak, frequency. Ezra toggled his comm back to general send as quickly as he could.

"IFF to blank," he said, and touched his own switch. If this was the mystery Ridzik, whoever it was didn't need to know that he had elements of three different factions waiting for him. None of the waiting 'Mechs had been broadcasting with more than a few watts; it was unlikely the newcomers could have IDed them. They'd know there were 'Mechs here, but not which ones, exactly.

A *skrick* of noise announced another entry into the conversation. "You're seeing this?" Elly Burton demanded.

"I am," he told her. "Anyone have IDs?"

"Not ours," Nathalie said.

"Not Tigers," Ezra said. "Not even fake ones, like last time."

"Not mine," Burton said. "Baranov?"

"Unlikely," Ezra said. "I didn't tell him we were coming out here."

"He could have had the idea on his own."

"I don't think Buddy Boy has many ideas of his own," Nathalie snapped. "I think these are our boys."

"New contacts," Sergeant Akhtar reported. "Looks like VTOLs."

"Not Baranov, then," Burton said. "He doesn't have any."

"Anyone got a count?" Ezra demanded.

"I get ten 'Mechs and a swarm of VTOLs," Nathalie said. "I can't tell how many flyers. Maybe half a dozen?"

"Same here," Burton said.

"Okay." Ezra looked around. The Dismal D 'Mechs that had gone into standby shuddered and came back up. The trio of Burton's Brigade 'Mechs moved to the center of the formation. He suddenly realized Brim had forgotten one very important thing when he arranged this little excursion: all three of them were captains, and no one knew who was in overall command.

His instinct was to take command himself, but he rejected that almost immediately. He was supremely confident of his skills, but there was no chance in any hell he could think of that Elly Burton would take orders from him. Nor would he accept orders from her, which left . . .

"Nathalie, you're in charge," he said.

She started to object, but Burton overrode her. "Can it—he's right. We're sure as shit not telling each other what to do."

Ezra felt a moment's grudging respect for Burton, but didn't linger on it. "We're pretty even," he said. "How do we draw them in?"

"We're a peaceful convoy caught unawares," Nathalie said. "We run for it."

"But not so fast we get away," Burton said hesitantly.

"Of course not," Nathalie said.

Ezra passed the orders to his lance and then keyed the private link to Nathalie. "Hey."

"Hey."

"After, okay?" he told her. "We'll talk after."

"It's a date," she said.

Ezra smiled and closed the channel. Then he opened another one. "Iqbal."

"Here, Six."

"As soon as we're engaged, get word back to Bravo Base."

"Roger, Six."

As fast as the new contacts were moving, it shouldn't take long.

Together, the Tigers lance and the others turned back north, as if retreating back the way they'd come. They didn't move very fast—they couldn't, not with Burton's big *Cyclops* and the Disinherited *Victor*—but they made a credible effort at trying to escape. The new 'Mechs turned to intercept them.

"Approaching 'Mechs, this is the Dismal Disinherited. Identify yourselves, over." Nathalie's transmissions went out at full power; a light flashed on Ezra's comm board as one of her MechWarriors sent a contact report to Rockfall Maze and the other distributed AMC stations.

There was no answer from the approaching 'Mechs.

"Identify, or we will fire on you," Nathalie insisted.

"Go ahead," a man's voice said. Ezra blinked. The *Crusader*'s computer painted one of the approaching 'Mechs as the sender. "We're here to fire on you."

"Identify yourself."

"Nikoli Ridzik," the man said.

"Nikoli Ridzik is dead," Nathalie insisted. "He's been dead for almost ten years."

"You're thinking of my brother Yuri," Ridzik said. "Baranov managed to kill him, but not me."

Nathalie didn't say anything else. Instead, she turned her column around to face the oncoming 'Mechs. There didn't seem to be much point in continuing to run, now that they knew who they were facing.

Ezra turned his *Crusader* around with the rest and eyed the land. They'd barely made it to the edge of the Hole. The battle would be fought on the open terrain there, which would be good. He looked at two more glowing carets on his strategic map and eyed the distances, then toggled his radio.

"Nico."

"Here, Six," Lieutenant Reynard replied.

"Feed incoming. Watch where they go and cut them off."

"Will do, Six."

Ezra nodded and switched channels. "Iqbal."

"The report has already been sent, Six," Akhtar said.

Ezra smiled. It was good to have efficient subordinates. He'd heard the colonel say that often, and he'd learned it was true as soon as he'd risen high enough to *have* subordinates. That it wasn't a new thought didn't make it any less a pleasing one.

"Get ready."

BRAVO BASE
HALL
THE CHAOS MARCH
19 AUGUST 3067

By the time Kirsten Markoja got to the TOC in the heart of Bravo Base, the alert signal had already wound down. Colonel Rauschenbusch stood near the center of the room, arms folded, watching the master display. It was showing a rebroadcast feed from a 'Mech's HUD. Kirsten checked the ID legend in the bottom left corner—it was from Ezra Payne's *Crusader*. She frowned and headed toward the colonel.

"Where is he?" she asked, stopping at the colonel's side.

"Camden Hole," Rauschenbusch said.

"What? What the hell is he doing way the hell down there?"

Rauschenbusch looked at her and smiled with an expression that mimicked the regiment's namesake. "He's about to put Nikoli Ridzik down."

Cold sweat burst out on Kirsten's back, between her shoulder blades, but she disguised her shock by looking back toward the screen. It was a poor-quality picture, being relayed so far, but it didn't show anything but a brown-green expanse of wide-open ground. The rising hallways of the desert painted the background, and the first stars were almost visible in the sky.

"How'd he catch him?" she asked.

Rauschenbusch laughed. "He's been working with the AMC."

Kirsten looked at him. "*What?*"

"He and that Brim character set it up, along with a company from the Disinherited. They made it seem like Elly Burton would be alone on the road to Rockfall Maze." He looked at Kirsten. "I could wish he'd cleared it with me first," he said, "but if it works, I won't argue."

"If it works . . ." Kirsten said absently. She looked back at the screen.

I should have seen this possibility, she raged at herself. She'd seen the communiqué about Burton's movement. She'd passed it on to her ersatz Ridzik immediately—it had been too good an opportunity to pass up. She looked to another screen, the strategic display. It showed a red force—Ridzik, her Light of Mankind team, and its attached mercenaries—moving toward a green force—Payne and his AMC allies. That was to be expected. But it also showed two more green forces out on the flanks.

"What's that?" she asked a nearby technician, pointing at the other contacts.

"Payne put two of his lances out on the flanks," the woman told her. "In case the marauders try and get away."

Smart. Damn him. Kirsten looked around. Her brother wasn't here, and neither were any of his officers. "Where's Mason?"

"I put the Panthers in the field," Rauschenbusch said. "They're moving south now. They'll get there long after this is all over," he gestured at the screen, "but in case any of them get away, they can help Ezra round them up."

Kirsten nodded, to show she understood and, she hoped, for the appearance of support. Inside, she was reeling. She wanted to retreat to her office, to try and warn the operative of what was coming, but by now he had to know. And anything she sent would be recorded. She'd be discovered.

Instead she stood there in the TOC, arms crossed, and hoped that the man pretending to be Nikoli Ridzik was as good a Mech-Warrior as the original had been reputed to be.

**BRAMPTON
HALL
THE CHAOS MARCH
19 AUGUST 3067**

"It's starting," Carlsson called.

Jacob Brim looked up from the map he was studying, trying to guess where the Ridzik 'Mechs had come from. Carlsson stood at Gallifrey's shoulder, looking down at the analyst's console. Jacob stood up and went to join them. He looked at each of his surviving analysts as he did. Each of them looked ready.

"Gallifrey?"

"I'm in every net that leads in or out of Fort Decker," the big man said. "If there are transmissions from anyone at the Tigers HQ that shouldn't be transmitting, I'll get them." He looked up at Jacob and nodded. "It's covered."

"Good." Jacob looked at the next tech. "Katie?"

Katie Loomis didn't look away from her console. "She's still in her apartment," she said. Loomis was responsible for watching Adele Estwicke. Jacob hadn't forgotten about her, but the Word agent hadn't done much of anything since the ambush on Alexander Avenue. She mostly stayed in her apartment.

"Keep on her," Jacob said. "If she moves—a centimeter—during this, I want to know about it." He looked at the next seat. "Ben?"

Benjamin Adams was a slight, spare man with a prominent Adam's apple and no hair. He was looking at a map display overlaid with glowing unit icons. "No movement from any of Baranov's forces," he said. He looked at Jacob. "I'm not sure they even know it's started yet, Jake."

Carlsson grunted. "We've got all the angles covered."

Behind them, the door to the small room opened and Colonel John Marik-Johns stepped inside. He nodded to Jacob, but didn't say anything. He just let the door slide shut and leaned against the wall next to it.

"All the angles we know about," Jacob said.

"Rumors have reached us today of accusations by the Allied Mercenary Command that the emperor's efforts to secure our annexation into the Free Worlds League are a ploy. The Free Worlds League, these accusations contend, is nothing more than a Word of Blake satrapy. These are the latest in a long line of increasingly paranoid statements from the AMC as they continue searching in shadows and under rocks for any evidence of Word of Blake collusion.

"No one disputes history: the Word of Blake did indeed seek shelter beneath the aegis of the Free Worlds in 3052. It was in the League that the Blakists, persecuted by their former ComStar brethren, found a bulwark to rebuild and retaliate. It was League factories that built their 'Mechs, League crews that salvaged the Star League-era WarShips only the Blakists knew about. It is true that Thomas Marik, the current captain-general of the Free Worlds League, was once a member of ComStar.

"But these accusations go too far. The Free Worlds League has existed—guaranteeing and defending the rights of its citizens—for much longer than there has been a ComStar, much less a Word of Blake. That it shelters those who flee persecution is a virtue, not a ploy to conceal conspiracies. The AMC refuses to believe this, and in doing so name themselves rumormongers and worse—persecutors."

–From the *Harney Evening Edition*,
HV Channel Six

CHAPTER NINETEEN

CAMDEN HOLE
HALL
THE CHAOS MARCH
19 AUGUST 3067

The first 'Mech Ezra saw from Ridzik's force was a battered-looking *Thunderbolt*. The sixty-five ton machine was considered one of the better brawling 'Mechs on the battlefield, and had been for centuries. It was tough and well-armed, and there were worse choices when you knew you were headed into a fight.

"Burn them down as they come in," Nathalie said. She suited action to words even as she spoke. Protective covers on her *Dervish*'s LRM batteries slid open and she sent a full double-barrage at the *Thunderbolt*. More 'Mechs moved into the field behind it, at least a lance.

"They won't just come in," Ezra whispered, but he raised the *Crusader*'s arms nonetheless. He didn't really care what tactics the marauders chose this time. He just wanted to end this. And he wanted revenge for Alexander Avenue.

The *Thunderbolt* stepped out of the path of Nathalie's missiles with a grace that belied its bulk. The barrel-like launcher on its shoulder spat its own missiles, more than one of the *Dervish*'s launchers could manage, but not as many as both together. Ezra didn't see which 'Mech it was shooting at.

A pair of VTOLs appeared out of the darkening sky. They flew without running lights, and if the *Crusader*'s sensors hadn't tagged them and thrown a caret up on his HUD, Ezra would have never seen them. The computer named them both Cavalry attack helicopters, making him cringe. Cavalrys were swift and deadly attack birds, with heavy SRM loads in their noses.

Both them swung around and dove at the *Crusader*.

Ezra's feet slammed down on his jump jet pedals even as his hands drew the *Crusader*'s crosshairs over one of the helicopters. His missile launchers were out of position; in the short time he had to fire, all he had were the paired medium pulse lasers in the *Crusader*'s chest. The night flickered with verdant laser fire as both beam weapons spit light at the rightmost Cavalry; at least some of his shots hit, ablating the thick armor over the helicopter's nose.

A dozen fat-bodied SRMs spun in on him in return.

The *Crusader*'s jump jets tried to fling his 'Mech out of the way, but he was too slow. Half the missiles impacted, striking it in the belly, chest, and left leg. The explosions rocked his 'Mech, leaving smoking divots in the *Crusader*'s thick armor. Even so, Ezra brought the 'Mech back to the ground in a crouch, breathing deeply.

A patch of ground two meters to Ezra's left exploded into a long furrow of dirt and rock. The *Crusader*'s HUD painted a new contact in the sky across the field and showed him an ID: a Hawk Moth gunship, another VTOL. This one carried a dangerous light Gauss rifle instead of SRMs.

"Lots of choppers," he said.

"Noticed," Hicks spat.

Ezra looked toward her *Centurion*. It was running full out behind the bulk of the lance. Its right arm was extended, and while Ezra watched her LB-X autocannon belched a canister round. Its flash lit the *Centurion* like a strobe light.

In the sky, sparks flashed off another VTOL. The *Crusader*'s computer had just enough time to identify it as a Mantis light attack chopper before it spun out of the sky. Hicks' shot had amputated two of its rotor blades.

"They're concentrating on Burton," someone called. It must have been one of the Dismal Ds; Ezra didn't recognize the voice. He looked on his HUD for the *Cyclops*.

The *Thunderbolt* was putting another batch of missiles into Elly Burton's armor. She twisted the big assault 'Mech, trying to get out of the way, but only partially succeeded. A third of the salvo tore into the armor protecting her right leg. She stumbled, and that put her into the path of the bright red beam of the *Thunderbolt*'s large laser. Behind it, a gangly *Starslayer* added its own lasers to the mix, burning at the weak patch of armor over the *Cyclops*' leg. Burton stumbled again.

"Give her some help," Ezra said.

"On it," Roses called.

Her *Hatchetman* spun out of line with the other Jaguar 'Mechs and dashed to the right, toward the Burton's Brigade cluster. Her autocannon spat rounds at its highest rate. Ezra didn't want to think what it must be like inside Roses' cockpit just then, with the jarring impacts of forty-five tons of 'Mech running and a high-speed autocannon slamming out shells at its maximum rate of fire. He was proud to see it, though.

Roses' fire slammed into the *Starslayer*'s side, rocking the medium 'Mech and making it turn toward her. It flashed a laser at her, but the shot missed wide. Roses kept on running, closing the range. If Ezra had been the enemy MechWarrior, he would have noticed the way Roses' hatchet swung when she ran.

But Ezra had his own battles to fight.

The Cavalry helicopters had passed overhead and swung their course around, never slowing down. The death of the Mantis would have reinforced that their only real defense was speed. Ezra tracked them, concentrating on the one he'd already hit, and raised the *Crusader*'s arms. When he saw gold, he fired.

The pulse lasers in the *Crusader*'s chest stuttered again, painting the Cavalry's side with red-hot damage. Ezra added his conventional medium lasers to the mix, too, this time. One of the beams zipped beneath the dodging chopper, but the other cut through the space where the Cavalry's rotor joined its hull. The helicopter fell as if cut from strings—and from a certain point of view, it had been—and impacted on the desert floor, where it exploded. The light threw the ground into stroboscopic relief.

The other Cavalry shot overhead, peppering the *Crusader* with more SRMs. Ezra rode the impacts out.

"'Mech," Akhtar said.

A marauder *Quickdraw* appeared out of the darkness. It belched a flight of LRMs that angled straight in and blasted armor from the *Crusader*'s chest. Without slowing down, it leaped into the air on jump jets and came down 150 meters to the left, breaking into a run almost immediately.

Akhtar fired at it, but his LRMs and PPC fell behind. Roses was out of position trying to support Burton, and Hicks was still tangling with VTOLs. Ezra bit his lip and tried to project its course—it was headed for Burton, just like all the others.

He had to give the marauders credit. They were dedicated to

their mission, though Ezra didn't understand why. The first rule of guerrilla fighting was to never hit something large enough to kill you while you were killing it. The marauders might—*might*—get through and hit Elly Burton hard enough to put her down, but they were already taking grievous losses.

Ezra's lasers chimed ready. He turned.

The Hellraiser *Stealth* appeared out of the darkness, sprinting toward the *Quickdraw* as if trying to cut it off. Missiles and lasers lit the night as it fired. The SRMs missed behind the *Quickdraw*, like Akhtar's fire had, but the lasers cut at the armor over the *Quickdraw*'s shoulder. It twisted at the waist and fired lasers back at the *Stealth*, but didn't connect.

The *Stealth* didn't veer off. It was trying to cut the *Quickdraw* off, make it turn aside.

Ezra saw the way the *Quickdraw* was moving. "No!" he shouted.

The two 'Mechs converged. They hit.

The *Quickdraw* had fifteen tons on the *Stealth*, most of it in armor and weapons. It was moving faster than eighty kilometers per hour. The *Stealth* was moving faster, but weighed less. Worse for the Disinherited MechWarrior, Ezra didn't think he'd really expected to the collision to happen.

It was clear that the marauder MechWarrior had *decided* to make it happen, as soon as he'd realized it was possible.

The *Quickdraw* dropped its shoulder at the last instant and hit the *Stealth* like a linebacker. Ezra grimaced in sympathy at the sound. The *Stealth* ricocheted off the larger 'Mech and collapsed into a skidding slide along the ground. The *Quickdraw* rebounded as well, but kept its feet and held it course. Armor plates fell from it like it was shedding scales, but it didn't fall.

"Ballsy," Hicks admitted.

"Not the first time he's done that," Ezra agreed. He turned his 'Mech that way, but as soon as he did, something slammed into the *Crusader*'s shoulder. The impact shoved the 'Mech around. Damage alarms screeched at him. The *Crusader*'s computer careted the firing unit.

The damned Hawk Moth.

"We need to deal with these VTOLs," he grumbled.

"No shit," Hicks said. A sizable flicker of light made Ezra look at the corner of his HUD. Another Mantis was tangling with Hicks' *Centurion*. Mantis' were dangerous in the same way the Cavalry was; it had a sizable armament up front, but where the Cavalrys were missile boats, the Mantis carried a battery of extended-range lasers.

That battery had just melted scars all across the *Centurion*'s back. None of the lasers were individually that powerful, as 'Mech-scale weaponry went, but the Mantis carried *a lot* of them.

"Iqbal," Ezra ordered, "deal with the Hawk Moth." The *Grand Dragon*'s ER PPC had the range to almost match the Hawk Moth's light Gauss rifle, and if it strayed too close, Akhtar could back it up with LRMs.

Ezra turned toward Hicks, intent on helping with the Mantis. He couldn't spare a second, just then, to do more than glance at the 'Mech battle raging around him. He only hoped Nathalie Ortiz and her MechWarriors would prove as adept at night fighting as they had been in the desert months before.

BRAVO BASE
HALL
THE CHAOS MARCH
19 AUGUST 3067

The images were grainy and poor, and every technician and officer in the tactical operation center leaned toward their screens, squinting. It was enough, though. A cheer went around the room as Aurel Hicks put another VTOL down with the LB-10X autocannon. Kirsten cheered along with them, even though she felt a little sick doing it.

"Status of Panther Battalion?" Colonel Rauschenbusch asked.

"Moving," a tech reported. An icon on a strategic map the left of the main screen blinked three times. "Panther Six reports no resistance, and no contacts."

"Very well," the colonel said.

Kirsten looked at the map. Of course there was no resistance—they were only twelve kilometers south of Fort Decker, skirting Harney proper as they moved toward the Helmand. There wasn't anyone out there to oppose them. Nor would there be, ever, unless the Dismal Ds turned against them, or a couple of the Ridzik force escaped from Ezra Payne.

She looked back to the rebroadcast battle feed in time to see a familiar 'Mech: the *Quickdraw*. She pressed her lips together and resisted the urge to look around furtively. She didn't want to see if anyone else recognized it.

Estwicke's contacts had provided more mercenaries willing to take a contract with the surprisingly-not-dead Nikoli Ridzik, but she'd been unable to secure a BattleMech to turn over to the Light operative pretending to be him. Kirsten had had to remove one of the 'Mechs from the Stealthy Tigers' own reserves and deliver it, and that hadn't been easy.

Not easy at all.

And now there it was, on the screens in the regimental TOC, for everyone to see.

She only hoped no one recognized it.

"Colonel," a technician called, "the gate is calling. They just passed Colonel Richardson through. He should be here in just a few minutes."

Rauschenbusch frowned. "Okay," he said. He looked at Kirsten. "He wasn't supposed to be here today, was he?"

"Not that I know of," she told him. "But . . ." she gestured toward the screens.

"Yeah." He looked around. "Captain Lisk." One of Kirsten's company commanders looked up from where she'd been leaning over a tech's shoulder, pointing at something on his console.

"Sir?"

"Get downstairs. Meet the colonel, offer him compliments, the usual, and put him in the main conference room."

"Yes, sir."

Rauschenbusch stepped closer to Kirsten while the captain left the room. "I'm going to go tell him what's going on," he said. "While I do that, I want you to stay here. Keep your brother appraised of what's going on, and if Ezra needs support, get it to him."

Kirsten nodded. "What will you tell Richardson?"

"The truth," the colonel said. His smile was craggy and showed age-yellowed teeth, but his eyes were strong and bright. "That we're finishing the job his emperor started a decade ago, and when the sun rises tomorrow over the Helmand, the Ridzik brothers will be dead or captured—again."

He touched her on the shoulder and stepped around her, headed for the door. He looked sideways at the screen as he walked and, if Kirsten had looked away a half-instant sooner, she would have missed it.

He did a double-take at something on the screen. Kirsten

glanced at the screen as well. It was the *Quickdraw*. Her blood cooled to ice. When she looked back, Rauschenbusch was moving toward the door again.

But his head was still twisted to the side. When he got to the door, he stopped and spoke quietly to the sentry. The sentry, one of Kirsten's MechWarriors, nodded at whatever the colonel said, and then pulled his comm out. Rauschenbusch disappeared through the door.

Another cheer rang through the TOC. Another of the marauder VTOLs was down.

Kirsten tasted bile in the back of her throat. What had the colonel seen? She wanted to call the sentry over, to ask who he'd called, but that would be out of character. Someone would notice. She'd have to wait until the right moment—and pray the right moment wasn't too late.

"Major?" a tech asked. "Can you take a look at this?"

Kirsten blinked and nodded. Whatever Rauschenbusch had seen would have to wait. She had a role to play now.

"What is it?" she asked the technician, leaning over the console to look at the small screen.

On the large screen, the *Quickdraw* body-checked a Disinherited *Stealth*, and the whole room groaned in sympathy.

It was all Kirsten could do to hide her smile.

CAMDEN HOLE
HALL
THE CHAOS MARCH
19 AUGUST 3067

A PPC shot passed the *Crusader*'s cockpit close enough that the HUD flickered, and Ezra swore he felt the hairs on his arms stand on end. The bolt took the marauder *Thunderbolt* in the shoulder. It turned away from pumping lasers and missiles into the Burton's Brigade *Guillotine* and faced Akhtar's *Grand Dragon*. The quiet MechWarrior followed his PPC with a flight of missiles, but they missed wide left.

Ezra turned his *Crusader* that way. Most of the marauders were still concentrating on Burton and her 'Mechs. They were nothing if not persistent. He thumbed the throttle forward, intent on closing the range so he could bring his MRMs to bear. The *Thunderbolt* had been tagged several times, but never once with a solid hit. Sixty medium-range missiles was a solid hit in anyone's book.

Roses was dueling the marauder *Starslayer*, and the *Starslayer* was getting the worst of it. While Ezra closed, he saw Roses feint toward the *Starslayer*'s left, reverse, and bury the *Hatchetman*'s hatchet in the *Starslayer*'s right shoulder. The marauder's entire right arm fell limp as Roses ripped the blade free, dragging sparking wires with it. She stepped clear and burned at the *Starslayer* with her single medium laser, but that was a desultory parting shot.

"Nice job," he sent.

"Thanks," Roses said. Her *Hatchetman* worked up to speed, but its insectoid head pivoted to face Ezra's *Crusader*. He waved the *Crusader*'s hand and kept his thumb on the throttle. He had a moment, so he checked the rest of the battle.

Burton's *Cyclops* was limping and looked like it didn't have a single undamaged armor plate anywhere, but she was still moving and firing. While Ezra watched she lit into a marauder *Shadow Hawk* with her big 200-millimeter autocannon. The giant weapon's fire buzz-sawed through the *Shadow Hawk*'s knee and dropped the 'Mech to the ground. It scrabbled with the stump of its left arm, trying to right itself, but Ezra knew that was a hopeless folly.

The *Guillotine* had been taking the worse end of the exchange with the *Thunderbolt*, but the Jaguars' efforts in distracting it allowed the *Guillotine* to spin and put some lasers into the downed *Shadow Hawk*.

Burton's *Charger* was sprinting toward the Dismal D lance. Ezra looked that way and frowned. Only three of Nathalie's 'Mechs were still upright, and her *Dervish* was limping on a lamed ankle actuator.

Her opponents were heavier and just as determined as the rest of the marauders. A *Zeus* was firing its autocannon at Nathalie's *Dervish*, but not connecting. Its companion large laser shot hit, though; even after the light beam faded, the armor gave off dull red light as it tried vainly to shed heat.

"Hicks," Ezra said, scanning the backfield, "support the Dismal Ds."

"On it," came the laconic reply.

"Iqbal, go with her," he said. "You two are the only ones fast enough to get there in time to do any good."

Akhtar double-clicked his mic. The *Grand Dragon* looped into a run and pounded after the speeding *Centurion*.

That left the *Thunderbolt* for Ezra. He looked at it just as the crosshairs flickered from red to green to gold and not-gold. Ezra mentally crossed his fingers and fired anyway, both arms.

Sixty MRMs flittered out of the launchers in under six seconds, washing the *Crusader* in flame and missile exhaust. He cleared the cloud in time to see his barrage fall on and around the *Thunderbolt*. Those 'Mechs were renowned for the amount of damage they could soak up, and this one did not disappoint. More missiles struck the *Thunderbolt* than missed, but the MechWarrior shook the damage off and stalked toward the *Crusader*.

"I think I just made you mad," Ezra whispered.

"ComStar hyperpulse stations along the Lyran Periphery report no contact with stations in the Circinus Federation for some time. Although the Word of Blake administers the HPGs on Circinus, regular communications would pass from those stations to the ComStar-operated bureaus in the Lyran Alliance. Reports of outbreaks of violence and the disappearance of the Black Warriors were the last reported news.

"The Black Warriors are what passes for a standard military in the bandit kingdom. Little more than pirates themselves, the Warriors constitute half the nation's combat power. The other half is gathered in the McIntyre Guard, the personal troops of President McIntyre. No word has reached ComStar about the fate of the McIntyre Guard; it is possible—even probable—that the pirates have fallen into fighting among themselves."

–From the *Daily INN Download,*
ComStar Hall Hyperpulse Station Harney

CHAPTER TWENTY

CAMDEN HOLE
HALL
THE CHAOS MARCH
19 AUGUST 3067

The *Thunderbolt*'s first shot was a flight of LRMs, which Ezra tried and failed to dodge. Only a handful of warheads struck, blasting armor from his left arm, but it was still not a good sign. He adjusted his course a few degrees off straight at his enemy and waited.

The range dropped, and Ezra triggered his paired medium lasers. One beam struck the *Thunderbolt* in the chest, but the MechWarrior ignored it. A trio of medium lasers replied, cutting at the *Crusader*'s protection, but thankfully the accompanying large laser passed harmlessly over the Mech's left shoulder.

Ezra triggered his MRMs again before they had even finished loading. The usual *ker-chunk* of the bins settling was lost in the *whoosh* of the missile thrusters lighting. His haste affected his aim—only one of his barrages connected. When the *Thunderbolt* emerged from the smoke cloud, its left arm moved awkwardly. Ezra relished the sight; it meant one or more of his salvo had breached the armor over its shoulder actuator.

The range between the two 'Mechs had fallen to under two hundred meters. It was close enough that Ezra could begin to count individual impact scars on the 'Mech's torso, even in the low light. He reversed his turn, hoping to throw off the *Thunderbolt*'s aim, but the MechWarrior anticipated him.

The *Thunderbolt*'s large laser lanced into the armor over the *Crusader*'s left knee. Its medium lasers hit two out of three, slicing at the protection over the 'Mech's heart. It didn't fire its long-range missiles. Ezra assumed that was because the range was so low, but it was slightly possible that the *Thunderbolt*'s pilot had exhausted his ammunition.

While the MRMs reloaded, he considered his next move. Had he been the *Thunderbolt*'s pilot, he would have already begun breaking off. He'd been engaged by at least three 'Mechs and put none of them down, and he'd taken damage to pretty much every part of his armor except his cockpit. Now, with a 'Mech his own weight coming at him, one that carried significantly heavier close-in weaponry, he was still fighting.

That meant he was either a zealot, more dedicated to his cause than his life, or a professional. Except professionals didn't fight when there was no chance of winning . . .

Ezra blinked.

Unless he's stalling.

He swept his sensors around, checking back the way the marauders had come. Nothing new. He toggled his radio.

"Nico, any contacts out there?"

"Negative," Reynard said. "We're two minutes out."

"Keep a watchful eye. I think they're stalling."

"Stalling for what?"

"I don't know," Ezra told him. He swept his sensors across the backfield, behind the line of Burton's 'Mechs. He got nothing . . . nothing . . . then something.

Then he knew.

"Saladins behind you!" he yelled. "Captain Burton!"

"What?" The *Cyclops* began to turn, but by then it was too late.

The Saladin was a light assault hovertank. It was little more than some fans, a bit of armor, and an autocannon to match the one on Burton's *Cyclops*. Three of them screamed out of the badlands behind Burton, less than half a kilometer away.

The Saladins closed that distance very quickly, almost quickly enough. Burton managed to get her *Cyclops* turned to get her heaviest remaining armor facing them, but that was it. Her other two 'Mechs were too far out of position, with their commander between them and the danger.

Ezra looked at the *Thunderbolt*. It was too close to ignore, and nothing he would do here could affect the Saladins and Burton. That was in her hands now. It had only been a few seconds—he felt the Shigunga missile launchers settle their bins. He fired.

The *Thunderbolt* should have run.

Almost every one of his missiles hit, a feat he was sure he'd never manage to repeat in his life. The *Thunderbolt* shuddered and fell, its right arm—and the large laser there—snapping free at the elbow. Its return fire, a flight of LRMs, smashed impotently against the *Crusader*'s armor, but did little additional damage.

Ezra looked back at Burton. The first of the Saladins had already passed her. Unlike many combat vehicles, Saladins didn't mount their weapons in a turret. Instead, the cannons were mounted centerline, with a fixed traverse and limited azimuth. They rarely fired from anything other than max speed because of that. From the smoking pile of debris behind her, the Saladin had missed its shot and blown up a goodly stretch of desert.

The next two didn't miss. The first one nearly vanished beneath the exhaust of its firing. The heavy shells smashed the last of the armor over the *Cyclops*' right arm and torso. The limb fell limp—still attached, but helpless since the control runs were cut.

The second of the two remaining hovertanks fired as well. It put its full cassette-round of ammunition into the *Cyclops*' chest. The ninety-ton 'Mech twisted and writhed, trying to avoid the fire, and lost its balance and fell. It was too far to tell for sure, but Ezra didn't think the shot would be fatal. *Cyclopses* were tough 'Mechs in their own right. They had to be—they'd been built as command 'Mechs.

The Saladins' appearance and attack was the signal the marauders had been waiting for. Once the third tank fired, every raider 'Mech started moving backward, obviously trying to disengage.

"Press them!" Ezra urged. He moved toward the *Thunderbolt.* The sixty-five ton 'Mech was struggling to rise, but as he got close Ezra saw that the 'Mech's cockpit canopy was starred; he'd hit it with at least one missile. As the *Thunderbolt* slipped and fell again, he knew he'd managed to wound the MechWarrior inside. He pressed closer.

Aiming carefully, Ezra burned at the *Thunderbolt*'s remaining arm, its left, with his medium lasers. The *Thunderbolt* tried to roll onto its side so it could fire its torso-mounted weapons at him, but Ezra sidestepped out of the line of fire. He fired his laser again, and was rewarded with a burst of smoke and sparks. He'd severed the 'Mech's elbow actuator.

The *Thunderbolt* fell on its stomach again, and its active sensor emissions shut down. It was shutting down. Surrendering.

Ezra didn't wait to confirm the kill. He turned toward Nathalie's lance and maxed his throttle. He looked back toward Elly Burton while he did. The three Saladins had gotten past her unhurt, but they'd had to run the gauntlet of her lancemates.

The *Guillotine* was chasing one Saladin with laserfire, but the MechWarrior's aim was off. He was leading the 'Mech as if he were using projectile weapons, and was missing ahead. Ezra didn't think that MechWarrior had been piloting that particular 'Mech for very long.

The *Charger* had gotten its revenge. Its Saladin was a smoking trail of wreckage spread across a hundred meters of desert. Ezra didn't have to guess what had happened; the *Charger* had hit the Saladin with its own autocannon, which was just as powerful as that carried by the *Cyclops* or the Saladin itself.

The third Saladin was already 200 meters past them and still going.

Ezra grinned and concentrated on where he was going.

Nathalie's *Dervish* was running, but it suddenly halted and turned. Its two derringer-like hands came up and burped a pair of short-range missiles each at a marauder *Zeus*. All four of the missiles hit, but the *Zeus'* armor was thick enough that they would only be an annoyance.

Akhtar's and Hicks' arrival changed the balance. The *Grand Dragon* put a PPC into the *Zeus'* side at range. The assault 'Mech turned to look at the heavy Combine-built machine, and Ezra could see the decision being made. The *Zeus* was powerful, but it was slow. Unless the Dismal Ds let the 'Mech get away, it couldn't.

And the Dismal Ds, damage or no, were still pressing forward.

The *Zeus* stopped retreating.

"Aurel," Ezra ordered, "ignore the *Zeus*. Hit the stragglers. I want as many of these bastards brought down as we can."

Hicks double-clicked her understanding. The *Centurion* bore away from the *Zeus*, launching its LRMs at a limping marauder *JagerMech* instead. The warheads punched through the support 'Mech's thin armor and detonated inside. On his thermal scanner Ezra saw the 'Mech's heat output suddenly spike; Hicks had hit its engine shielding.

"Good idea," Nathalie sent. "Help me with the *Quickdraw*?"

"Roses, help Akhtar," he said. He settled his sights on the *Quickdraw* and waited for the range to close. He was only a hundred meters away from being able to fire.

The *Quickdraw's* MechWarrior could do the geometry as well as the rest of them. It saw itself as one corner of the steadily shrinking triangle between Ezra's *Crusader*, Natalie's *Dervish*, and itself. It unloaded on Nathalie's *Dervish* and leaped backward on its jump jets.

Nathalie cried out in pain. Ezra looked in time to see her *Dervish* fall, one of its legs stiff with actuator damage. There was a yelp when the *Dervish* hit the ground, and then nothing.

"Nathalie?"

No reply. Ezra changed channels. "Captain Ortiz?"

Nothing.

"She's down," one of her MechWarriors said. "Let's get this over with so we can check on her, hey?"

"That's my plan," Ezra said. He looked at the *Quickdraw*.

The 'Mech's leap had carried it more than 120 meters backward, but that wasn't far enough. Ezra cut the corner and got into range, and he fired. Sixty MRMs erupted at the *Quickdraw*, one for each ton of the marauder 'Mech's mass.

The *Quickdraw* had been fighting hard, but a wave of sixty warheads was a torrent it couldn't endure unscathed. The 'Mech didn't fall, but its speed dropped dramatically as one of Ezra's missiles clipped its hip. Ezra crowed in triumph and kept coming. He'd be in laser range in just a second.

The *Quickdraw* didn't intend to go down easily. It leveled its arms and dialed two medium lasers at Ezra as soon as the *Crusader* was in range, and both struck. Fresh alarms rang as one of the lasers removed the last of the protection over the right side of his torso, but Ezra ignored it.

He'd take this 'Mech down or fall trying.

His own mediums cut at the *Quickdraw*, capitalizing on the damage his missiles had done. A flash of actinic light foretold the destruction of one of the enemy 'Mech's power conduits. One of its lasers was out of action. Hobbled, it continued lurching backward. Ezra slowed his 'Mech, adjusted his aim, and toggled his MRMs to his primary trigger.

Then he blew the *Quickdraw* off its feet.

BRAVO BASE
HALL
THE CHAOS MARCH
19 AUGUST 3067

Kirsten Markoja knocked on the door to the conference room once and stepped inside. As she opened it, she was surprised meet Charles Monet coming out. He nodded to her and stepped past as she made way for him. Neither of them spoke, and she watched him until he turned the corner and was gone. Then she stepped inside.

She found the colonel sitting at the head of the table, alone. There was no sign of Colonel Richardson. She glanced around and raised an eyebrow at the colonel. "Did I miss him?"

"He's down the hall," Rauschenbusch said. "Status?"

"Payne is mopping up."

"Did he get him?"

"It's too early to tell," Kirsten said. She'd seen the *Quickdraw* go down, but she wasn't going to count a Light of Mankind operative out until she saw his body cold on a slab. She pulled out one of the chairs near Rauschenbusch and sat down, her left hand rubbing at her right palm.

"Losses?"

"Light, so far. A couple of the Dismal D 'Mechs went down, but it looks like the jocks are okay. The rest of Payne's company is about to mousetrap what's left of Ridzik's force, but they should do okay."

"Good."

Kirsten watched the colonel. He had his hands on the holo controls and was looking at a display keyed to his station only. She saw the holo projected, but it was just a scattering of light. Only the person sitting at the controls would be able to read it. He hadn't met her eyes since she entered the room.

"Should I see to Colonel Richardson?"

"He'll be fine," Rauschenbusch said. "I'll just be a second more."

Kirsten shrugged. She waited while he tapped keys. Finally he grunted and sat back. He collapsed the hologram and looked her in the eye for the first time.

She almost recoiled from the rage she saw there.

"Why?" he asked. His voice was tight with anger, and his skin flushed red. It contrasted sharply with his white hair.

"Why what?"

Rauschenbusch didn't speak. Instead, he toggled a control,

and the wall screen lit up with a recording of the battle from ear-lier. Kirsten watched the *Quickdraw* put a brace of lasers into a Dis-mal D *Dervish* and felt the pit fall out of her stomach. Her fingers massaged her right hand in ever-faster circles.

"This is from earlier tonight," the colonel said, "and this—" A new image appeared, another *Quickdraw*. "—is not." It was day-light, and Kirsten recognized the background as the final mop-up of Critchley's Cavaliers.

"That's my gun camera footage," Rauschenbusch said. "From my *BattleMaster*." He froze it, then replayed a stretch. "Pay attention to the way the hips move." The *Quickdraw* advanced a few steps. Now that she'd been warned, Kirsten saw the hitch in its steps.

"The techs say that's an intermittent fault in its thigh myo-mers," Rauschenbusch said. "I asked them when we salvaged it."

Kirsten looked away from the screen and back at the colonel. "Okay. What does this have to do with me?"

Rauschenbusch switched the displays. The *Quickdraw* Ezra Payne had just shot down had the same hitch in its step. He didn't look at the screen. He looked at her.

"According to our inventories," Rauschenbusch said, "that 'Mech is still in our bays." He snorted. "Or at least, that's what the computers say."

"Is that where you sent Monet? To check himself?"

"He brought me the footage from last year," Rauschenbusch said. "Now answer my question. Why?" He leaned forward, slam-ming his hands on the tabletop. His face was bright red. "*Why?!*"

A sense of calm filled Kirsten at the colonel's outburst. Her fin-gers made a specific pressure on her fight hand, and she pulled her hands back to her lap. It was like a weight had been lifted, or a veil that had been hanging between her and the real word had been parted. She regarded Rauschenbusch almost without emotion.

"Because it's my mission," she said.

"Your *mission*?" He sputtered. "Betraying your *family*?"

She laughed. "You're not my family, Yuri. You never were."

"Mason," he said. "Mason is with you? Of course he is . . ." He sat back. He was sweating.

"Of course he is. We're twins."

"Who are you working for?"

"Isn't it obvious?"

"The Word?" Rauschenbusch looked like he was going to be sick. "Oh, God. You've been here all along, haven't you? All the way back to Aswan on Caph. Did they place you here?" He frowned. "Is *anything* you've done honest?"

She smiled. "Of course. But honest to myself."

Before he could react, she leaped. She slid down the meter of the table or so that separated them and grabbed at his throat with her right hand.

Despite his years, Rauschenbusch was a fit man and in training. His left hand came up to block her strike, which was all she'd wanted in the first place. She twisted until she could grip his wrist in her hand. Then she squeezed.

He flinched.

She let go and slid backward. The smooth tabletop didn't impede her at all. A moment later, she was back in her chair.

Rauschenbusch gobbled and rubbed his wrist where he'd touched her. "It burns," he muttered. He looked at her. "What did you do?"

She stood. "Peace of Blake be with you, Yuri," she said. Her left hand was manipulating the controls just beneath the skin of her palm. She felt the feathery prickle as the nano needles withdrew into her fingertips.

"You—you . . ." His words slurred. His face turned bright red, and he clutched at his chest. "Ack!" He thrashed in the chair, but the movement was tetanic, not conscious. His feet kicked, futilely drumming against the floor.

"It's a poison from the world of Jardine," she told him. "You've never heard of Jardine. No one has. But I've been there, with Mason. We were *selected.*" She rubbed her hand, ignoring the pins-and-needles sensation of her nerves realigning. "We were *ascended.*"

Rauschenbusch looked at her in horror, but she could already see the light fading from his eyes. She knew the poison was undetectable; it metabolized even as it worked, and the blasts of hormones the body released as it fought against death would mask what few traces remained. It didn't so much *look* like a heart attack as *cause* one. That's what the medics would say when they examined the colonel's body.

Speaking of which . . . Kirsten rolled her head around on her shoulders and took a couple deep breaths. She walked to the door and keyed it open. Then she screamed.

"Dear Christ, someone get a doctor! *It's the colonel!*"

Hopefully no one would notice the smile she couldn't quite hide.

The Tikonov Free Republic will never die. Cut off our heads, new ones will grow. Stab our hearts, fresh ones will beat to life. You can't kill freedom. You can't kill liberty. So long as the people of Hall suffer under the thumb of outsiders, we will never go away. Look for us in the sky, in the stars, and in the halls.

–Excerpt from a recruiting advertisement
on the Hall planetary net, August 3067

CHAPTER TWENTY-ONE

Nathalie Ortiz came out of her *Dervish* spitting mad. "Where is he? Did you get him?" She stepped past two of her own MechWarriors to stand in front of Ezra. "The *Quickdraw*. You got him?"

"I got him."

"Good. Where?"

"I was just about to go see about cracking him open," Ezra said. He gestured behind her. "Are you okay?"

Nathalie turned and, if Ezra was any judge, really saw the damage to her 'Mech for the first time. He would have thought having had to be pried out of her cockpit would have been sufficient notice, but seeing the *Dervish* lying on its side, awash in the harsh lights of 'Mech searchlights, seemed to do the trick. She looked all along its length, then held one hand to her mouth. She walked back over and touched one of the gashes, then turned to look at Ezra. She was still covering her mouth. She didn't speak.

"I know," he told her. He wanted to say more, but not in front of everyone.

She walked back to him, lowering her hand as she approached. Her hair was matted with sweat and from being smashed under a neurohelmet. She wore baggy battledress pants and her cooling vest. A revolver was in a belly holster across the front of her vest.

"Where is he?" she asked.

Ezra jerked a thumb over his shoulder and turned to walk with her. "I left a 'Mech to watch him, but when I left, no one had come out." He shrugged. "He's either jammed up like you were, or unconscious."

"Or dead," she said.

"Or dead," he agreed.

A few steps later she touched his arm. "Burton?"

"Alive," Ezra told her. "Her 'Mech might be a little worse than yours, but she's okay. I heard her on the radio to her son a couple minutes ago, and one of her 'Mechs went with Nico Reynard to chase down the rest of these people."

"How many did we get?"

Ezra's mind went back to the battle for a second. He saw the stroboscopic flashes of light that meant weapons firing. He saw the blurry edges of his HUD that he could only see at night. He saw the VTOLs sparking and crashing into the ground. He blinked and shook his head.

"We got seven," he said, "not counting the VTOLs. Four here, and Nico's accounted for three more so far. They're still running them down."

"The *Quickdraw*?"

"Me," Ezra said.

"Thank you." He shrugged. "Are any of them claiming to be Ridzik?"

"Not yet," he told her. "The *Zeus'* pilot is dead—Iqbal hit it with a PPC." They climbed up a low, sandy rise, struggling with their heavy boots in the loose sand, and he pointed to a lit area ahead. "It could be him, I guess."

Before them lay the fallen *Quickdraw*. It was smashed and battered, with broken armor across most of its body. The critical strikes had been his last round of missiles—they had penetrated into its chest and smashed its gyro. Without the massive contraption, it was impossible to balance the sixty-ton 'Mech on its feet. Still, the *Quickdraw's* pilot had been crawling the 'Mech away until Roses had arrived with her hatchet.

Then it had collapsed, and not moved since.

"The other pilots we've recovered are mercenaries, hired on personal retainer with Nikoli Ridzik. Or so they say." He looked at her and raised his eyebrows. "We'll know more when you get them back to Jake and let him work them over."

Roses' *Hatchetman* stood over the fallen 'Mech like a policeman over a suspect; the *Quickdraw* lay face-down on the sand. The *Hatchetman* stood behind it, bent at the waist so its autocannon muzzle was aimed at the marauder 'Mech. And if that wasn't enough, Roses had extended her 'Mech's right arm. The large hatchet blade rested against the back of the *Quickdraw*'s cockpit. Spotlights in the *Hatchetman*'s armpits illuminated the scene.

"I hope it is," Nathalie said.

The *Hatchetman*'s head twisted to the side to watch them as they walked up. A bleep of static announced Roses opening her external speakers. "All quiet here, Six."

Ezra waved to show that he heard her, and then pulled Nathalie around the edge of the *Quickdraw*'s foot. At the 'Mech's head stood Iqbal Akhtar, wearing khaki battledress and an infantryman's helmet and holding an AX-22 assault rifle.

Nathalie looked at him and then gave Ezra a side-eye. "I thought you didn't carry any infantry."

Ezra smiled at his MechWarrior. "Iqbal has a rich fantasy life," he told her. Then, speaking to Akhtar, "Anything?"

"I have heard nothing," he said. "The mechanism looks undamaged, but I have not yet tried it."

Ezra looked at Nathalie. "Shall we?"

"Let's."

Ezra looked at Iqbal. "You keep that cannon aimed at the hatch. I'll work the mechanism." He pointed Nathalie back. "You stay behind us, out of Iqbal's line of fire, okay?"

Nathalie drew her revolver and stood behind and to the side of Akhtar. "Do it," she told him.

Ezra nodded, got a nod back from Akhtar, and then turned to the hatch mechanism. BattleMech security was some of the strongest in the Inner Sphere, but most of that was electronic. Hatch access had to have some vulnerability to allow for rescue. 'Mech armor was, by definition, nearly impossible to cut through. Usually a 'Mech's rescue features kicked in when it took disabling damage, such as gyro destruction. That was what Ezra was counting on now.

The hatch cycled before he could touch it. He stepped back, hand dropping to the automatic he wore on his thigh, but he didn't draw it.

"I'm coming out," a man's voice called from inside the dark cockpit.

"Throw out your sidearm first," Ezra said.

A small laser pistol hit the sand at Ezra's feet. He bent to pick it up, then looked at the dark hatch. "And your backup."

A knife hit the sand next to the pistol. Ezra picked them both up. "All right," he said, stepping clear, "come on out."

A man climbed carefully through the sideways hatch. He held his left arm stiffly against his side, and the side of his head was bloody. He wore a cooling vest, and MechWarrior boots. His holster was on his vest, and it was empty. He looked from Ezra to Iqbal to Nathalie, then back at Ezra.

"I surrender," he said.

"Who are you?"

"Nikoli Ridzik," the man said.

"Bullshit," Nathalie spat.

The man shrugged, or tried to. His left shoulder didn't seem to work. "I'd show you my ID," he said, "but I left it in my other 'Mech."

"Nikoli Ridzik is dead."

The man just held up his right hand. "I'm doing a hell of a resurrection impression, then."

Ezra frowned. "Who hired you?"

"No one hired me," the ersatz Ridzik said.

"Who sent you after us tonight?"

"I came for Elly Burton," he said. He looked at Nathalie again. "You're not her. Did my tanks get her?"

"No," Ezra said.

"Pity."

The four of them stood staring at each other for a long moment. Then Ezra shook his head and slapped his thigh with his free hand. "All right. Let's get back to the others. Maybe one of them will shed some more light on matters."

Akhtar motioned with his rifle back the way they'd come. The MechWarrior nodded and turned. He trudged slowly, taking small steps, as if he were having trouble with the sand. Nathalie was still holding her revolver. She frowned.

"This is going to take forever," she said quietly to Ezra.

Ezra looked at her and gave a Gallic shrug. "It's a nice night," he said, giving her a smile. She smiled back, and holstered her revolver.

The prisoner stumbled and fell to one knee. His right hand went out to catch him before he fell any more. He tried to move his left, but flinched and yelped in pain.

Ezra handed Nathalie the man's weapons and stepped forward. "Here, let me help—" was all he got out.

From the ground, the man's foot lashed out, catching Ezra in the pit of his stomach. He saw it coming and tried to dodge, shouting, but the man was too fast. His boot drove the breath out of Ezra's lungs, turning his warning into an incomprehensible *urk*. The man recovered his foot and spun. His right hand came up full of sand and hurled it at Akhtar, who took his rifle off aim to try and block his eyes.

Ezra fell to his side, trying and failing to cough. He knew he wasn't going to suffocate. This wasn't the first time he'd had the breath knocked out of him. But knowing was different from feeling, and right now it didn't feel like he'd ever breathe again.

Iqbal dropped to one knee, blinking furiously, trying to bring his rifle back around. Ridzik, or whoever he was, lurched upright and charged toward Iqbal and his rifle. Ezra saw him, but couldn't move.

A single shot boomed. Nathalie Ortiz stood with her revolver in one hand, the MechWarrior's laser pistol forgotten in her left hand. The shot took the MechWarrior in the shoulder and spun him, but he didn't fall. He stuttered a step or two, and then straightened up. He looked at Nathalie. He took another step.

Boom.

Nathalie's revolver was a large caliber, ten or eleven millimeter, from the sound. Her second shot took the MechWarrior just over the bridge of his nose and blew out the back of his head. The large bullet scooped out most of his brains with hydrostatic shock and spread them across the landscape.

Across Ezra, who was just starting to lie on his side and wheeze weakly.

Light flashed as Roses swung her *Hatchetman*'s head around. The 'Mech's body twisted to follow, bringing its powerful spots around. A moment later the scene was lit better than daylight, though with harsh white actinics rather than the natural yellow of sunlight.

"Six?" Roses shouted through her speakers.

Ezra sat up. He still couldn't breathe, but he waved at Roses. Akhtar was back on his feet, standing over Ridzik's body, rifle leveled. Nathalie was still standing where she had been, revolver leveled at where the MechWarrior's head had been. She wasn't moving. She wasn't blinking. If it hadn't been for the slow rise and fall of her chest, Ezra would have taken her for a statue.

He climbed to his feet.

"Nathalie . . ." he wheezed. She didn't look at him. Whatever she was seeing, it wasn't something in the world with Ezra. He stepped to the side, well out of her line of fire, and stepped closer. "Nathalie?"

She blinked and lowered her arm. The laser pistol and knife fell out of the other hand. If she even noticed, she gave no sign.

Ezra stepped close and touched her on the arm. "Are you okay?" she asked him.

"Fine," he said. "Are you okay?"

"Fine," she said. She looked down at the body. "At least this time there's a body."

A group of people came running over the dune from back toward Nathalie's *Dervish*. Several of the Disinherited MechWarriors had their sidearms out, and Ezra bit back a frown when he saw Elly Burton with them. She trailed the group, with a burly MechWarrior that must have been one of her Brigade.

While Nathalie reassured her people, Elly Burton came to stand near Ezra.

"Payne," she said.

"Captain."

She indicated the body with her chin. "Who's that?"

"Nikoli Ridzik, he claimed."

"Huh." She leaned down, peered at what was left of his face, then straightened. "I'll take your word for it." She looked around until she saw the gun in Nathalie's hand. "She do it?"

"Yeah."

"Huh."

Ezra suddenly wanted very badly to be anywhere else in the world than standing next to Elly Burton in the desert. He looked around. The Disinherited *Stealth* limped up to stand near Roses' *Hatchetman*. Even in the terrible light, Ezra could see its entire shoulder assembly had been ruined by its impact with the *Quickdraw*.

"Thank you," Burton said suddenly.

Ezra frowned and looked at her. She was looking at the sand between them, not meeting her eyes. "For what?"

"For the warning, about the Saladins."

"It was nothing," he said. And it wasn't. He hadn't thought about shouting the warning. He had just done it. He hadn't thought about it since, either, until Elly Burton mentioned it.

"They'd have gotten us in the ass if you hadn't said something," she said. She looked up suddenly, her face clouded with anger. "I needed to say that," she said, then turned and walked away.

Nathalie excused herself from her MechWarriors and walked over to stand next to Ezra. She looked after Burton, then met Ezra's eyes. "Anything you need to talk about?"

He indicated Burton with his chin. "I saved her life, apparently."

"The Saladins?"

"Yeah."

"She's probably right."

"Maybe." He grimaced and clutched his side. He'd tried to take too deep a breath. His probing fingers found tender flesh, but no sharp pains. So the worst he'd have in the morning—*later* in the morning—was a nasty, boot-shaped bruise.

"You going to live?" Nathalie asked, looking at his midsection.

"Doesn't feel a lot like I should want to, just now," he allowed.

"Maybe you should sit down."

"Maybe," he said. He held out his hand, and she took it, and despite the pain and the tiredness and both of them stinking to high heaven after a battle in 'Mechs' cockpits, he felt the old electric tingle when his skin touched hers.

From her expression, she felt it, too.

"Maybe," he said again, and looked down to see what he'd be sitting on.

"Six!" Roses shouted. Or rather, her 'Mech shouted. The volume was far too loud. Everyone within earshot jumped. Weapons were trained outward. Nathalie's revolver was back in her hand and half-raised. Ezra just flinched, then groaned and held his stomach at the pain the flinch caused, then looked up at the *Hatchetman*.

"What is it, Jessica?" he called.

"You need to get on your comm, sir!" She sounded like she had a lot more to say, but didn't want to. There was something in her voice. "Signal from Bravo Base!"

Ezra reached into his webbing and pulled out his comm, but it was broken. Ridzik's boot had broken it against his stomach. He held it up and shook it. "Can't," he told her. "Relay it."

"Maybe you should wait until you get back in your 'Mech, sir," Roses said.

Ice bled into Ezra's veins. He stood up a little straighter, his pain forgotten. He took two steps, then realized that was stupid.

He turned to Akhtar. "Iqbal?"

Akhtar reached into his own webbing and pulled his comm out. He tossed it underhanded to Ezra, then went back to covering the dead body on the ground. The expression on his face was set, and fierce. Ezra knew from experience that meant Akhtar felt like he'd failed at something.

Catching the comm, he keyed in an officer's override and called up his message queue. Most of them looked like standard message traffic . . . but there was one new priority message blinking. He swiped it open and frowned. The sending code was from Kirsten Markoja . . .

Then the words on the screen registered.

The pain in his stomach vanished. An entirely new kind of pain, throughout his entire chest, replaced it. He couldn't breathe. He couldn't balance. His legs folded beneath him and he half-sat, half-collapsed.

"Ezra!" Nathalie shouted. She knelt beside him. "Ezra, what is it?"

Ezra couldn't speak. He tried to raise the comm, to show her the message, but his arm wouldn't work. He tried to look down at it, to find out why, but his head wouldn't turn. He felt like he was outside his body, watching himself.

"Erza!" Nathalie took his face in both of her hands. He felt the sand on her palms rub against the stubble on her face.

"Ezra, talk to me! Are you hurt?" Her hands probed at his stomach, but he didn't feel them. The words he'd read scrolled over and over in his head. He wanted to stand up, to scream, to kick the dead man's body and the downed *Quickdraw* and anything else he could reach. He wanted to hurt himself. He wanted to do anything. Anything that would make the feeling in his chest go away.

Anything that would take away the sudden, familiar, unending feeling of loss that washed across him.

The comm fell out of his hand. Nathalie saw it, picked it up. The screen was still lit. She read the words still displayed. She hissed. She looked at Ezra's face, then back at the screen, then up at the others.

Then she stood. "I need transport back to Harney ASAP," she said to one of her MechWarriors. "VTOL, blower, I don't care. Call a DropShip if you have to. We have to get back right now!" People scurried to do as she said. They didn't know any more than he did—less, far less than he knew—but they reacted to the sound of command in her voice.

Ezra sat in the sand of the Camden Hole. He was hundreds of kilometers away. He wanted to tell her that it didn't matter, that there was no longer any reason to rush.

Yuri Rauschenbusch was already dead.

Nathalie stepped aside, and Ezra could suddenly see the body of the Ridzik imposter.

A sob tore up out of his tortured gut. Then another one.

And after that so many that he didn't bother to count.

"With the death of Colonel Yuri Rauschenbusch of the Stealthy Tigers, command of the mercenary regiment passes to Colonel Mason Markoja, who had served as the previous colonel's executive officer. The emperor's press office assures us it has complete confidence in Colonel Markoja, and that the Stealthy Tigers remain committed to Hall's security and the security of its people."

"We mourn Colonel Rauschenbusch," the emperor said during a rare public appearance in Harney, *"along with his soldiers and staff. He was a brave man, a courageous leader, and a tenacious fighter. Hall would be a much more violent, much more bloody place if it were not for Yuri Rauschenbusch. His sudden death is a tragedy for all of us."*

–From the *Harney Morning Edition*,
Harney HV Channel Six

CHAPTER TWENTY-TWO

BRAVO BASE
HALL
THE CHAOS MARCH
21 AUGUST 3067

Ezra Payne was numb.

Around him, the business of the Stealthy Tigers went on without pause. Many of the other faces around him showed the same shock that he felt, but they were soldiers. Mercenaries. Death was a constant and dear companion to people in their profession. People died around them, or because of them, every time they climbed into a 'Mech's cockpit to go and face an opponent.

But that was it, Ezra realized. *They expected death in the cockpit.*

They didn't expect death in bed.

Or in a conference room.

The colonel's funeral had been yesterday; it was quiet and private. Only the regiment had been welcome. The emperor's representatives had been confused, but not really offended. They'd only come because they thought they had to. None of the Tigers had cared, and the representatives had said all the right platitudes at the reception following the funeral.

Now Ezra sat with the rest of the regiment in the Panther Battalion 'Mech bay, waiting for the majors Markoja to appear and tell them what would happen next. He sat with the rest of Jaguar Company, near the two battalion rows, but not really a part of them. Most of the regiment was present, including the technical staff.

Sergeant Major Halleck sat down next to Ezra. Ezra looked at the grizzled black man, nodded, and went back to staring at the back of the folding chair in front of him. He didn't want to look at the pain in Halleck's dark eyes, or see the exhaustion lurking in his face or the set of his shoulders.

"Don't seem right," Halleck said quietly.

"Isn't right," Ezra said back.

The space around them rustled with similar whispers. When Ezra looked to his left, he saw Captain Heather Hargood looking at him. He nodded at her. She frowned and looked away. Ezra wondered what that was about, but put it down to grief.

Yuri Rauschenbusch had led the Stealthy Tigers for more than thirty years. In a very real sense, he *was* the Stealthy Tigers. The regiment had been around for over a century. They would survive. Losing the colonel was wounding, sure, but wounds healed.

Ezra snorted softly. He was repeating the mantras he'd forced himself to say to his company that morning. He wondered if they believed them any more than he did.

Wounds healed, true. But they left scars.

Ezra didn't look forward to rubbing this scar for the rest of his life.

The whispering stopped. Ezra looked up into the silence, and movement caught his eye. Kirsten and Mason Markoja were walking toward the front of the assembly. Behind them came Wesley Eberhardt and Colonel Richardson, from the emperor's staff.

Ezra felt his breath catch in his throat. He'd forgotten about that—how had he forgotten about that? There was only one Major Markoja now.

Mason Markoja was colonel of the Stealthy Tigers, by the grace of his commission as *de facto* executive officer and with the blessing of Emperor Baranov, through the office of his liaison officer, Colonel Richardson.

"Bastard," Ezra heard Halleck mutter.

Three days ago, Halleck would have knocked to the floor anyone who showed Yuri Rauschenbusch such disrespect. Now he was swearing at the colonel's replacement. Ezra knew he should say something. They didn't have to like their new commanding officer. They were professionals. They were Raiders. They should be able to get past it. Ezra knew that.

But, like the speech he'd given his company that morning, he didn't believe it.

Truth be told, he agreed with Halleck's sentiment.

Mason reached the lectern that stood at the front of the assembly. He was dressed in duty utilities, brown-and-red khaki battledress. It was too far for Ezra to read the collar flash on his blouse, but he knew what he would see: colonel's insignia.

"I don't have a speech for you," Mason said. His voice was deep and carried easily across the entire space the regiment occupied. "Our colonel is dead. I didn't want to lead this regiment this way." He frowned and looked down. "But we don't always get to choose." He glanced at his sister.

"Major Markoja will take over as XO," he said.

Of course, Ezra thought bitterly.

"I've also chosen a new commander for the Panthers," Mason continued. He turned and gestured Eberhardt forward. "Wesley Eberhardt is hereby promoted to major, and command of First Battalion."

Chairs scraped against the cold ferrocrete of the floor. No one spoke. No one leaped to their feet. But when Ezra looked again at Heather Hargood, she wouldn't meet his eyes. *She knew about it beforehand,* he realized. *That's why she'd looked away.*

"I know you'll do a good job," Mason said to Eberhardt. The former captain—*and current stooge,* Ezra's mind filled in—stepped forward to take his commander's hand. Then he grinned and took the lectern.

"Like the colonel said," he began, but Ezra tuned him out.

Yuri Rauschenbusch was the colonel. Not Mason Markoja.

Ezra wasn't ready to accept any other reality than that one. He closed his eyes and stared down, toward where his hands were clasped between his knees. Both his feet bounced on the floor. He squeezed and released his fingers. Squeezed and released.

The pain was back in his chest. He opened his eyes and looked at Robert Halleck. Then he stared, because Halleck was *shaking.*

The sergeant major was looking straight ahead. His eyes were unfocused, but his hands were balled into fists, resting on his knees. His back was ramrod straight, as if he were trying to sit at attention.

Every part of him trembled.

"Bob?" Ezra whispered. His own malaise was forgotten. "Are you okay?"

"Sixty-eight, sir," Halleck gasped.

"You don't look sixty-eight, Sergeant Major," Ezra said.

"I'm good."

"Bob—"

Something snapped in Halleck's expression. He looked at

Ezra suddenly, his eyes sharpening into focus. Ezra watched the man's pupils dilate as they focused on him. "It's not right," he whispered through gritted teeth. "Ezra. It's not *right!*"

"Bob—" Ezra said again, but Halleck shook his head.

"No. *No!*" He faced the front again, where Eberhardt was still speaking. "None of them up there are Raiders. It isn't *right.*"

Ezra didn't disagree, but just then he couldn't quite feel that strongly about it. He couldn't quite feel that strongly about anything. His mind kept going back to the day before, when they'd put the colonel into the furnace. He closed his eyes and tried to think about something else. When Eberhardt stopped talking, he looked up.

Colonel Richardson took the lectern. "I don't presume to intrude upon your grief," the Tigers' liaison officer said. *Except you're here, intruding,* Ezra thought. "My emperor sent me here to assure you that he retains the highest confidence in Colonel Markoja and the Stealthy Tigers. Your regiment is a critical and valued part of the peace every citizen of Hall now enjoys . . ."

Ezra tuned him out as well. He could already tell it was going to be nothing but the usual platitudes. Long series of words that ultimately said nothing. Instead he looked around the crowd. He wasn't ready to argue with Halleck yet.

Heather Hargood still wouldn't meet his eyes. She sat, hunched over, chewing on the tip of one finger while her foot tapped on the floor. When she glanced up and down Ezra saw the light reflect from her Raider pin. He frowned, suddenly afraid that he'd forgotten to put his on. Their colonel would rip him a new one . . .

Ezra swallowed.

He kept looking, now for other Raiders.

Ervil Gam glared at Markoja with unbridled hatred. He wasn't making any attempt to hide it. Sergeant Liam Porra, sitting next to him, was sitting stiffly in his chair, hand tucked into his armpits, as if he expected to be doused with cold water at any moment. Two rows behind them Lieutenant Branden Roth rubbed his hands together. Ezra couldn't see his hands, but he could see the big man's shoulders working.

On the other side of the group, Charles Monet wasn't even looking toward the front of the room. He was looking at Ezra. When Ezra met his eyes, he jerked his head to the side, toward the Jaguar Company hangar two kilometers away. Then he tapped the Raider pin on his collar.

He wants to meet.

Ezra nodded.

Monet looked back to the front. His hands moved, and a message vibrated into Ezra's comm in his pocket. He slipped the device out far enough to see the words: *PAYNE'S, RIGHT AFTER.*

The head of every Raider turned to look at Ezra at the same time.

They all want to meet.

Great.

By the time Ezra got to his office, it was overflowing with Raiders. A half-dozen people stood outside the door; through the open door he saw the backs of at least that many more. He sighed and started making his way through the press of bodies to his desk, but gave up halfway there. He didn't want to be in that small space with that many people.

"Everybody," he called, "let's do this out here." He backed up until he was a couple meters from his door. "Come on."

The Raiders filed out the door and fell into loose ranks in front of his office. Ezra looked around the cavernous, empty bay while they did, but all was quiet. None of the 'Mechs were being worked on, and there were no techs in sight.

The last person out of the office was Heather Hargood. She must've been the first person in, to get out that late. She ignored the grouped others and walked straight up to him. "I didn't find out until just before we sat down," she said. "Ezra, I'm sorry."

"It's nothing," Ezra said. It wasn't nothing, but there was nothing she or he could do about it now.

"I didn't want you to think I knew and didn't tell you," she persisted.

"Heather." He gripped her shoulders and stared at her until she met his gaze. "I understand." He waited until she nodded, then lowered her hands. She stepped back with the others. Ezra looked at a couple of them, waiting.

"We're not going to take this," Lieutenant Roth said. Murmurs of assent whispered through the group.

"Yes, we will," Ezra said. "What else?"

"That's it?" Roth asked. "The colonel is dead, and the new colonel isn't a Raider? None of the battalion commanders are Raiders?" He gestured between Hargood and Ezra. "Only two of the company commanders?"

Ezra looked at him without reacting. Nothing Roth had said was incorrect, but he knew he had to let the big man come to his own place of stopping. His emotions ran hot, but he was a good man. There wasn't a more loyal man in the Stealthy Tigers. He was proving that right now, just not to the right people.

"It's not right," Roth said. He looked down, then back up.

"The only difference between today and three days ago is that the colonel is dead," Ezra said. "We only have one less Raider than we did then."

"But it's the *colonel*—" Roth persisted.

"No, it's not," Sergeant Major Halleck said. He stood near the edge of the group. He still looked furious, but his anger had turned cold. Ezra saw it in the set of his shoulders and the balls of his fists. "The colonel *is* dead," he said, "and we can't hide from that. But the new colonel isn't a Raider, and that has never happened since there's *been* Raiders."

"No regulation that says the colonel has to be a Raider," Ezra said. "It doesn't feel right, but it's not illegal."

"Legal don't mean right," Sergeant Vann grunted.

"No, it doesn't," Ezra agreed. "But the only other option is mutiny. And I'm not dishonoring the colonel's memory by throwing away everything he worked to build for the past thirty years."

Some of the Raiders looked nervous at that.

"Look around," he told them. "There's less than twenty of us." He looked several of them, including Roth, in the eye. "The regiment doesn't exist to serve us. We're a part of it. The best part of it, for my money. All we can do is continue to be the best part of it. We can continue to lead by example, and we can continue to do our duty." He waited half a beat. "Sixty-eight."

"*Sixty-eight!*" they chorused back.

"Then you all have duties."

Most of them nodded and began stepping away. Ezra waited, but no one said anything more. He stepped past them and into his office, but didn't close the door behind him. Three people followed him inside: Halleck, Hargood, and Charles Monet.

Ezra sat down behind his desk. Hargood and Monet sat in his two chairs; Halleck stood. He folded his hands across his belly and looked at all of them, waiting.

"You didn't really mean all that," Hargood ventured.

"Of course I did," Ezra said.

"But . . ."

"Look," he told them, sitting forward, "at the end of the day, it doesn't matter. Do the math. There are seventeen of us. We make maybe a company. The regiment is bigger than that, and unless we bring some new people in, we'll be an even smaller drop in the bucket when they bring Three Batt online."

"If they bring Three Batt on," Halleck muttered.

Ezra looked at him. "Of course they will. We have the 'Mechs, and Mason will need to put his stamp on the regiment as quickly as he can. Putting together another battalion—especially when he can say he's done something the colonel didn't—is the easiest way to do it."

"We don't have the MechWarriors," Halleck grumbled.

"Of course we don't," Ezra said. "Haven't we spent the last year on Jaguar Company? He won't care."

"He's already floated it to me," Hargood said quietly.

"Floated what?" Monet asked.

"Three Batt," she said. She looked up and met Ezra's eyes. "He offered me command."

"Command of what?" Monet asked. "A desk? He may have the plan, but he doesn't have the working 'Mechs or the people to drive them."

"That's what I told him."

"What'd he say to that?" Halleck asked.

"He said I should be patient," Hargood said. She glanced at Halleck and then back at Ezra. "And he said I should remember where my loyalties lie."

Halleck came off the wall like a rocket. "That son of a bitch!" he shouted.

"Which is more or less what I called him," Hargood said.

Ezra didn't move. He couldn't. He was too deep inside of himself just then, relishing the bloom of incandescent fury he found there at Hargood's words. The idea that Markoja would try and turn one of the Raiders against the others—

Ezra blinked. His fury turned ice cold.

That's what happened—he tried to turn her against us.

He sucked in a deep breath.

He's actually working against us. Against me.

"Charlie," he said. No one heard him. Halleck and Hargood were going back and forth.

"*Charlie!*" he shouted. Everyone stopped talking. "Where are you on the task the colonel asked you about?"

"Which one? The Word files, you mean?"

"What 'word files?'" Hargood asked. "The Word of Blake?"

Ezra looked at her, then at Halleck. He nodded. "The money used to hire us came from Terra," he said.

Hargood stared at him. Her mouth opened and closed. She looked at Monet, who nodded. Halleck nodded when she looked at him. "Wha-what?" She looked back at Ezra, and he saw the first traces of anger there. "Say that again?"

"The Word of Blake subsidized our hire here," Ezra told her. Then, before she could wind up again, "Charlie figured it out. The colonel told us to keep it close to our vests."

Beside Hargood, Monet nodded.

"Who else knows?"

"No one."

"What are we doing about it?"

"Nothing."

She sputtered. "Nothing!" She started to say something, then stopped. She closed her mouth. Ezra watched her get her temper under control. It looked like it took both hands.

"Why aren't we doing anything?" she asked calmly.

"Because we can't prove it," Ezra said.

"But Charlie—"

"Is sure. But there's a difference between knowing something and being able to prove it." Ezra cleared his throat. "And, in the end it doesn't really matter. The contract is the contract, no matter where the cash comes from."

"I'm not sure—"

"It was the colonel's position," Ezra said softly. "Maybe it was the wrong one, but it's done, and we're here today."

Hargood looked like she wanted to argue, but Halleck coughed quietly and, when she looked at him, shook his head. She looked at the sergeant major for a second, then turned to Monet. "Okay, Charlie. Answer the captain's question."

Monet grinned at her. "The trail is cold," he said. "No new data, and I can't make the data I have perform any differently." He shrugged. "I'd hoped there was something in the 'Mech data, something I'd missed and the colonel picked up on, but then he . . ." he shrugged again.

"'Mech data?" Ezra asked.

"The other day," Monet said, "probably just a couple minutes before his heart attack. The colonel asked me to pull him the maintenance and repair logs for the 'Mech graveyard. What 'Mechs were where, in what stage of repair, things like that."

"Why?"

"I don't know. I just dropped it off. He had a meeting with Kirsten Markoja right then." Monet looked at the floor. "He never came out of that meeting, so if he found anything, he didn't get a chance to tell me what it is."

"I want to see all of that data," Ezra said. "If there's a clue in there, we need to find it."

"Sixty-eight," Monet said. He stood to go.

"Go," Ezra told him. He nodded to Hargood and Halleck too, and all three left.

Sixty-eight, he thought. *That's only four months away.*

"With the apparent demise—again—of Nikoli Ridzik and his Free Tikonov Republic movement, the emperor has again called on the Allied Mercenary Command to admit defeat and withdraw from Hall. Citing the coming annexation by the Free Worlds League, the emperor has declared the AMC's mission null and void, and ordered them off-world."

"There can only be one reason these mercenaries remain," the emperor wrote in a prepared statement. *"That reason is greed. They hope to keep us from joining the Free Worlds, from expressing our will and our independence. Jaime Wolf and the rest of his ilk are desperate to keep the worlds around Terra independent and fighting. That means more contracts for mercenaries, more money for the Mercenary Review and Bonding Commission, more work for Outreach's administrators and trainers and manufacturers."*

"No response has been received from the local AMC headquarters in Rockfall Maze."

–From the *Harney Morning Edition*,
Harney HV Channel Six

CHAPTER TWENTY-THREE

HARNEY
HALL
THE CHAOS MARCH
21 AUGUST 3067

Jacob Brim sat in a groundcar, watching the door to Adele Estwicke's apartment building. He sat in the passenger seat with his feet up on the dash, hunched down for comfort. He could just see over the windowsill to keep an eye on the door.

He was bored.

He knew he was wasting his time, and that didn't help. There was next to no chance Estwicke would return to her public home. He hadn't been able to learn exactly what had been said between she and Baranov, but he did know they had spoken. None of Burton's sources were close enough to Baranov to have heard the words, and he hadn't been on-world long enough to build that kind of network.

Still . . . it was better than being back in Rockfall Maze.

He'd returned there to oversee the interrogation of the captured MechWarriors from the battle at Camden Hole, but hadn't learned anything new. They were mercenaries, as he'd expected, hired to support the faux Ridzik. So far as they knew, he *was* Nikoli Ridzik. It didn't matter if Jacob or the others told them he was an imposter. They didn't know anything to hide.

It was a dead end.

Colonel Marik-Johns hadn't taken that well. He was getting off-balance looking for the Blakist connection. No one doubted it was there. No one didn't believe in the mission. But with the FedCom Civil War ending, there were too many open slots in the interstellar news. The AMC couldn't afford—Jaime Wolf couldn't afford—any bad publicity, not with the Star League conference on Tharkad looming. News took time to percolate around the Inner Sphere, even with hyperpulse generators, but a bad reputation lingered far out of proportion.

Being seen as the regiment that forced little old Bud Baranov to admit to a fabricated story about the Word of Blake wouldn't improve the AMC's reputation. Nor would being the force that kept the Free Worlds League from gaining a peaceful member-world that was begging to join.

Neither of those things would be the truth—but the news hadn't been about the truth for centuries.

Which meant Marik-Johns was leaning on his intelligence section to find the link they all knew existed, and produce the indisputable link to Terra that not even Jerome Blake himself could disprove.

No pressure.

He'd tried going to the Stealthy Tigers colonel's funeral to say something to Ezra Payne, but like everyone else, he hadn't realized it was a private event. He'd waited outside the gate, and then gone to Marko's. None of his messages to Payne had been returned, but Jacob didn't blame him. He wouldn't be very communicative if Jaime Wolf dropped dead. It would take time.

A woman walked up to the door of Estwicke's building. Jacob leaned up to look, but she was too tall, too blonde. He slouched back down. Another dead end.

The car rocked as the driver-side door slid open. Jacob lurched upright. His feet slammed down on the floorboards and he stifled a groan; his feet had fallen asleep. He bounced them, cringing at the acute pins and needles sensation as fresh blood flowed back to his toes, and glared at the woman who sat down.

"So this is a stakeout?" Nathalie Ortiz asked. She looked around the car. "It looks dirty." She sniffed. "And smelly."

"I've been here for ten hours," Jacob said. "You sit in one place for ten hours and see how ripe you get."

"I've been in my 'Mech's cockpit for a day straight before," she said. "I don't think I smelled this bad after that."

"It gets hot in a cockpit," Jacob said. "Probably kills all the bacteria. Or maybe your sense of smell." He wiped his hands on his shirt and frowned. She was probably right. His skin felt oily from sitting too long and eating crappy food.

"Maybe," she said. She looked past him at the entrance to the building. "Seen anything?"

"Lots of people who aren't Adele Estwicke," Jacob said. "What are you doing here?"

"I learned something interesting today," she said, "from the colonel?"

"Oh?"

"You think the Markojas are Blakist collaborators."

"Ah."

Ortiz looked at him like his trainers had when they were disappointed in him. "Tell me."

"I saw them talking to Adele Estwicke," he said. "Near Fort Decker. Both of them, at the same time."

"What does Ezra say?"

Jacob grimaced. "I haven't told him." He didn't want to have this conversation alone with her. The relationship between Ezra Payne and her wasn't secret, but they didn't advertise it, either. To his certain knowledge, outside of contact in the line of their duties, they'd only seen each other socially once after the colonel had rescinded Payne's liaison status, and that meeting had likely been the "we shouldn't meet anymore" meeting.

But that didn't mean he wanted to tell her alone that he was keeping sensitive information from her boyfriend. It was hard enough to look himself in the mirror. He considered Ezra Payne a friend.

"What? Why not?"

"Because he's not one of us."

"How can you say that?" She glared at him. "I've fought with him twice. Even without . . . even without anything else, I would trust him just for that."

"I'm not saying he's not good people," he said. "I'm saying he's an officer of a rival mercenary group, under contract to allies of our enemies, and possibly under the direct command—now that his colonel is dead—of people I'm fairly sure are in the direct employ of our enemies." He bounced his eyebrows. "I want to tell him, even. But I can't. Not until I can show him proof."

"What proof?"

Jacob looked back to the apartment entrance. "Damn little, so far," he told her. "I can't find the thread from this end. If I could get Estwicke's databases, I could find the trail that leads to Hall, and trace it that way." He shrugged. "But I can't find them or her."

"So you're wasting your time out here." It wasn't a question.

"I'm wasting my time on a long shot," he corrected her. "Everyone makes mistakes."

"Well, I think this one is one of yours." She held out her hand for the ignition fob. "Let's go. Where are your people holed up in the city?"

He handed her the fob and gave her the address. Moments later, she was accelerating into traffic.

"I told the colonel much the same thing on a different topic," she said. "We don't have time for this. The League will be here any day."

"Okay . . ."

"You can't wait for this Estwicke woman to appear. You have to flush her out."

"And we do that how?"

"Easy. We tell Ezra about the Markojas."

The chair squeaked when Jurowicz spun around. "He's gone."

"The Dragoon?" Estwicke asked. She sat at the small table in the kitchen, reading Kirsten Markoja's mail.

Jurowicz had finally cracked the Sixth of June's encryption, which had given her access to the few hidden files she'd found on the Tigers' servers. There weren't many. Jurowicz suspected, and Estwicke agreed, that Kirsten must keep a separate, offline database of files somewhere. They'd probably never get access to that.

"Yeah," Jurowicz said. "A woman got in the car with him and they drove off."

"Who was the woman?"

"Looked military," she said. "Probably AMC."

Estwicke turned in her chair so she could see Jurowicz. "Probably?"

Jurowicz shrugged. "I can keep looking for Sixth of June files, or I can track down one mystery woman."

Estwicke turned back to her reading. "Keep digging."

Over the last month, she and Jurowicz had changed safe houses twice. She'd only had contact with Markoja once, right after the Tigers' colonel had died. It had been a short message: *go to ground, but be ready.*

Ready for what? That was the question. Markoja had declined to share her plan, and as the days ticked by and the League failed to show up, Estwicke began to get impatient. She began searching through the files Jurowicz had uncovered, trying to divine the major's plan, but none of the data was coming together into a useful form. It hadn't helped that the AMC had stepped up its game; one of the two safe houses they'd abandoned had already been blown, and Jurowicz had almost been caught twice trying to crack the AMC data security.

The logic was simple, especially with the Tigers' colonel out of the way. Now in command of a regiment of BattleMechs, the Markojas had far greater options. Blake's Blood, they could just openly move against Baranov now if they wanted to. The AMC would stand aside, and Baranov's pathetic military couldn't hope to stand against the experienced mercenaries. It would ruin the Tigers' reputation, but Markoja would be able to find employment with the Word.

The Word was already paying for their contract, after all.

"Interesting," Jurowicz said.

"What is?"

"New traffic on the Tigers' net," the hacker said. "Someone knows about the Markojas. Someone inside the Tigers."

Estwicke turned away from her reader and stood up. She walked into the other room and leaned over Jurowicz's console, trying to make sense of the four screens of data the other woman was looking at. "What are you talking about? Who knows?"

"One of the Tigers, I think," Jurowicz said. She used her fingertip to trace a moving line of code before it blinked and vanished, then pointed at another one in another quadrant. "This is doing the same kind of searching I am, looking for access points to Kirsten Markoja's databases."

"You can tell that?" Estwicke asked.

"Sure. Once you know the environment, it's easy to see what the code is doing."

"And you can't tell who it is?"

"Not yet," Jurowicz said, cracking her knuckles. "But I can find out."

Estwicke straightened up. "Do it." She turned and went back to the kitchen and her reading. As she sat down, Jurowicz cleared her throat.

"Are we going to tell her, if we find out who this is?"

Estwicke looked down at the mass of data in front of her. She thought about the condescending way Markoja treated her, and the sneer on Baranov's face when he'd told her about the Free Worlds deal.

"That depends on who it is," she said.

MARKO'S DELI
HALL
THE CHAOS MARCH
21 AUGUST 3067

"You're insane," Charles Monet said.

"And what if I'm not?" Ezra asked.

The two of them were at Marko's. Nathalie and Jacob Brim had left a half-hour earlier. Ezra had called Monet and told him to meet him at the deli before the conversation was half-over. Then he'd spent the last thirty minutes going over the story in his head, distilling it down to the simplest possible explanation so he could explain it to Monet. Which he had. Which had then prompted Monet to question his sanity.

"You want me to believe that the CO and XO of our regiment are Word of Blake agents?"

"Maybe not agents. Maybe just on the payroll. Informants, maybe."

"So you don't know," Monet said.

"I thought you'd be on board with this, Charlie," Ezra said. He looked around the deli, suddenly conscious that they were sitting in the same place where Brim had caught the Markojas talking with the Word of Blake agent. Any of the people sitting around them eating could be agents of one kind or another.

But that's true of anywhere, he told himself. Paranoia wasn't going to help anyone.

"It's one thing to know the money for our contract came from the Word," Monet said. "It's a whole other thing to think they're directly running our regiment." He looked around, too. "Do you think the colonel knew?"

"Of course not."

"I didn't think so either," Monet said, "but at least he never found out."

Ezra didn't want to think about Rauschenbusch just then. It was still an open wound for him. It probably was for Monet, too, he realized, which could be why he felt a little off his game.

"What do we do?" Monet asked. "Denounce them?"

Ezra shook his head. "We can't."

"But—"

"It's the same thing as the money," Ezra said. "We don't have proof. We have the word of a spy from the AMC that he saw our commanders sitting in a booth with a known Word of Blake agent. I happen to trust that spy, but I can't go to the regiment and say 'this guy I know . . .'"

"Right . . ."

Ezra looked around again. He wasn't so much looking for anyone as just finding an excuse not to look at Monet. A woman at the counter was eating a sandwich and leaning over her young son. She whispered something to him, and he laughed, and she sat back up and went back to eating.

"So what happens now, then?" Monet asked. "We play a long game of 'they don't know that we know?'"

"More or less." Ezra rubbed his hands together. "I want you to start digging into the Markojas. Concentrate on Kirsten. If she's dirty, she'll be the brains behind it. Mason is certainly in on it, but we both know he's not doing the heavy lifting in the intelligence department."

"I can do that," Monet said.

"I'll talk to Halleck and Captain Hargood," Ezra said. "Don't tell anyone else."

"Of course not."

"And keep your ear to the ground," Ezra told him.

"What if I find proof?" Monet asked. "What will we do then?"

Ezra didn't have an answer for that. "The right thing," is what he told Monet, and sent him on his way, but he stayed in the booth for another hour, trying to figure out what that 'right thing' might be.

He could denounce them in front of the regiment. He could call on them to resign, to be imprisoned. He could turn them over to the AMC. All of those were possible things, but they ignored a great many things. A great many realities. For one thing, it wouldn't just be the Markojas.

Say Monet found the proof. Say Ezra could get the regiment together and present that proof. Who would enforce it? Him?

He was a captain. He didn't have authority over anyone in the regiment except Jaguar Company. Removing Kirsten and Mason Markoja would put a more senior officer in place. Ezra took it as a given that he'd have to arrest Wesley Eberhardt, too. He may not be dirty, but he was 100 percent a Markoja man, and making him colonel by default would shatter the regiment. It would have to go to the next most senior captain. Right now that was Captain Wa, from Panther Battalion, and Wa was not someone the regiment would follow. Best case, there'd be a mass exodus as some of the regiment left rather than stay under his command. Mercenary regiments were cults of personality: it took a charismatic leader to keep them together.

Worst case, there'd be actual fighting. The lore of the Succession Wars was filled with tales of mercenary units destroying themselves in internecine combat. When you were a soldier, and you solved your problems with a 'Mech, soon enough every problem looked like something that took a 'Mech to solve.

He could ask the Raiders to enforce it, but Raiders had no more authority than their ranks conferred. They were excellent soldiers, top-notch mercenaries. But they were few and scattered, and if the last few months were any indication, waning in even social authority. The death of the colonel had put the entire regiment into flux. Mason Markoja was too new to his command to be able to bring everyone together, even if he could.

What scared Ezra more than the knowledge that Kirsten and Mason Markoja might be bought and paid for by the Word of Blake was that he couldn't, for the life of him, come up with a scenario for removing them that didn't result in breaking the regiment. And he didn't want to do that—couldn't do that. Yuri Rauschenbusch had devoted his life to making the Stealthy Tigers one of the preeminent mercenary regiments in the Inner Sphere. His *life*.

Ezra would be damned if the first thing he did after Rauschenbusch was gone was take that regiment and break it like a piece of obsidian against granite.

"The emperor's press office has confirmed the news: Jump-Ships of the Free Worlds League Military have entered the Hall system at the nadir jump point. Pennon codes are for the Fourth Oriente Hussars, a storied regiment. No incoming messages have been received yet, but the emperor's staff believes this regiment is proof of the League's commitment to Hall.

"No comment has yet been received from the Allied Mercenary Command, but no one doubts they must soon pack up and leave Hall."

–From the *Harney Morning Edition*,
Harney HV Channel Six

CHAPTER TWENTY-FOUR

BRAVO BASE
HALL
THE CHAOS MARCH
4 OCTOBER 3067

By the time Ezra Payne reached the tactical operations center, someone had already turned the alarms off. He strode through the armored hatch and looked around until he found the cluster of officers around Mason Markoja. Setting his jaw, he walked over, trying not to stare at Kirsten Markoja with each step. She saw him coming, met his gaze, and looked away without reacting. Which pretty much exemplified the entire last month.

Monet hadn't found anything. Nothing.

Hargood and Halleck's reactions to the news that Kirsten might be in bed with the Word of Blake had been more or less exactly what he'd expected, but they were both pros. They knew he was right; they couldn't just accuse the Markojas without proof. Not right then.

Especially not right then.

Besides, even with more time, Ezra hadn't found a good way to remove them. If he even could.

A couple of the Raiders had taken Ezra's point about how few they were to heart. They'd started looking for more Raiders. They'd started the talks, taken the straw polls. An invitation had been floated. Ezra had made it personally; he was the most senior Raider. It was his duty, and even if his heart hadn't been fully in it, he'd always been one to do his duty.

The MechWarrior had declined.

Ezra had just stared at her. In a century, no Tigers MechWarrior had *ever* declined to become a Raider. Not once. There wasn't even an established protocol for a refusal. Ezra knew the acceptance forms, knew the words to say, and the promises to make. He didn't know what to do when the woman said no.

"It's not for me," she had said after Ezra had approached her in the 'Mech hangar, away from her lancemates. "I don't want anything to come between me and the regiment."

Ezra had thanked her, and walked away.

I don't want anything to come between me and the regiment.

He didn't even know how to process that.

In his entire professional life, no one had *ever* tried to put any distance between the regiment and the Raiders. Not once. It had been the opposite, in fact. You were part of the regiment because you were a Raider. No, more. You were the best of the regiment because you were a Raider. Like he'd told the Jaguars all those months ago: every Raider was a Stealthy Tiger, but not every Tiger was a Raider.

Afterward, Halleck had argued it was the Markojas, meddling. He tried to tell the rest of them that the twins hated the Raiders because they weren't a part of it. Hated them because they couldn't control them. Ezra hadn't weighed into that conversation. He was still trying to process too much.

"I don't want anything to come between me and the regiment."

The Raiders were about nothing if not professionalism, duty, and getting the job done. For thirty years, there had been no higher ideal in the regiment.

Walking up to the clutch of officers now, all whom he knew, but felt he didn't, Ezra realized those thirty years might be over.

"The League is here," Mason Markoja said. He didn't look up as Ezra arrived. Instead, Mason met the eyes of every other officer around him. Both his sister and Wesley Eberhardt were present, representing First and Second Battalions. He was there for Jaguar Company, the only independent company stood up so far. The rest of the company commanders were present, but only Heather Hargood looked up to see Ezra. And she looked nervous.

"What do we do?" Captain Wa asked. Wa was a squat man from New Samarkand who led one of the First Battalion companies. He'd never been considered as a Raider candidate, since he was a gambler. Not in the field, but personally; the regiment had lifted ahead of local bookies several times that Ezra knew of. He also knew Colonel Rauschenbusch had tolerated it because

Wa was a crackerjack MechWarrior. Ezra wondered why—or how long—Mason Markoja would.

"We're going to wait and see," Mason said. He looked at his sister. "Kirsten?"

"Our contract is with the planetary government of Hall," she said to everyone. "That is, with Emperor Baranov. He was the one who invited the Free Worlds League to take possession of Hall; we should all be on the same side here."

"And if we're not?" Heather Hargood asked.

"We are," Kirsten told her.

"Do we know who it is yet?" Heather Hargood asked. "Which regiment, I mean?"

"Fourth Oriente Hussars," Kirsten said.

Ezra had to think for a moment. There were more regiments in active service than most people could remember off the top of their heads; he saw several people looking down at their comms or full-size noteputers. The Fourth Oriente was a good regiment, but it had a bad attitude. Many of its officers were openly critical of the Free Worlds League government, and the Marik ruling family in particular.

The same Marik family that John Marik-Johns was distantly related to.

Ezra frowned. That could be trouble.

"I want two teams," Mason Markoja said. "Team one, led by Major Eberhardt: you're on planning integration with the League forces. They're on our side, though they'll probably say we're on theirs. We need to be ready to work with them, especially if it comes down to them and us against the AMC."

"You really think that's likely?" Captain Wa asked.

"I do," Mason told him. "Likely enough that the second team's job, under my sister's direction, is to start planning what the AMC might do." He looked across the faces of the officers, blinked across Ezra's, and kept going. "I want to start predicting what they might do, in case we have to get in front of them."

Both Eberhardt and Kirsten started indicating officers as the meeting broke up. Ezra hadn't said a word, and no one had spoken to him. Much as the staff meetings had been for the last month. He was a captain and a company commander; they couldn't exclude him. Everyone in the regiment knew Rauschenbusch had been grooming him for the next battalion commander's slot, but Rauschenbusch was dead.

Wesley Eberhardt had gotten it instead.

Someone touched Ezra's elbow. He turned. It was Sergeant Major Halleck.

"You needed here?" he asked, indicating the group of officers. Ezra looked around. No one was looking at him. "No." Halleck led him back out the room. He glared back through the hatch as it closed, then pulled Ezra aside, out of the flow of traffic in the corridor. "What's up?"

"Fourth Oriente is in-system," Ezra told him.

"AMC's going to love that," Halleck said, snorting. "Their CO has the wrong last name for that group."

"Yeah."

"What's the plan?"

"Planning," Ezra said. He sketched out Mason's two groups. Halleck frowned at him.

"Shouldn't you be in the AMC one?" the sergeant major asked. "You know them better than anyone else. If anyone can read Marik-Johns' mind, it'd be you."

"Think about who's in charge," Ezra said with a shrug. "What'd you need, Bob?"

"You got a message," Halleck said.

Ezra waited. "From?"

"The missus." He held out a local disposable comm.

Ezra took it with a puzzled frown. He put the earbud in, then touched the "play" control. There was moment's hiss as the recording started.

"Ezra," Nathalie Ortiz's voice said, *"you know the League is here. Jake says our time is up. It's now or never."*

The line clicked off. Ezra looked down at the comm, but that was the only message. He pulled the earbud out and handed it to Halleck.

"Listen," he said.

Halleck listened. Then he frowned, pulled the earbud out, and slid it back into the holder on the comm. "Short," was all he said.

"Yeah."

"What's it mean?"

Ezra looked up and down the corridor. "It means the gloves are about to come off."

**ROCKFALL MAZE
HALL
THE CHAOS MARCH
4 OCTOBER 3067**

Jacob Brim had just spent a dozen hours in a vibrating hovercraft, racing south from Harney to meet with the AMC leadership in Rockfall Maze. He hated blowers, and having his bones vibrated for so long had put him on edge, so when the colonel asked him a stupid question, he gave a stupid answer.

"Yes," he told Marik-Johns, "I've had the proof for months. I've just been waiting for the right time to give it to you." He regretted the words as soon as he said them. "Sorry."

The whole staff of the Dismal Disinherited was assembled, either in person or via videoconference, in the staff hall. The colonel sat at the head of the table, with majors and captains around him. At the other end stood Jacob Brim, feeling like the entire weight of the intelligence operation on Hall was resting on his shoulders. Probably because it was.

"The League is here," Marik-Johns said. "In a week, they'll be on the ground. So when I say we're out of time, you understand my urgency."

"I share it," Jacob said.

"We need that evidence."

"Yes, we do," Jacob said.

"What do you need to locate it?"

Jacob shrugged. His temper was still there, and though he had a better hold of it, he could still feel in burbling in his core like an angry volcano. "I need them to make a mistake," he told the colonel.

"A mistake," Major Fletcher said.

"That's right," Jacob told the head of the Disinherited intelligence shop. Fletcher may not be a complete moron, but his vaunted shop had been less than worthless, and Jacob didn't care what he thought.

"How do we force them to make a mistake?" Fletcher asked.

"I've been pressing every way I know how," Jacob said tiredly.

"We know about Estwicke," Colonel Marik-Johns said. "What if we go public with that?"

"With what?" Jacob asked. "We tell the world that the local Word of Blake attaché is a Word of Blake *agent provocateur*? Of course she is. That's her expected role. She doesn't even deny it in anything more than a pro forma manner."

"It will get people looking at the Word," Marik-Johns insisted.

"To what end?" Jacob wanted to throw up his hands. "We're a single jump from the Word of Blake Protectorate. On a Chaos March world that's been killing itself for a decade, that has just asked for and received annexation into the Free Worlds League." He looked across the sea of faces, local and video, trying to find someone whose face showed enough understanding that he could get *them* to explain it. He certainly wasn't finding the right words.

All the faces were stony.

"We can't just say 'It's the Word.' Maybe it is. We all think it is. I'm pretty damn sure it is, but the Free Worlds League thing makes it even muddier."

"We have to do *something*," Marik-Johns said. "We were sent here to make sure that the people of Hall get a free chance to decide their own destiny. To ensure they weren't being manipulated in the background by the Word of Blake." He looked around at his officers. "That's why there's an Allied Mercenary Command in the first place."

"What do we do when the Fourth lands?" an armor officer asked. Jacob hadn't learned his name.

"We keep on," Major Fletcher said, before the colonel could speak. "Our contract is clear. They don't have any reason to interfere with us."

"Except that they hate the Mariks," Captain Ortiz put in. She was on a video screen; her company was still north, near Holden, where they'd first captured the forces pretending to be Nikoli Ridzik's. "And, all due respect, colonel—"

"I know my own name," Marik-Johns said. He looked around the room, then back at Jacob. "If it comes to a fight . . ." He shook his head. "This is the endgame, Sergeant Brim," he said. "Is there anything—*anything*—I can give you that might move the needle?"

"Give me an infantry company," he said. "A blower company, and let me call Captain Ortiz if I need her."

"Done."

Jacob blinked. He'd just listed those things because he knew an answer was required, and whether or not the colonel haggled would tell him just how desperate Marik-Johns was getting. The fact that he hadn't even hesitated told Jacob enough.

The colonel was serious.

"We're done here," Marik-Johns said. "Brim, Ortiz, you stay. Everyone else, give us the room." A couple of the majors looked like they might argue, but Marik-Johns ignored them until the room was empty.

"What if we publish the Markoja link?" he asked once the door was closed.

"Sir," Jacob said, glancing at Ortiz's image, "we can't say for sure our comms aren't tapped—"

"Don't care. What about it?"

Ortiz shrugged. "Does it change anything?"

"It's another link in the chain," the colonel said. "We have Estwicke, the public agent. We can put her with the Markojas, and now with them in command of the Stealthy Tigers we can say the Word has both influence with Baranov and controls his largest military force."

"It sounds convincing," Ortiz said.

"I hear a but coming," Marik-Johns said.

"But," Jacob said, "we don't have any evidence."

"You *saw* them, Brim!"

"Yes, I did," Jacob said. "I, a serving noncommissioned officer of a mercenary unit known to be all-but-at-war with the Word of Blake, saw two other mercenaries meet with a woman I know to be a Blakist agent. At a deli. With sandwiches." He resisted the urge to wave his hands in the air. "That's about as far away from 'disinterested witness' as it's possible to get."

"They had to meet somewhere," Marik-Johns insisted.

"That was not, in fact, my point, sir.

"I didn't think so." He clasped his hands together and looked down at them for a second. His knuckles were white. "I think it's enough. I think a reasonable person—"

"Sir, all due respect, stop right there," Jacob said. "We're not dealing with reasonable people. We're dealing with *people* people. People who watch HV news, who decide on international issues across the Inner Sphere based on a twenty-second news snippet or a crawler on their flatscreen. Reasonable people might well make the leap of belief you wish, but reasonable people don't make decisions."

He frowned. "We could announce everything we know, right now. I could do the press announcement from here. But it wouldn't matter, because we don't have anything *convincing*. People who already think Baranov is in bed with the Word of Blake will crow and shout 'finally, the link is revealed,' while people who call us Blakist alarmists will wave the data away with an 'anyone could have manufactured that.'"

"Then it's hopeless," Marik-Johns said.

"I'm not giving up, sir," Jacob said. "They might be in-system, but they're not on the ground yet. We have a few days, at least."

"What good will days do when we've squandered *months* on this?"

"The Fourth Oriente's arrival is a catalyzer, sir," Captain Ortiz said from the screen. "Not just for us. The Word of Blake element here will be moving, too. If giving the planet to the Blakists isn't the Leaguers' plan, the Word will be just as desperate as we are."

Marik-Johns looked up at that, as if someone had poked him. "We've been assuming Baranov called the League on his own," he said. "That the Word was here all along, but that Baranov snaked them, too. What if that's not it? What if bringing in the League was *his* plan all along?"

Jacob frowned. "Sir, we examined and discarded that plan already. They could have put that into effect any time in the last few years."

"McNally was here," Marik-Johns said. Jacob tried to ignore the quiet desperation in his voice.

"The League could have crushed McNally like a grape," Jacob said. "He wouldn't have stopped them."

"Then it's us," the colonel said. He pressed his hand back against his own chest. "*We* weren't here. They were waiting for us."

"Sir—" Captain Ortiz started, but Marik-Johns held up a hand. There was mania in his face, but Jacob let him talk.

"Not us, specifically. Not the Hellraisers. But someone. Someone from the AMC. Someone they could blame for pushing Hall into the League. It hurts us—the whole AMC—because we failed. And after the news from Keid, we don't need any more bad press."

"With all due respect, sir," Jacob said. "That's reaching."

"But possible. Right?"

"Barely."

"Even if it wasn't their primary plan, Hall entering the Free Worlds League helps the Word of Blake. It gets them feet on the ground, running the HPG. And in a few years, who knows? If their Protectorate keeps growing, the people of Hall may just vote to leave the League and join the Protectorate."

"Thomas Marik will never let them do that," Jacob said. If there was one constant among Successor lords, it was that they never—ever—relinquished a world gained unless you pried it out of their hands with a few 'Mech battalions.

"He's former Word of Blake himself," Marik-Johns said. He stood. "There could be something here." He looked at Jacob. "You keep doing what you're doing. I need Estwicke in the bag, with all her data." Then he looked at Ortiz.

"Be ready for a call, Captain," he said. "If the Fourth Oriente wants a fight, then a fight they'll get."

"The mercenary regiments of the Northwind Highlanders have activated the escape clauses of their contracts and begun the journey back to Northwind from garrison stations in the Draconis Combine and Chaos March. Few of the Highlander officers have deigned to speak with INN, but we were able to get this exclusive data from one source: the Highlanders are returning home to vote on new Clan elders.

"This comes on the heels of the accidental death of yet another elder of the Highlanders in recent months. Though no foul play is suspected, many on Northwind are looking askance at the Highlanders. Though the escape clauses built into Highlander contracts is fairly standard, and their withdrawal is completely legal, many wonder how this will affect the Highlanders' future hiring.

"No doubt the situation on Northwind requires the attention it is receiving; but the threats the Highlanders were hired to face don't go away just because their BattleMechs withdraw."

–From the *Daily INN Download,*
ComStar Hall Hyperpulse Station Harney

CHAPTER TWENTY-FIVE

BRAVO BASE
HALL
THE CHAOS MARCH
10 OCTOBER 3067

"The emperor," Colonel Richardson said smugly, "has been in contact with the incoming League commander, Colonel Fleur Lewis. She feels, as we do, that we can't trust in the mercenaries meekly drawing away."

Even through the video, Ezra could see the shit-eating grin on Richardson's face.

He couldn't see the rest of the table, though.

Because he wasn't there.

Richardson had arrived an hour before, and declared he had new orders for the Stealthy Tigers. Mason and Kirsten Markoja had called for Major Eberhardt and closeted themselves with the liaison officer. None of the company commanders had been invited. It wasn't technically improper, but Ezra had always been a part of such meetings when Colonel Rauschenbusch had still been alive.

But this was now.

Once he realized the meeting was taking place and that he wouldn't be there, Ezra had called Charles Monet to his office. A few minutes work with his desk console had been enough to let them listen in, even watch the meeting through the videoconference software. Monet swore he was the only one who'd be able to tell the console was active from within the conference room, and Ezra believed him. He didn't have a choice.

"That's good," Mason told Richardson. "Better to get in front of it, rather than wait to see what happens once the Fourth lands."

Monet, standing behind Ezra's chair and watching with him, snorted. Ezra didn't react.

"We believe the mercenaries will fight," Richardson said. "They can't do anything else."

"They haven't fought us," Kirsten said, "and we've been here for most of a year with them."

"You're not taking the world away from them," Richardson said. "Thus far the AMC has declined to heed the emperor's entreaties that they should leave Hall. Our analysts believe that once the League is on the ground, the AMC will have to decide." He paused. "Our analysts believe Colonel Marik-Johns will choose to fight."

"He'll have to, if we go after them," Monet said.

Ezra considered. He was the only person in the office—including the people he was watching on the screen—that had spent any real time around John Marik-Johns. It was entirely possible that he would react the way the emperor's staff believed he would. He was under enormous pressure, whether he admitted that or not. He didn't want to go back to Outreach a failure. Who would?

But failing to uncover the Word of Blake was a different beast than attacking a regiment of the Free Worlds League. The Allied Mercenary Command might be backed by the Northwind Highlanders and Wolf's Dragoons, two of the most powerful mercenary organizations in the Inner Sphere, but the Free Worlds League could swat both of them like flies, if it came down to it.

"So he fights," Mason said. "What's the plan?"

"We crush him," Richardson said. "Depending on the trigger, we'll sally the Republican, your Tigers, and the Fourth Oriente at the greatest AMC concentrations together in one unstoppable wave. The emperor has indicated that he will take the field personally to insure the destruction of the mercenaries."

"Wow," Ezra said. Baranov hadn't climbed into his *Zeus* in years, not even for the last battle, where the Tigers had killed Count McNally.

"That's quite an escalation," Kirsten said, but not in the tone of an objection. It was more like admiration.

"The people of Hall asked to join the Free Worlds League," Richardson said. He was obviously going for quiet dignity, but he didn't have that much gravitas. All he was accomplishing was preening pomposity. "The League has seen fit to send a regiment here to insure that claim. The emperor can do no less."

Kirsten Markoja waited in her brother's office—the colonel's office—and tried not to rub her hand. The cybernetics tingled. She'd known they would—they had after every use on Jardine, when she'd had them implanted and learned to use them—but the tingling had never lasted this long before.

Mason was escorting Colonel Richardson off the base. She'd ensured Eberhardt was out of the way. One of Richardson's orders had been for the Tigers to take over garrison of the Lexicon PowerCorp facility near Fort Lexington; she'd sent Eberhardt and his company out to take over that position. It got the supposed battalion commander out of the way, and put Mason in line to take direct command of Panther Battalion if it became necessary.

Kirsten smiled. It would be necessary. Very soon.

Her plans had been working perfectly, no matter how much that whiny bitch Estwicke complained. The colonel's death had gone smoothly. No one suspected a thing. Mason's elevation, her own rise to XO . . . it was all perfect.

Even Payne, the insufferable jackass, had taken to moping around the base as if he still mattered. He and his little band of Raiders. She already knew how she was going to deal with them. The next contract, she'd make sure Mason disbanded the little secret club. There wouldn't be Raiders this time next year.

Assuming any of them survived the next week.

The door slid open and Mason stepped inside. He unsealed his battledress blouse as soon as the door closed and pulled it off. It flopped onto the couch behind Kirsten as he stepped around the desk and sat down.

"It's working," he said.

"Of course it's working," she told him. "Why wouldn't it?"

"Estwicke—"

"Estwicke worries too much," Kirsten said. She sat down on the couch next to his blouse, fingers clasped. She rubbed her hands back and forth against each other. Her foot tapped. Her whole body tingled now, she was so excited.

"You think it'll be a fight?"

"I have no doubt," she said. "Lewis—" The Oriente colonel. "—hates the Marik family. I don't know if the Order colluded to have that regiment sent, or if it's Blake's own luck, but there's no way she'll avoid fighting an AMC regiment commanded by someone with Marik in his name."

"And when that happens . . ."

"Then we strike," she said. "We make sure, no matter what happens, that Baranov goes down in the fighting. We make sure he dies, and that the fight goes on long enough that the Hussars get mauled. Even if we lose, the AMC loses. And Baranov will be dead."

"I don't understand."

"That fat bastard is the glue holding all this together," Kirsten told her brother. "If he dies, the idea of League annexation dies with him. The nobles will go back to feuding before Baranov's 'Mech stops smoking. And if the Hussars are hurt badly enough, the League will recall them and paint Hall as a bad investment."

"The Disinherited will get hurt between us and the Hussars," Mason said. He wasn't as stupid as most people made him out to be, but he was a slow and methodical thinker. Leaps Kirsten made intuitively, he had to muddle through. He always made the connection, eventually, but sometimes . . .

"No Baranov," he said. He looked up at her, smiling. "No AMC. No League. Hall will be all alone, especially now that the Com Guards have pulled out of the HPGs. They'll be all alone, fighting each other . . ."

"The perfect atmosphere for someone—perhaps the colonel of a mercenary regiment, whose contract is about to end, but who'd given the world's previous leader good service?—to suggest the planet look to Terra for guidance." Kirsten's grin was a voracious shark's smile.

"And when that happens, *we'll* have done it, not that twat Estwicke." Mason smiled back at her.

We will have done it, she told herself. The news of that happening would travel all the way out to Circinus, if necessary. The Master himself would know the value of her service. She looked down at her hand and made a fist, ignoring the constant pins-and-needles sensation.

He would know he'd made the right choice, all those years ago.

"How do we do it?" Mason asked.

"We let the fighting start," she said. "With the Disinherited spread to hell and gone across Farnorth, it won't be difficult. We'll put the Panthers out to support the Republicans. The League will side with them, you can count on it. Politics will mandate it, even if the military situation doesn't."

"Okay," Mason said. She saw his mind working.

"At some point, the Disinherited will feint around the emperor's flank," she said. "When that happens, I'll lead the Leopards—"

"How do you know they'll do that?" Mason interrupted.

"Because if I have to, I'll drag them by the nose," Kirsten told him. "When they go, that will draw off the League regiment. I'll lead the Leopards to pursue. You'll keep the Panthers on the other flank, in case there's another feint."

"Will there be?"

"There could be," she said, "but that's not the point. The point is the Republicans will be weakened. I've already made sure the news that the emperor's *Zeus* is being readied has been leaked to McNally's old network. That will draw out Elly Burton."

"Her."

"Her," Kirsten said, nodding. "She'll find him on the field. Even if her little company isn't enough, Marik-Johns will send enough force with her to do the job. She'll kill the emperor. We, alas, are too far away, on the flanks of the battle, and cannot return in time. A terrible tragedy for Hall." She smiled.

"What next?"

"Next," she told her brother the colonel, "we pound the AMC into the ground."

Now Mason's smile mirrored her own.

HARNEY
HALL
THE CHAOS MARCH
10 OCTOBER 3067

"Sergeant?" Gallifrey called.

Jacob looked up from the map he was studying. He'd been noting distances between Estwicke's known apartment and the two discarded safe houses they'd already uncovered, and comparing those distances to the HPG facility and the government building downtown. It was probably a fool's errand—thus far, Estwicke had shown better tradecraft than that—but it was all he could do.

The Wolfnet team had relocated *en masse* to a safe house Jacob had set up in Harney. All the main Disinherited field bases were too far from the city, and with the fighting and bombings, rent was cheap here.

"What do you have?" he asked, standing up.

"Maybe something," the analyst said. He waited until Jacob came to stand next to him, then pointed at the screen of his console. "I just copied a data packet from Bravo Base, headed south."

"What's in it?"

"Don't know yet," Gallifrey said, "but it went through two of the channels we've already IDed as Blakist."

Jacob frowned. "Which channels? And in which system?"

"One in Bravo Base and one in South Harney," Gallifrey said. South Harney was a suburb of Harney. He read off the data packet IDs, but they meant nothing to Jacob.

"Markoja and Estwicke," Jacob breathed. "They're talking. And we're seeing it." He spun. "Carlsson!"

"Yeah, Jake," his XO said, lurching up from where he'd been sleeping on the sofa in the corner.

"Gallifrey is going to send you a message we intercepted. I need to know the contents."

"Can do," Carlsson said. He sat back down and reached for the noteputer on the floor by his boots. Across the room, one of the bedroom doors opened, and Dooley looked out. The forensic accountant had clearly been sleeping; his hair was mussed, and his glasses were crooked on his face. Jacob shook his head—he didn't need him yet.

"Show me South Harney," Jacob said to Gallifrey. The analyst already had a map screen up, with a series of pulsing locations. "What are those?"

"Locations the data passed through."

"All of them?"

"Yes."

"What are they?"

Gallifrey overlaid a map schematic. Names and descriptions appeared. "These two are self-storage facilities," he said, "this one is a data service provider hub, and this one—" he tapped the screen, "—is an apartment building."

Jacob swallowed. "Can you get in?"

"I'm already in," Gallifrey said with an air of pardonable pride. "I'm sucking everything electronic dry as we speak."

Jacob slapped Gallifrey on the shoulder. "Dooley!" he yelled. A moment later the sleepy, tousled head appeared again. "Get in here—Gallifrey has something for you."

"Jake," Carlsson called, "I don't have the details yet, but I have the header. It's going to the McNally network. I recognize this name—it's one of the ones Burton's people turned over to us."

"Why would she be talking to them?" Jacob asked.

"Give me time, and I'll find out."

Jacob nodded, then looked at the floor. He needed to think. It was possible they were getting the evidence they needed, literally at the eleventh hour. He needed time. Time to get Dooley moving on uncovering exactly what they had, for Gallifrey and the others to start putting the pieces together. Time for Carlsson to figure out what Markoja was saying to McNally's people.

Time. Time time time.

The door to the apartment slid open. Jacob looked up, surprised, as Captain Sand of the Disinherited stalked inside. She stopped at the edge of the room and put her hands on her hips. "Time's up."

"What?" Jacob blurted. "I haven't even told you what we have." He was vaguely conscious of the number of times he'd said "what" in the last few minutes.

"Doesn't matter," Sand said. Jacob saw the tension in her face, heard it in her voice. "The Hussars are down, and shots have been fired." She looked around the room. "Pack it up. The colonel wants us back in Rockfall Maze, getting ready to support the field battalions."

"No," Jacob said. "We can't leave."

"Brim—"

"No, Captain, listen." He sketched out what Gallifrey had found. "This is *exactly* what we've been looking for."

"You think," Sand said. "You said yourself you don't know yet. It could be someone's laundry list."

"Yes, it could," he said. "If someone were encoding their laundry in a known Word of Blake cipher, transmitting it on known Word of Blake pathways, and routing it to the other side of the desert." He looked at Carlsson, but his XO just shook his head. He was still working.

"Okay," Jacob said, mind racing. "Let's call in the infantry and go hit these places."

Sand stared at him. "You want to take armed soldiers into

South Harney. On a mission."

"You said shots were already fired—what harm can it do?"

"It can get us all killed," Sand ground out. "The colonel—"

"—is busy." Jacob spread his hands, pleading. "This is what he sent us up here for: proof. If he trashes the Hussars and Baranov, this will be the evidence that makes it the right decision. And if he loses . . ."

"The colonel doesn't lose," Sand said stubbornly

"If he loses, then this will be the salve for the AMC's wounded pride." He stared at Sand, trying to make her understand.

If she was right, and the Hussars and the AMC were already shooting, then she was probably right: it was too late. Given the attitude of the Hussars and the desperation Marik-Johns had for uncovering the Blakist operation on Hall, there was little to no chance either side would back down now.

But if he could get the evidence out, there was a chance he could serve the larger mission: stopping the Word of Blake from gobbling up more worlds in the Chaos March. It might not save Hall, but it could save the next world.

"How long would it take?" Sand asked, and Jacob knew he'd won.

"I'll tell you on the way," he said. "How soon can you get the infantry the colonel sent with us up here?"

"An hour or two," she said. Reaching into a pocket on her combat suit, she pulled out a small black comm and turned away to speak into it. That gave Jacob an idea.

"Carlsson," he said, "give that packet to Gallifrey to work on. Get our kits."

"Right," his XO said. "We're going?"

"Just you and me. Everyone else stays here and keeps working."

"Got it."

Jacob pulled out his own comm and dialed a combination. "Ortiz."

"We need to get in touch with Ezra Payne," Jacob said.

"Jake, it's not a good time," Captain Ortiz said. From the sound Jacob could tell she was rebroadcasting to her comm from inside her 'Mech's cockpit. "We've got shooting in the Austin Badlands, and the colonel has called the alert. The whole regiment is gathering."

"I can tell them where to go," Jacob said. "But we need to talk to Ezra."

"What? Why?"

"I've got the location of several Word hard targets. We can take them down. But we need Ezra to run interference in his regiment."

"Jake," Ortiz said flatly, "you know there's no way in hell he'll move with us against his regiment."

"He will," he told her.

"I—" she stopped. "I don't have time. What's the message?"

"I'll send you the packet once I've got it decrypted," Jacob said. "In the meantime, I have to get my kit on. We're moving on the safe houses now."

"Where?"

"South Harney," Jacob said. "Tell everyone. The Word of Blake is in South Harney."

"The peace on Hall was broken this morning when elements of the Allied Mercenary Command's Third Dismal Disinherited failed to accede to the lawful orders of the Free Worlds League to withdraw from Hall. In the scrub outside the Austin Badlands, the Dismal Disinherited had established a field base to support one of their companies. The newly arrived Fourth Oriente Hussars sent a lance to check that the AMC force had withdrawn, and was instead fired upon."

"*We have no choice but to conclude that the AMC intends to contest Hall's peaceful entry into the Free Worlds League,*" said Colonel Fleur Lewis, commander of the Hussars. "*We will react accordingly to protect the rights of every League citizen on Hall.*"

"The emperor's office confirms that the Fourth Republican and the Stealthy Tigers are mobilizing to enforce Colonel Lewis' orders. According to the emperor's office, '*no threat to the people of Hall or the security of our world will be tolerated.*'"

—From the *Harney Morning Edition,*
Hall HV Channel Six

CHAPTER TWENTY-SIX

HARNEY
HALL
THE CHAOS MARCH
11 OCTOBER 3067

Estwicke looked up in surprise when Jurowicz burst into her bedroom. She snatched the pistol on the nightstand, but recognized her supposed assailant before she had the gun half-raised off the polished hardwood. Glaring, she let herself flop back down on the pillows.

"Get up," Jurowicz said. The muscular woman went to Estwicke's closet and keyed the door open. The small light over the hung clothes came on automatically. She grabbed the first thing she saw and tossed it onto the bed.

"What's going on?"

"There's a hit team coming here. We have maybe twenty minutes."

Estwicke sat bolt upright. *"What?"*

"Markoja screwed us."

Estwicke rolled out of bed and scrambled for the closet. She shouldered Jurowicz out of the way and spoke while she dressed. "How?"

"She leaked some information about Baranov," Jurowicz said. "But she used channels and codes the AMC had already cracked. They've got the connection between us and the Tigers, if they can get here in time." She cursed, low and guttural in a language Estwicke didn't speak. "If they can get us, I mean."

"But the data—"

"Is wiped. But I was too late."

"Too *late?*"

"They got in last night, past me. They have the backup. And the addresses to the warehouses and the holding points." For a moment, she looked guilty. "We're burned, Adele. The League is here, the AMC knows about us, and if they can get their hands on us to tie it all together, they'll drag the whole thing into the light."

Estwicke slid the pressure seal of her blouse closed and looked around the room. Her pistol was already in her pocket; there was nothing else she needed in the entire apartment, and neither of them had brought anything in except the specialized equipment built into the console. And Jurowicz was already seeing to that.

It was time to go.

The future of Hall was in Kirsten Markoja's hands now.

Estwicke inhaled sharply. She felt like a weight had been lifted. She had failed—finally, and for certain. Even if Markoja somehow pulled it out, the success would be hers, not Estwicke's. It would be success for the Sixth of June, not the True Believers. Estwicke would have to go back to Terra—to Blane—and report her failure, much as she had been fearing for months.

But it was no longer an uncertainty.

There was no longer any chance of success for her.

And that was liberating. She could finally stop worrying about it.

"Let's go," she said. "We want to get in front of the 'Mechs."

"It's not 'Mechs."

Estwicke paused at the door and looked back. "What do you mean?"

"The 'Mechs are busy with the Oriente Hussars," Jurowicz said. "We've got infantry and hovertanks coming."

Estwicke pushed off the doorway. "Then we really need to hurry."

From outside came the rumbling thunder of weapons fire. She didn't look back to see if Jurowicz was following.

"Damn it!" Jacob shouted.

He sat in the gunner's station of the wheeled APC he and Carlsson had boarded. The small screen wasn't good, but it was enough to show a low-slung Myrmidon medium tank in the colors of the Fourth Republican blocking the intersection. The PPC in the Republican tank's turret spun to the left. The shot was a sizzling wash of static on Jacob's screen, but the APC wasn't the target.

A shocking *boom* and the rattle of metal-on-metal from the roof overhead told him the Myrmidon hadn't missed its shot. He jerked the gunnery controls to the right, aiming the paired machine guns at the tank, and held down the triggers. The big tribarrel weapons spun up and spit out heavy 12.7 millimeter rounds. Ricochets sparked and *whizzed* away from the Myrmidon's armor.

"Not enough," he muttered, but he didn't stop firing.

He'd hoped they could sneak into the city, but with the fighting down south that hope had been dashed almost immediately. They'd come in under cover of darkness, but the Republicans were alert and had patrols out. Captain Sand had tried to decoy around them, but the Reps were on strict positional defense. They weren't getting drawn off, which meant the captain had had to switch to a different tactic.

Frontal assault.

The two platoons of hovertanks she'd brought with her smashed into one of the Republican positions, annihilated the pair of Manticore tanks stationed there, and drove deeper into the heart of Harney. It was a masterful display of speed and firepower, and if Sand and her tankers made it back out of the city, Jacob would buy them all the drinks they could handle.

While that went on, though, he took command of a platoon of APCs and a Hetzer wheeled assault gun the infantry had captured and moved toward the safe house. Gallifrey had called in that he'd been detected, but that was thirty minutes ago. Jacob chewed on his lip and fretted, desperately hoping they could get there before Estwicke cleared out.

Taking a captured Blakist agent back to Outreach would almost redeem the hellish fighting he knew was going on behind him.

With Jacob's news in hand, Marik-Johns had assembled his forces and sprinted north. 'Mech companies had assembled into battalions and driven remorselessly through the rocky hallways of the Helmand. The few outriders the Fourth Oriente and the Republicans had thrown out had been crushed or driven off.

In not more than a few hours, there'd be what one of Jacob's trainers had always called a "motherin' great battle" going on more or less where he was sitting.

The right-side machine gun jammed and stopped. Jacob snapped his attention back to the present and let up on the triggers. He toggled the jam-clearance gear, pushing the rotating barrels forward and backward, but the jam indicator stayed on.

"He's coming around," the APC driver called.

"We're almost there," Carlsson yelled. "It's only a few blocks—let's hoof it!"

Jacob snarled and reached for his belt release. "Let's go!"

The rear door of the APC collapsed down into a ramp with a *clang*. Disinherited infantrymen clambered out, Carlsson behind them. Jacob lurched out of his seat and clapped the driver on the shoulder.

"Come on," he shouted. "That PPC will go through this thing the long way!"

The driver was already half-out of his bucket seat. "Out of the way, trooper!"

Jacob grinned, spun, and dashed backward.

"Look out!" someone cried just as his boot touched pavement. He cursed and threw himself to the side, up on the sidewalk. Hard concrete skinned his elbows and shins through his fatigues, but he ignored it. If the Myrmidon was about to light the APC up, he didn't want to see it. He curled into a ball.

The growl of a big diesel engine made him look up. The captured Republican Hetzer rumbled past. It's blunt prow crunched into the wreckage of the APC that had absorbed the Myrmidon's first bolt. Forty tons of armored car pushed those few paltry tons of wreckage aside with contemptuous ease. The thick composite pseudo-rubber tires groaned disgustingly as they gripped the pavement.

"Odin's frozen balls," Jacob whispered. Still on his side, he looked from the Hetzer to the Myrmidon. Then back. Then he tried to curl into an even smaller ball.

The Myrmidon fired first, the blue-white of the PPC stinging Jacob's eyes despite being scrunched closed tight. He saw the veins of his eyelids as afterimages, and twisted to look despite himself. The sound of the shot was physical, a kick to his whole side, as if someone had hit him with a mattress. The *whip-crack* of air displacement was thunderous. His ears rang.

It was nothing next to what came next.

The Hetzer absorbed the blast on its thick glacis. Armor exploded away, but the thickest part held. Purple-white static traceries spidered across the front of the tank, and Jacob swore he heard a sickening *squelch* as the tires lost their grip on the road for a few decimeters. The tank's scratch crew cranked the steering wheels around and lined up on the Myrmidon. Then the giant Crusher 150mm autocannon cut loose.

The Crusher was a reliable, high-rate gun, and the crew held the trigger down. Where the PPC had been one hellacious smack, each report of the Crusher was punishing. The cannon *boom-boom-boomed* through its cassette round. Windows across the street cracked and collapsed from the pounding. Jacob yelped and flinched as heavy glass fell across him.

The autocannon fire ate through the Myrmidon's side armor. The tank's crew had halted it across the intersection and cranked the turret around, and the Myrmidon's side protection was thinner. The explosive shells pocked that armor first, then smashed it open. The final few rounds detonated inside the tank's body. A burp of fire lifted the Myrmidon's multi-ton turret off its ring and settled it off-kilter. Smoke billowed from all around it.

Jacob heard savage cheering from the infantrymen around him. He joined in.

Carlsson appeared and lifted Jacob to his feet. He had his rifle presented and pointed toward the wreck of the Myrmidon, but Jacob knew no one would be escaping from that pyre.

The Hetzer grumbled forward. Its exhaust, hot and black and acrid, washed across the two Dragoons.

"We're close," Carlsson said.

"I know." Jacob shook himself. He knew he'd have some bruises from the glass, but nothing felt broken. His ears were ringing, and he felt his elbows bleeding, but he ignored that. His Striker was still strapped to his chest by its sling. He gripped it and pushed it out to present, then let the sling take it back, testing. "Let's go."

Estwicke stopped at a corner two blocks down from the safe house. Past the next door, a wrecked Republican tank belched black smoke into the air, but when the wind gusted she saw men and women in tactical gear starting down the street toward them. She didn't look away—she was just one of dozens of bystanders doing the same thing, watching the tank burn.

"We should go," Jurowicz murmured, just loud enough to hear.

"Wait."

The infantry stopped in front of her building and began stacking to do the door. She watched long enough to see them go in, then turned away. She started walking, trusting Jurowicz to follow. There'd be a train in the station three blocks ahead in ten minutes. That would get them to the spaceport.

Numbered accounts would do the rest.

BRAVO BASE
HALL
THE CHAOS MARCH
11 OCTOBER 3067

Ezra sat in his *Crusader*, the other eleven 'Mechs of Jaguar Company around him, watching the backs of the Panther Battalion BattleMechs recede as they headed south to link up with the main body of the Fourth Republican. None of the Jaguar 'Mechs were going. Mason Markoja had claimed that right for his battalion, saying they had to get their vengeance for the attack on Major Eberhardt's lance.

Eberhardt's garrison post at the Lexicon power facility had been struck without warning before dawn. Eberhardt had called in the attack and then gone off the air—and never come back up. That never boded well, and the Disinherited had been jamming most channels wherever they advanced. Civilian comm channels were still open, but all the bands reserved for military use were full of hash.

"We should be going with them," Hicks growled.

Ezra didn't disagree.

"We're the reserve," he said instead. "Somebody has to be."

His comm chirped. He looked at the ID code when it flashed on his HUD, and frowned. He worked his jaw, both wanting and not wanting to answer it. From a certain point of view, answering it would be treason against the Stealthy Tigers. It was undoubtedly treason against their employers. But he could say that about a lot of things he'd been doing lately.

He hit the connect button on his control console. "Nathalie."

"Ezra."

"Not a good time," he said. He wanted to say more, to say something different. He wanted to ask her to leave all this behind and leave with him. He wanted to ask if they could just sit the fighting out in a hotel in Rockfall Maze. He wanted to ask if Elly

Burton had been hit by a bus. He wanted ask her anything except what he knew he had to ask, because he was still an officer of the Stealthy Tigers, no matter what that meant lately.

"For me, either," she replied.

There was silence for a moment.

"Are my people alive?" he asked.

"What people?"

"Your lot hit one of our lances at the Lexicon plant a few hours ago. We haven't been in contact with them since." He looked at the still-moving forms of the Panther Batt 'Mechs. Any one of them could be shooting at Nathalie's *Dervish* before the end of the day.

"That wasn't me," she said quietly.

"I didn't say it was," Ezra said. "Are they alive?"

"I'll find out."

"Thank you."

Another silence. Ezra didn't break it this time. He just watched the 'Mechs walk away. Clouds moved across the sky. The *Crusader* trembled with the restrained power of its fusion engine. Then there was a sound. A cleared throat.

"Jake Brim told me to call you," she said. Now there was steel in her voice.

"Okay."

"He said to tell you he has proof, or shortly will."

Ezra started. "What proof? What's he talking about?"

"I—" she stopped. "I can't tell you that, not today. He said he'd leave it somewhere your man Monet could find it. But it links the woman to the club. That's as clear as I can be."

Ezra's mouth went dry. The woman was Kirsten Markoja. The club was the Word of Blake. If Brim had proof . . . Ezra had to pull his hands back from the controls. His fingers twitched to put the *Crusader* into motion right then and charge back into the base. He made a fist and relaxed it, over and over again.

"Nathalie—"

"Be careful today, Ezra," she said. "This isn't Caph."

The line clicked closed. A red icon appeared on his HUD as a visual cue. He stared at it until it vanished. Then he stared at the spot where it had been, and felt something suspiciously like loss inside when he realized what he was doing.

His fingers were shaking. He was suddenly cold, and his fingertips tingled. It was adrenaline. Proof. *Brim thinks he has proof.* Something that would tie Kirsten to the Word. And it was enough that he asked Nathalie Ortiz to contact him, discreetly, on the same day that the Disinherited moved against a Tigers lance.

He looked around, letting the *Crusader*'s sensors wander around the landscape. Jaguar Company had come out as the reserve, partly as a reaction force in case the Disinherited tried to ambush Panther Batt as they left Bravo Base. But the Panthers were far enough away now, almost out of sight . . .

"Anyone got any contacts?" he radioed. All the Jaguars signaled negative. "All right, back to the barn. Two Lance, you're on alert. The rest of us, five-minute standby." That meant Two Lance was staying in their cockpits, while One and Three Lances could dismount, but had to be able to reach their 'Mechs in five minutes or less. Which meant they weren't leaving the hangar.

As he turned the *Crusader* back through the gate, Ezra keyed his comm. He was careful to make sure it wasn't transmitting through the *Crusader*'s commo, but using the separate civilian network. He keyed in Monet's code.

"Monet."

"Charlie, are you up or down?" Meaning, was he in his 'Mech's cockpit or dismounted.

"Down."

"Get online. Someone left you a present." He didn't want to say more—there wasn't more to say.

"A present."

"Find it," Ezra ordered. It felt like the first order he'd given since Yuri Rauschenbusch died. "Find it, and then set up a Raider call. I want to get every Raider who's not blacked out on the line. Thirty minutes."

"On it," Monet said, and clicked off.

An alert chimed. Ezra looked—it was a strategic download from the emperor's command post in Harney. The small map display on the side of the *Crusader*'s cockpit flickered and reformed. New red icons appeared in the northern reaches of the Helmand. Enough red icons for two or more battalions of BattleMechs.

The Disinherited were heading north.

Ezra licked his lips. He hoped thirty minutes would be enough time for Monet.

He stared at the advancing red icons.

He hoped he could give Monet the whole thirty minutes.

"Late last night, an AMC strike force hit the Kallon Industries warehouse district in Keid City, destroying millions of C-bills of technology and equipment. During the attack, the mercenaries touched off a seven-bell fire that engulfed four high-rise apartment buildings, burning them to the ground. As of press time, the death toll sits at 312, and is still rising as emergency crews search the smoldering wreckage for survivors."

—From a Voice of Truth *transmission dated 31 September 3067, from the planet Keid*

CHAPTER TWENTY-SEVEN

It took Monet seventeen minutes to find the present, and two to parse it out into the data Ezra needed. Unfortunately for him, Kirsten Markoja called him and the Leopard Battalion company commanders to the Leopard hangar in only fourteen minutes. His comm chirped to acknowledge receipt of Monet's message, but it was too large to read on the comm's small screen. It would have to wait until he got back to his *Crusader*.

For now, he stood with the other three captains at the foot of Kirsten's brown-and-red *Nightsky*.

"The Dismal Ds are coming out," she said without preamble.

"Wasn't that why we sent the Panthers? To meet them?" Captain Elinor Lisk asked. She was a tall, brown-haired woman with a permanent frown and saggy cheeks. She wore her hair short, with bangs, and worked out religiously. She was probably in better shape than Ezra was.

"We did," Kirsten said, nodding, "but the whole regiment is coming, plus Elly Burton's Brigade. It's the whole AMC—in a way, the final battle for Hall starts today."

"Then what's the plan?" Lisk asked.

"We're going out," Kirsten said. "The Leopards will move up along the Panthers' flank, and help support the Oriente Hussars while the Panthers secure the Republicans." She looked each of them in the eye, finally settling on Ezra. "Captain Payne."

It might have been the first time she'd spoken directly to him since Rauschenbusch died. "Major."

"Your Jaguars will remain here," she said. "Hold the base, in case any of this is a feint."

"All due respect, ma'am," Ezra said, "but you need my 'Mechs out there if the whole regiment of Dismal Ds is coming."

"We have an entire regiment of the Free Worlds League Military on our flank," Kirsten said. "With the Republicans, we'll outnumber them two to one already. One more company won't make a difference."

"Ma'am," Ezra said, inclining his head. None of the other captains looked at him.

"If there's no other questions?" she asked. There weren't. "Then let's go."

Ezra watched them walk toward their 'Mechs for a minute, then spun and started walking back toward the exit to return to the Jaguar hangar. He wanted to turn, to shout, to tell the other captains that their battalion commander was a pawn of the Word of Blake. But he hadn't seen the evidence.

Right then he hated himself, because he was sick of waiting for evidence. He was sick of waiting for irrefutable proof, sick of taking shit orders from someone he *knew* wasn't working for the regiment's best interests. He was sick and tired of being sick and tired. But he kept walking.

Because someone had once taught him an officer doesn't act from his heart. He acts from his mind, because acting from the heart will get you killed. Ezra remembered the knowing grin Yuri Rauschenbusch had given him the first time he'd given Ezra that advice. *"It's going to be hard to swallow, but it's the right move,"* the colonel had said. And he was right.

He walked a little faster. Because evidence or no, if Kirsten Markoja came back to Bravo Base after today, he was going to deal with her once and for all.

On that, his head and heart agreed.

"It's gold," Monet said when Ezra walked into his office. "Pure gold. We have the bitch."

Monet was in his 'Mech—he was a lance commander in Leopard Battalion, after all—but he was broadcasting securely to the wall screen in Ezra's office. It wasn't quite like he was there, but it was close.

Ezra perched on the edge of his desk. "Tell me." He crossed his arms and squeezed his elbows; as Monet spoke, the short, fact-filled sentences packed with nothing but the information Ezra needed to make a decision, he squeezed harder and harder. When Monet finished, Ezra took a deep breath.

"It's good?" he asked. "We could put it in front of anyone, and it won't mean anything else?"

Monet shook his head. "Unless every single bit of Brim's early work is wrong, and there was never, ever a shadowy Word of Blake operation on Hall, it can't mean anything else. He has the times and dates. And besides," he grinned, "what possible reason could there be for our executive officer to warn the opposition that the one person they want most to kill on the planet will be present during a battle, in a BattleMech, where they can reach him?"

Ezra didn't have one. He lowered his hands and wiped suddenly sweaty palms on his trousers. It felt like he'd exchanged one crushing weight for another. "How do we tell the Raiders? Hell, what do we tell the regiment?" Ezra looked at the wall clock. By now the Leopards were out of the gate and moving south. The Panthers were on the other side of Harney. If the battle hadn't already started, it soon would.

"We use the Raider call to tell the Raiders," Monet said, "and then we cut the bitch off at the knees."

"Charlie," Ezra said, "you're walking with her into combat. I can't just pick up the all-regiment channel and shout that she's a Word of Blake plant." He licked dry lips. "The Dismal Ds would cut you down if you're even a little distracted." He stepped away from his desk and sat down on the small couch against he wall.

"Ezra—" Monet began, but Ezra cut him off.

"No—what's her plan? Why did she tell Burton about Baranov?"

"So Burton would come kill him," Monet said.

"Right—but why does she want that? Baranov is her employer. He's just taken the planet into the Free Worlds League. That gets the world into the Word's clutches, if indirectly."

"Maybe she was supposed to get the world into the Protectorate," Monet said. "Or maybe she just wants Baranov out of the picture, so the League has an easier time of it." Ezra couldn't see it, because he was sitting beneath the wall screen, but he heard the sneer in Monet's voice. "Does it matter?"

"No," Ezra said, as the realization came to him. "It doesn't." He stood up. "Here's what we're going to do."

**SOUTH HARNEY
HALL
THE CHAOS MARCH
11 OCTOBER 3067**

Jacob Brim was on his last magazine.

He knelt at the corner of a warehouse, breathing deeply. A Hellraiser infantryman with a long-barreled Federated Long Rifle stood above and behind him, reloading. Jacob looked over his shoulder. The Hellraiser slapped the magazine into place, nodded once, and snugged the rifle into his shoulder.

"Okay," Jacob whispered. He seated his own rifle, then leaned around the corner.

A squad of Republican infantry had been working its way up the street. He sighted on the squad's point man and caressed his Striker's trigger. The carbine spat out six rounds in less than a second; the point collapsed, his body armor shattered. Above him Jacob heard the slower, heavier fire of the Federated rifle. Another of the infantrymen shouted and collapsed. Jacob slid back out of sight as rounds began glancing off the ferrocrete in front of him.

"That should slow them down," he said. Two more Disinherited infantrymen ran up behind them. Jacob nodded to the first one and stood. He slapped the original trooper on the shoulder and stepped around him. The command post—such as it was—was at the other end of the block.

Carlsson looked up when Jacob walked up. He held out a radio headset. "The colonel," he said.

"Sir."

"Brim. Did you find it?"

"Yes, sir," Jacob said. The safe house had been a dead end, but the Blakists hadn't had time to clear out the warehouses. There was material there—incriminating records, financial transfer documents, the works. Even a cache of small arms that Gallifrey was certain he could trace back to Terra. It would be enough to refute the Word's protestations of innocence, if they could get it clear of the fighting.

"Good," Marik-Johns said. "I'm sending a company toward you, but you may have to self-extract."

"That will be problematic, sir," Jacob said. "Our escorts are down, and the Republicans are pressing hard."

"They're pressing everywhere," the colonel said. "Just hold on." Fresh firing erupted back where Jacob had been defending the corner. He twisted to look, but the Disinherited infantrymen were reloading, not falling back. He had a few more minutes, at least.

"Tell them to hurry, Colonel," he said into the headset. "Out here." He pulled the headset off and tossed it back to Carlsson. "Get back inside," he told his XO. "Help them get it sorted." He looked at the cluster of Disinherited NCOs that were all that remained, so far as they could tell, of Captain Sand's company.

"Sergeant Greer," he called. A short, heavyset man with a shock of thick, gray hair looked at him. "Any contact with your company?" Greer shook his head. "Okay. Detail a squad to get us some wheels."

"Sergeant?"

"We're leaving, Sergeant Greer," he told the man. He told all of them. "If your captain can't make it back to us, we have to egress on our own. That means vehicles, civilian ones. Enough to carry us, and as much of the loot as we can load." The sergeant looked around, then back at Jacob and nodded. He stood.

Jacob looked around. He was torn. There were more Blakist holdouts nearby, but the Republicans were closing in. He didn't have the strength or ammunition to resist them. Or the demo to blow them, if it came down to it.

No. Their only chance now was escape.

OUTSIDE BRAVO BASE
HALL
THE CHAOS MARCH
11 OCTOBER 3067

"No one will react," Ezra said. "That is an order."

"Sir?" Sergeant Major Halleck asked.

"I need a readback," Ezra said. He waited until every Raider on the comm channel confirmed his order, then looked ahead of him. He was in his *Crusader* moving south, at the head of Jaguar Company. He had all the Jaguars on the channel as well, though none of them could send. They needed to hear this, too.

"Lieutenant Monet has placed a data packet in each of your 'Mechs' computers," Ezra began. "It's for if you want to confirm what I'm about to tell you after I'm done talking. You won't be able to open it without a key that Charlie will send you as soon as I'm done, so don't try now."

"What's this about, Ezra?" Heather Hargood asked. She was with her company in South Harney with Panther Battalion. They weren't engaged, but that had been as recently as an hour ago.

Branden Roth was dead, killed in the fighting. The Panthers had already tangled with one of the Disinherited battalions. The Hellraisers had been trying to screen around them, and Roth's lance had blunted the attack, but it had cost the big Raider his life.

The tension in Ezra's shoulders threatened to cramp. He should have said something sooner—even an hour might have saved Roth. "Charlie and I have been chasing something down," he said carefully, "something the colonel asked us to look into before he died." In the distance, he saw the tall buildings of downtown Harney on the horizon. "We've been building a case for months, and today the AMC gave us the last pieces of evidence."

"The AMC?" Sergeant Gam asked. "You mean it's true, what they've been saying on the boards?"

"Let the captain talk!" Sergeant Major Halleck barked.

Ezra looked in his HUD at the bullet-shaped *Jinggau* marching with Two Lance. Mason Markoja hadn't wasted any time transferring Halleck out of his new command lance. Ezra had been disappointed for his friend, but he hadn't been disappointed to get the elite MechWarrior back into his company.

"Monet sent you the evidence," Ezra said. "But the short version is this: Kirsten and Mason Markoja are in the Word of Blake's pocket."

There was silence.

And then there wasn't.

Shouts filled the comm line. Curses, questions, comments—all of them overrode each other, stepping on transmissions, cutting each other off. Ezra just let them talk for a minute, the waved the *Crusader*'s arm.

"*Ten-hut!*" Halleck yelled. The Raiders were in shock, but they were trained soldiers. They shut up.

"Today the why doesn't matter. The how doesn't matter. If you get ten free minutes, read Charlie's information. What matters now is what we do about it. Because Kirsten sent McNally's people a note telling them Baranov would be on the field in his *Zeus*. That means Elly Burton and her company will be gunning for him, and the Markojas are going to let them go right by."

"But we didn't!" Hargood said. "For God's sake, we lost Branden stopping a push by the Dismal Ds an hour ago!" Her voice contained as much shock as everyone else's, but two other Raiders in her company chimed in to support her.

"Is the day over?" Halleck asked. "No. There will be other opportunities."

"We have to tell the whole regiment," Sergeant Vann said. "Jesus, I'm looking at the rest of my lance and none of them know anything. I can *hear* the LT talking to the colonel right now, on another channel!"

"We will," Ezra said. "But first we have to be clear on what we're going to do."

"Which is?"

"The Markojas have to go."

"Damn straight," Halleck growled.

"But that means command passes to . . ." Heather Hargood said, but her voice trailed off. "Eberhardt never came back from Lexicon."

"That's right," Ezra said. "So it goes to Wa."

"Fat chance," Ervil Gam said. "I wouldn't follow that bastard to water in the desert."

"Then it's you," Hargood said to Ezra, "or me."

"Yeah."

No one spoke for a minute. "You know what you're saying," Sergeant Vann said. "You're saying you want to cut our head off in the middle of a battle."

"You see an alternative?" Ezra had already gamed it out every way he could in his head. He could let the Markojas stay in command, but that meant the Tigers were working toward whatever secret plan the Markojas and their Blakist secret masters had. It might be benign. It might not.

So far, it involved betraying their employer to his enemies.

Monet had argued that wasn't true, that just because the Word had ultimately financed the Tigers' contract, they could order the regiment to do what they wanted. Not even Monet liked that line of reasoning, however. He hated the Blakists. He just didn't want a leadership vacuum at the very top of the regiment during a pitched battle.

But Ezra had prevailed. It was pretty much the worst situation he could think of—he was asking every Stealthy Tiger to fight their own battle. If there was one time a commander could not be uncertain, it was during combat. Yuri Rauschenbusch had hammered that into Ezra and every other Tigers officer. Right decision, wrong decision, just *make* one. A MechWarrior had to know he could trust his officer to make those decisions. To give good orders.

He was going to rip that away from every Tiger when they needed it most.

Ezra worked his jaw and swallowed. He had to. The only other option was to not—and that would pervert everything Rauschenbusch had built.

Everything the Stealthy Tigers were.

"I'll make the announcement. I'll tell them to look to their company COs, to their lance commanders. Heather, you try and rally the Panthers. I'll take the Leopards."

"There's no way this works," Hargood said.

"You got another option, say it!" Ezra shouted. "We are *out of time*. The shooting starts up again, those two are in charge, then we're fighting against our contract. We're fighting for the Word against Baranov. We're *breaking our contract*."

No one said anything against that.

"This is the worst possible time to do it," Ezra said. "Except for any other time."

"Do it," Sergeant Major Halleck said. His immediate support carried a lot of weight, Ezra knew. "You announce it, I'll get on the back-channel to the NCOs. I think most of the regiment will see the right way. It's still the colonel's regiment." Ezra knew he didn't mean Mason Markoja.

"What if they don't?" Monet asked. "It's only me and Jenny here in Leopard." He didn't sound scared—no one who'd seen Charles Monet in combat would think he could be scared—but he was right: Kirsten had weeded all but two Raiders out of her battalion.

"I'll be there in less than an hour," Ezra told him. "I'll announce as the Jaguars come into range. Then I'll make my play for them."

"She won't take that well," Monet said.

Ezra thumbed his throttle forward another notch. The *Crusader*'s gait lengthened as its accelerated, still turned south.

"I really don't care."

"This is, without a doubt, the largest battle that has taken place on Hall in centuries, ladies and gentlemen. From the south march the BattleMechs of the Allied Mercenary Command, supported by the dregs of the rebel McNally's army and Burton's Brigade. Arrayed to meet them are the Fourth Republican, with the emperor himself at their head, and the Fourth Oriente Hussars of the Free Worlds League. The Stealthy Tigers, mercenaries in the employ of the emperor, are moving to support them.

"If you're in South Harney, get out. Get out now.

"Already we have reports of small-scale fighting inside the city precincts. Infiltrators entered the city before dawn, no doubt hoping to get into position to ambush the loyal forces when the AMC arrived. It was only the vigilance of the Fourth Republican that prevented the cowardly mercenaries from launching such an ambush.

"There have been clashes, but our sources say the main battle hasn't yet come. It can't be long, though. Again—if you're in South Harney, and you're hearing this, get out now."

–From the *Harney Morning Edition* Special Report,
11 October 3067, Harney HV Channel Six

CHAPTER TWENTY-EIGHT

Kirsten Markoja stared at nothing in her HUD. She would have stared at the speakers in her cockpit, but they were invisible to her. Payne's words refused to register with her conscious mind; that mind was too overtaken with emotion.

Disbelief, at the sheer gall of the statement.

Rage, at the timing.

Fear, irrational that it was, that she had been found out.

And here he was, saying it all out in the open, in front of the whole regiment. In front of the whole world! He'd come south, against her direct orders, and brought his entire damned company with him!

"She's betrayed the regiment," Payne went on. "She's betrayed the emperor. She's betrayed our contract." There was a pause. "And she's betrayed all of us. She and her brother both."

Kirsten looked around at the 'Mechs nearest her. They were from her own company of Leopard Battalion, men and women she trusted implicitly. Lieutenant Ames' *Enforcer* had its head twisted to face her, but it wasn't moving. Sergeant Grazer's *Anvil* hadn't moved.

She couldn't see the rest of her battalion, but the lack of movement in her direct sight was a good sign. If the Tigers were prepared to believe a word Payne said, she'd have seen some evidence of it. She'd spent a lot of time over the last few months undermining him; undermining his Raiders, spreading rumors about him, excluding him from staff meetings, not seeking his opinion. He'd been Rauschenbusch's fair-haired boy for too long.

The Markojas had no use for him. They'd made that plain, and if she had learned just one thing from Yuri Rauschenbusch, it was that the attitude of the commander became the attitude of the regiment. What she didn't know was whether or not the few short months she'd had were enough.

"We're Stealthy Tigers," Payne went on in that stupid, condescending tone he had. "We keep to our contracts. Defend the emperor, do your duty—but don't do it for the Word. And don't fight for Kirsten or Mason Markoja."

A light lit on her comm panel: Mason. She ignored it. She grabbed her emotions by the throat and forced them down, all except the rage. She opened her mouth, then closed it. She thought about what she should say. Deny it? Embrace it? Ignore it? A cold smile came to her face. *No.*

She toggled her mic. "Captain Payne," she said, "you're relieved of command." She took a breath. "Obviously the strain of command and the colonel's death has been too much for you. Lieutenant Reynard—" Payne's XO in Jaguar Company. "—take command and escort the captain back to Bravo Base."

More lights lit on her comm board. She toggled Mason live.

"Kirsten," he hissed, "what the hell? How did they find out?"

"It doesn't matter," she said. "In a couple of hours the battle for Hall will be over, we'll have won, and we'll put Payne and his Raiders in the ground if we have to." Speaking of Raiders . . . she toggled a different channel. "Lieutenant Monet?"

There was no response. She didn't expect one, not from the seniormost Raider in her battalion. But she had to make sure the forms were followed. "Lieutenant, I know you look up to Captain Payne. Why don't you return to Bravo Base as well?" She smiled. "In fact, any Raider in Leopard Battalion that wishes to return to Bravo Base may do so. I know you're all close . . . " She almost choked on the saccharine tone she had to force into her voice.

"Kirsten, what are you doing?" Mason demanded. "You can't let them go—"

"We don't take orders from you anymore, bitch," Monet growled.

Kirsten luxuriated in the hate in the man's voice. It was exactly the response she'd hoped for. She knew one of the Raiders would break, would do something that couldn't be ignored. It couldn't be better if he had fired on her.

"Charlie—" she started, trying not to laugh, but he cut her off.

"Shut up," Monet said. "You're a disgrace to the regiment."

"You're relieved, Monet," she snapped. She'd let him say enough. If anyone reviewed the tapes later, they'd see that she'd reacted calmly to the attempted mutiny—yes, that's what they'd call it—until it couldn't be ignored. "You will power down your BattleMech and remain there until we can come back for you."

"What do we do?" Halleck asked.

Ezra's mind raced. He'd hoped the whole regiment would turn against the Markojas. With Eberhardt out of the picture, either he or Hargood had a good chance of taking command. No one would follow Wa, and in the midst of fighting there wouldn't be time for any kind of conclave to choose a new colonel. One of them would get the slot by default, just because they were giving orders.

He toggled the Raider frequency. "Heather? Status?"

"No one's shooting yet," she said, "but I've got a lot of 'Mechs looking at me. Mason and his lance are headed toward you."

Ezra looked around. "Make your pitch," he told her.

"Okay, but it'll have to be fast. We just got a signal from the Hussars—the Disinherited is coming this way."

"Out here," he said, toggling the Jaguar channel. "Listen up: if this gets to shooting, screen Monet and Jenny Caruthers out and we'll pull back."

"Roger," Halleck said.

"I've got a signal here saying the Dismal Ds are moving this way," Nico Reynard said. Ezra looked at his *Enforcer*. Of everyone in his company, he worried the most about Reynard, the only other officer. If he supported Ezra now, the rest of the Jaguars would.

"Then we'll move fast," he said. He switched to the Leopard Battalion channel.

"Listen up, Leopards. This isn't our fight. This is Kirsten's fight. She brought you here, against our contract, because she has another agenda. That's not our mission. That's not our contract. We need to move toward the emperor. He's our contract." He gestured left with the *Crusader*'s arm. "Listen to your captains, and let's get over there. The AMC is coming, right now."

"Payne," Kirsten growled, "I'm warning you—"

"I know it's hard," Ezra said, ignoring her. "It goes against what we were taught. But we're Stealthy Tigers. We're professionals. We're Ra—"

He stopped. He never imagined in his life he'd ever feel wrong saying "we're Raiders," but here it did. *"I don't want anything to come between me and the regiment,"* he remembered the MechWarrior saying.

"We're Rauschenbusch's boys and girls," he said instead. *Tie it to the regiment.* "He taught us all what it meant to be a part of this regiment. Don't throw that away."

Comm lights lit on his console. He toggled them to read as text displays on his HUD. He couldn't afford to switch between channels, not when he was talking to the whole battalion.

EVIDENCE BETTER HOLD UP–KUZNETZOV. That was one company.

BAD TIMING–BOYLE. That was noncommittal, but Ezra would take it.

Alarms screamed to life in the *Crusader*'s cockpits. Targeting sensors were painting his 'Mech.

"Six," Hicks muttered. He still had the Jaguar frequency on listen-only. It wasn't only his 'Mech.

WRONG MOVE–LISK.

"Don't shoot!" he yelled.

"You will withdraw," Kirsten Markoja ground out, "or I will put you down, you mutinous bastard."

Ezra looked at her *Nightsky.* It was too far away for her to shoot him directly—not even her large pulse laser would reach that far—but Lisk's company was closer. Her shooters could reach him. He licked dry lips and took his hands off the controls. There was only one way this worked . . .

"Not for her," he whispered into the sudden loaded silence.

The *Crusader* rocked and red-tinged light flickered in the canopy. A large laser had just cut at his chest armor. He didn't move, except to adjust the 'Mech's stance with his foot pedals so it wouldn't fall over.

"I didn't come here to fight you," he transmitted.

"Six—" Sergeant Major Halleck started, but Ezra cut him off.

"The fight's over there," he said.

In the backfield, Captain Kuznetzov's company twitched, as if someone had prodded all of them at once, and then broke into a trot in the direction Ezra had indicated. Several of the 'Mechs in other companies turned to look, then twisted back on their fellows.

"Get back here," Kirsten said.

If there was a response, Ezra didn't hear it.

Six more 'Mechs took off after the first company. Then two more.

Ezra felt his stomach clench. It was working.

"You're all going to hang for this," Kirsten said. Her voice was a little less steady.

Charlie Monet's *Phoenix Hawk* stepped out of ranks, but instead of moving toward Ezra and Jaguar Company, he spun and raised his 'Mech's arms. Two extended-range large lasers pointed directly at Kirsten Markoja's *Nightsky*. "You need to shut down," he said, broadcasting in the clear, "or I will *put* you down."

Ripples walked through the remaining Leopard Battalion 'Mechs. Three of Lisk's 'Mechs turned back to face Monet's 'Mech.

"Charlie—" Ezra started, but then it was too late.

Kirsten Markoja's *Nightsky* leaped into the air on jump jets. Monet must have been distracted; only one of his lasers hit, painting the 'Mech's left leg as it rose.

Kirsten was a skilled MechWarrior; she landed only a handful of meters from Monet's *Phoenix Hawk*. The underarm hatchet that made the *Nightsky* such a dangerous in-fighter gleamed as she spun into a reverse, extending the 'Mech's arm to give the hatch greater velocity.

The reinforced edge of the melee weapon penetrated the cockpit armor of Monet's 'Mech like it wasn't there. The *Phoenix Hawk* flinched as its control runs were severed, then it dropped.

Every remaining 'Mech on the field opened fire.

Except for Ezra.

He wanted to be sick. Charlie Monet was dead, and Stealthy Tigers were shooting at each other.

And it was all his fault.

It wasn't supposed to be like this.

Kirsten ripped her hatchet out of the wreckage of Monet's 'Mech and straightened up. Around her, the three MechWarriors of her command lance and Captain Lisk's company were lighting up Payne and his Jaguars. She looked around for Jenny Caruthers'

Hercules, but that bitch was already sprinting toward the Jaguars, trying to open the range.

"Stop!" Payne yelled.

Kirsten grinned. "What's the matter, Payne?" she taunted. "Don't have the stomach for the big decisions?"

Across the field, the *Crusader*'s arms came up and it lurched into motion. She bared her teeth and thumbed her own throttle forward. The sooner she put Payne down, the sooner this would all be over. The comm light indicating Mason calling blinked at her, but she ignored it. Mason could handle himself for few minutes it would take her to kill Ezra Payne.

"Tell me why," he said.

She laughed. "You didn't seriously just ask me that."

The *Nightsky* was up to its top speed, just under 100 kilometers per hour. Her jump jets were recharged, and she leaned into the turns necessary to thread between the 'Mechs from Lisk's company shooting at the Jaguars. Her pulse lasers were powerful, but short-ranged. She had to get in close to do any real harm.

Just like she had with Rauschenbusch.

The hatchet on the *Nightsky*'s right arm swung in time with her steps. She liked the feel of that, they way the 'Mech pulled just a little farther on the downstroke when it ran. It matched the tingle in her right palm. It made her feel closer to her 'Mech, almost like she was a part of it.

She relished that feeling. Jerome Blake had taught them that technology was the key to mankind's future and survival. Feeling closer to the technology at hand was as near a religious experience as she'd had since leaving Jardine.

Payne's *Crusader* came to meet her.

Kirsten wrapped her tingling palm around the right-arm controlled and held her course. That was exactly what she wanted. She toggled her comm system.

"Mason."

"Kirsten! What's going—"

"What's the Panthers' status?"

"I don't—"

"Mason, I don't have time to explain," she said.

"They're coming apart," he said. "Hargood tried to turn them against me. I was coming to help you, but I had to turn around.

"Hargood?"

"Dead, along with all the other Raiders in my battalion," he said. "We're consolidating now." He paused. "The Dismal Ds are coming, Kirsten."

"How far?"

"A couple minutes. Their outriders are already skirmishing with the Republicans."

Kirsten glanced at the strategic map. Baranov and his Republican battalion were in South Harney, half-hidden among the buildings and houses. If the Disinherited wanted to dig him out of there, it would come at a horrific cost in destroyed property and, more than likely, civilian casualties.

It was perfect.

"Go support the Hussars," she told her brother.

"But—"

"Go, Mason," she said. "Remember the plan." She looked around the field, at the few 'Mechs that remained. "And if you see Kuznetzov or Boyle or their companies?"

"Yes?"

"They're traitors, too."

"Got it."

Ezra swallowed as the range fell. He was focused on Kirsten Markoja, but his eyes kept showing him horrific sights: Halleck's *Jinggau* putting a Gauss slug into the guts of a Leopard Battalion *Archer*, staggering the heavy missile-support 'Mech. He saw Hicks dodge a burst of autocannon fire from a Leopard *Clint* and pivot to blow a Leopard *Wasp* off its feet with her own autocannon.

He saw Stealthy Tiger killing Stealthy Tiger.

"Jaguar Six!" a panicked voice shouted. He didn't recognize it.

"Six, go," he sent.

"Sir, we're getting murdered here!" The *Crusader*'s computer helpfully threw up a comm code: Sergeant Jensen, from Captain Hargood's company. "The captain's down, the LTs are down! The battalion—they turned on us. Colonel Markoja came back and gave the order, and we couldn't stand against them—" the sergeant's voice cut off mid-sentence.

"Jensen? Jensen!"

"Sounds like your mutiny is going worse than you thought," Kirsten sent. Ezra clenched his fists around his controls and snarled at the image of her *Nightsky*, still pounding closer.

"You did this," he told her. "You twisted the soul of this regiment enough that it's willing to kill itself. A year ago these people were brother and sister. The colonel would never have let you—"

"The colonel," Kirsten spat. "I'm so sick of hearing about your precious colonel."

"He was—" she interrupted him.

"A good man, right? The best of us? A father to you?" She laughed, harsh and cold and without any amusement. "He was in my way."

Ezra's blood froze. "What did you say?"

"He was in my way," she said. "And then he wasn't." The Nighsky raised its right-arm hatchet, then lowered it. "Chop. Problem solved."

The *Crusader* stumbled. Ezra was thrown off-balance by Kirsten's words enough that his discomfort transmitted to the 'Mech's DI computer via his neurohelmet. He had to throw its arms out, out of battery, to keep it on its feet and moving.

Kirsten Markoja had been the only person in the room when Yuri Rauschenbusch has suffered his heart attack.

Problem solved.

Pieces clicked into place in Ezra's mind, pieces he'd had all along but couldn't put together, because he couldn't believe that even Kirsten Markoja could be so venomous. The colonel had asked for 'Mech records, during the fight in the desert. He'd seen something on the screen.

Kirsten Markoja had been the last person to see him alive.

Just seconds after Charlie Monet delivered 'Mech records to him.

The *Quickdraw*.

Ridzik.

She was behind *all of that*.

She had given Ridzik that 'Mech. Out of the Tigers' own stocks.

The colonel had recognized it. And confronted her.

And she'd murdered him.

Ezra blinked and swallowed his gorge. He wanted to throw up, but he couldn't. Cold sweat chased goosebumps down his arms and up his legs, despite the heat in his cockpit. He stared at the *Nightsky*, and his vision condensed down to just one red-tinged tunnel.

"You killed the colonel," he whispered.

She said nothing. Ezra didn't care. Around him, the rest of the Tigers fought one another unabated. It was too late to stop them. It was Raider against Tiger; Jaguar against Leopard. It was old against the new. It was the soul of the regiment against the young sinew, straining the seams.

Ezra didn't care if she admitted it. He didn't care if he never found evidence to back up his sudden insight. He'd spent much of the last year avoiding decisions, prolonging conflict, waiting and searching for *proof*. All of those precautions had been for nothing—the colonel was dead, and here they were, fighting. Fighting each other, fighting the AMC. Somewhere out there, Nathalie was shooting at and being shot at by a Stealthy Tiger, for all he knew.

This time, he would act. He had the power. His hands were locked on the *Crusader*'s controls in a death grip. He didn't need proof. There was no one left to convince. He knew all he needed to know.

The range fell, and his crosshairs turned green.

"You're a dead woman."

"We're getting unconfirmed reports now that the emperor himself has engaged the rebels and their AMC lapdogs in the streets of South Harney. Our broadcast crews aren't able to enter the combat zone, but we do have this footage of the emperor's *Zeus* marching with the rest of his Republicans earlier this morning.

"The Fourth Oriente has been sparring with the Dismal Disinherited all morning, and early reports put the 'Mechs of Burton's Brigade, the mercenary company commanded by the late, rebellious Count McNally's former lover, in the center of the Disinherited lines.

"The Stealthy Tigers are strangely quiet."

–From the *Harney Morning Edition,*
HV Channel Six

CHAPTER TWENTY-NINE

**SOUTH HARNEY
HALL
THE CHAOS MARCH
11 OCTOBER 3067**

For Ezra, it was as if the rest of the fighting fell away. He saw nothing but Kirsten Markoja's charging *Nightsky*. He watched every step of the fifty-ton BattleMech coming at him, saw the way she planted her feet, watched the way she swung the 'Mech's arms. He knew to the last meter the distance between them without checking the rangefinder.

He heard the shouting of the combat between Stealthy Tigers on his radio. He switched the radio off.

He saw the motion of other 'Mechs in his peripheral vision. He ignored it.

There was nothing else in his universe except him and her and their 'Mechs.

The crosshairs had turned green when the *Nightsky* had entered the range of his MRMs. Now they flickered green and gold as the *Crusader*'s computer tried for a lock. The *Nightsky* was fast, and Kirsten a good pilot, but Ezra Payne was no slouch as a Mech-Warrior himself.

The crosshairs turned gold. He fired.

The *Crusader* rocked as both Shigunga launchers cycled. Sixty medium-range missiles erupted from the cylindrical launchers, rippling around the circumference of the launcher as fast as possible, but just slow enough that the missiles didn't interfere with each others' flight. The wash of exhaust was, as always, blinding, but the fast-moving 'Mech ran out of its own smoke cloud in two or three steps. For a split second, it was like a cloud of glowing beetles all charging downrange.

The *Nightsky* twisted, trying to avoid the fire, but Kirsten couldn't dodge all of it. The missiles were too well aimed. Warheads pounded the armor protecting the 'Mech's chest and arms. Ezra thought he might have seen one hit the *Nightsky*'s cockpit canopy, but he couldn't be sure. If he had, it didn't seem to affect her—the *Nightsky* stumbled beneath the impacts, but stayed on its feet, still advancing.

The MRM launchers cycled, but Ezra ignored them. He pressed hard on the right foot pedal, turning the *Crusader* that way without slowing it down. All sixty-five tons of 'Mech twisted. He knew he couldn't hold the range open, but if he could slow the rate of closure . . .

The *Nightsky*'s large pulse laser was a dangerous and powerful weapon, but it was short-ranged. MRMs had a longer range, but at the speeds BattleMechs often fought at, the distance between "short" and "medium" fell away quickly. He had a small advantage, and he would lose it if he let the *Nightsky* get too close. It was smaller, yes. And carried less armor.

But it was faster, and it had the five-ton hatchet that had just crushed the life out of Charles Monet on its arm. If Ezra let her get too close—he shook the thoughts off. All of this flashed through the gestalt of knowledge, training, and experience that was his mind in a second or less, but it didn't linger.

All that lingered was the white-hot, boiling rage at what Kirsten Markoja had done.

Ezra Payne was no berserker—he wasn't going to charge in blindly and just hammer at her until he or she died. But he wasn't going to sit on the edges of the fight, hoping she'd make a mistake.

Twisting the *Crusader*'s torso to keep his weapons bearing, Ezra eyed the range between his 'Mech and hers and judged the rate at which the Shigungas were recycling. Sixty missiles was a lot of mass to move from the big magazine in the *Crusader*'s left chest, along the feed tubes in the 'Mech's arms and into the launcher. It was a cycle time measured in seconds, but he didn't know if he had that many seconds.

He did, but just barely. The launchers chimed loaded.

The crosshairs burned gold.

He fired.

Green-tinged laser light flashed like lightning in the cloud of his missile exhaust as Kirsten found the range and fired. Ezra didn't feel the *Crusader* take a hit, but he couldn't tell. It was still shuddering from the missile launches. He didn't glance at his damage schematic. It didn't matter whether he'd taken a hit or not, not yet. The *Crusader*'s armor would hold.

Or it wouldn't.

His missiles chased the *Nightsky* as Kirsten tried to evade them again. But again, she was only partially successful. More armor was battered on the 'Mech's chest. Ezra ground his teeth and grunted in satisfaction.

The MRM reload cycle began again. The pain in his chest, in his soul, tingled and cried out in agreement. He wanted vengeance on Kirsten Markoja, and the ghosts in his soul felt the same way.

Kirsten worked her tongue around her mouth and swallowed, ignoring the gorge-raising taste of copper from her bleeding cheek. The *Nightsky*'s damage schematic was more yellow than green, punished as it had been by the *Crusader*'s damned missiles, but the damage wasn't catastrophic yet. But soon it would be.

Time to end this.

She was already in range of her large pulse laser, and the mediums would range soon. The *Crusader* had medium lasers, too—both standard and pulse varieties—but the real threat was its missiles. She had to find a way to get Payne to use up his missiles without getting hit by them. He'd already fired a quarter of his total magazine space. If she could run that down, and then close with the hatchet—

"Kirsten!" Mason's voice was loud in her helmet speakers.

"Not now!" she told him.

"Hargood is dead. I had to put most of her company down, too, but it's done. There's not a Raider left alive in Panther Battalion."

"Good," she said. *You already told me that, idiot.*

Her large pulse laser chimed ready. She jerked her controls, twisting the *Nightsky* back in a reversal of its previous course, and fired as the crosshairs slipped over the *Crusader*. The stuttering green lasers dotted the armor over the *Crusader*'s right thigh, but didn't penetrate.

"Are you okay?"

Kirsten groaned and ignored him. She thumbed the throttle forward to its gate, pushing the *Nightsky* up to its top speed after her turn.

Red light flashed in front of her cockpit—Payne had fired his medium lasers, but missed.

"Kirsten?"

"Baranov?" she asked. Her eyes took in the range and the relative speeds as she talked; two more volleys, and she'd be close enough to bring her hatchet into the game. She wouldn't normally take her 'Mech against one fifteen tons heavier, but Payne was too good a gunner to let this play out at range.

"I don't know," Mason said. "Burton and her people were pressing him—"

"Then find out!" she snapped.

"What about you?"

"I'm . . ." She looked around. And what she saw was enough to break her out of the rageful focus she had on Ezra Payne.

The fighting around her had ended. The remnants of Lisk's company stood in a clump a half-klick back. Payne's Jaguars were in a similar cluster. Both of them were watching the drama play out between them.

Fine. "I'm finishing off Payne," she told him. "Then we'll get back to Bravo and get started."

"Started?"

"Building the regiment we were always supposed to have," she said, and clicked the channel closed. Her crosshairs flickered gold— she was in range of her medium pulse lasers. She fired both, and laughed as they savaged the armor over the *Crusader*'s right chest.

Her right hand tingled even more at the anticipation of bringing her hatchet into play.

"Ezra," Sergeant Major Halleck said.

"Not now," Ezra said. He set the *Crusader*'s right foot and pivoted, then squeezed the trigger. The paired medium pulse lasers in the *Crusader*'s chest fired. One missed behind the *Nightsky*; the other ate at the armor over its right elbow.

He touched the MRM trigger, but let off. He couldn't get a lock.

"It has to be now," Halleck said. "Baranov is dead."

"What?"

"It's coming in on the Republican channels. Him and Elly Burton both—they got into it near one of the Blakist warehouses in South Harney. The warehouse exploded—he's dead. They're finding pieces of his *Zeus* scattered across three blocks."

Ezra blinked, and suddenly saw the whole field again. No matter what else had happened, no matter what else did happen, the Stealthy Tigers' contract on Hall was over. The man they were contracted to serve was dead. They could pull back, let the League and the AMC fight it out, and wait for the dust to settle.

There was a way out for the regiment.

Kirsten's *Nightsky* moved across his field of vision, and Ezra's focus narrowed back down. A small, officer-trained part of his mind was considering what the regiment might do next—but the immediate part of his mind still felt the gaping hole where Yuri Rauschenbusch had been, where the honor of the regiment had been, and only saw the woman who had single-handedly ripped those holes in his being.

"After," he told Halleck.

The *Nightsky* fired again, all three lasers. One of the mediums missed, but the other combined with the large pulse laser to gut the armor protecting the *Crusader*'s left arm. Another couple strikes there, and he could lose the entire limb—and its MRM launcher.

Possible decisions fell away from the tactical computer that was Ezra Payne's mind. He had been husbanding his missiles, waiting for Kirsten to get close enough that he couldn't miss, that she couldn't dodge. But the last exchange changed the calculus.

He was getting very close to use it or lose it.

He aimed and fired everything.

His lasers cut at the armor over the *Nightsky*'s leg, and the fifty-ton 'Mech nearly vanished beneath explosions as sixty missiles angled at it. Some missed, but not many. The *Nightsky* stumbled and fell to one knee, shaken off balance by the pounding.

Ezra didn't hesitate. He changed his course and charged toward the 'Mech.

Kirsten worked her controls hard, trying to get the *Nightsky* back on its feet. The seeming wall of explosions that had enveloped her

'Mech had been too much for even her. She found the 'Mech's balance and stood, but alarms screamed at her. Her armor was savaged. Targeting sensors were painting her. She glared at the HUD.

Payne sprinted right at her. The *Crusader*'s every footfall raised a cloud of dust.

"Come on!" Kirsten screamed. She raised the *Nightsky*'s right arm and pushed her throttle forward to meet him. If he was stupid enough to come into range of her hatchet, she would let him.

"Payne!" Hicks screamed, but Ezra ignored her.

Less than 200 meters separated the two 'Mechs. Ezra kept a firm grip on his controls, his feet light on the pedals. His lasers recharged and he fired them, all four. Coherent light spent itself against the *Nightsky*'s armor. Kirsten's return fire did the same—neither of them did critical damage.

The MRMs reloaded. He raised the *Crusader*'s arms, but Kirsten leaped aside—he let up, trying to adjust his aim. Only one of his arms—the left—would bear on the *Nightsky*, but she was too quick; all thirty medium range missiles rocketed past the 'Mech. Ezra cursed and tried to turn. They were down to a hundred meters apart.

"Six," Sergeant Roses said, "get clear and let us—"

Ezra clicked the channel closed.

Sixty meters.

The *Crusader*'s lasers recycled, but he held his fire. The 'Mech shivered as missiles traveled down to the launcher in his left arm. It would only be a second . . . maybe half a second . . .

Ezra snarled at the image of the *Nightsky* and stomped hard on both foot pedals. The *Crusader* lurched into the air on its jump jets.

It was a short hop—just the last forty meters or so. He barely got more than a dozen meters high, but it was enough. Red and green laser pulses flashed beneath him as Kirsten failed to anticipate his leap.

At the apex of his jump, the MRM launcher reloaded. He pointed the *Crusader*'s arms down and squeezed both triggers. Missile exhaust blinded him as the launchers cycled, spitting another full sixty missiles out before he touched the ground. He landed with a crash, off-balance, but didn't fall. He looked for the *Nightsky*—he was close enough that the smoke from his own warheads was blinding him.

Kirsten lurched out of the smoke and flames, actuators sparking, smoke pouring from rents in her 'Mech's armor. The *Nightsky* moved with a limp from a lamed ankle actuator, but it was still as fast as the *Crusader*. The hatchet was already raised and coming down. Ezra twisted, but his 'Mech was too far off-balance. He couldn't get out of the way. The hatchet came down with a shocking impact on the *Crusader*'s shoulder, where the armor had already been weakened by laser fire. The last of the armor there collapsed, and the hatchet sunk deep into the shoulder's internal structure. The feed line for his missile launcher crimped and cut—thankfully there were no reloads traveling in them at that moment—and his laser dropped offline as the companion power cables were sliced in half. The *Crusader* lurched again, alarms screaming, as Kirsten ripped her hatchet free and raised it gain.

"My turn," Ezra said. He kicked his foot pedals until the 'Mech was upright, then fired the medium laser in his remaining arm. The ruby beam cut like a knife into the *Nightsky*'s belly.

The paired medium pulse lasers in the *Crusader*'s chest also strobed into the 'Mech's armpit, exposed by the raised arm. Light flashed inside its torso as those lasers cut something vital. The *Nightsky* staggered backward.

"Not so fast," Ezra muttered. He took three quick steps, wound up, and threw out a kick that caught the *Nightsky*'s left shin. The limb flew out from beneath the fifty-ton 'Mech, and Kirsten collapsed. She fell hard, shattering armor on her left side. Heat bloomed on Ezra's IR sensors as the *Nightsky*'s fusion containment was hit.

"Give up," he radioed. The heat in his cockpit was baking him, but he ignored it.

"Go to hell," Kirsten spat.

The faceplate on her neurohelmet was cracked. Kirsten scratched at it until her fingernails caught the edge, then pried the broken transpex out of its frame. Scorching hot air from her cockpit scalded her face, evaporating the sweat beaded on her forehead and cheeks, but she ignored it.

The *Nightsky* labored to move. Heat and damage were collaborating to hobble it, but Payne wasn't backing off, and her hatchet-arm still worked. She worked the medium 'Mech to its knee and then up, lurching to the side, off-balance. It was pure luck that Payne's lasers burned at the space she had just left—she hadn't been dodging.

There was still time. She would gut Payne's *Crusader* with her hatchet. The other Raiders would be too shocked to stop her, and she'd get away. Her right hand was throbbing now—not just a tingle anymore. In the deep recesses of her mind, she heard the whispers of the trainers on Jardine, warning her against getting too excited, of what extremely high blood pressure would do to her implants, but she ignored them.

There was still time.

"Kirsten," Mason's voice said, its calmness at odds with the fury of her cockpit, "Baranov is dead."

Hope burned brighter at Kirsten's core. Her plan was working. Now all that was left was to make sure the Fourth Oriente paid such a price that Thomas Marik would withdraw his offer of annexation from the newly-leaderless people of Hall. They would cast about, looking for support, and the Word would be there.

It would be the last piece in Kirsten Markoja's ascension puzzle. It would be the key.

Light moved on her HUD. Payne's *Crusader.*

Her lips drew back in a sneer and she lurched forward, hatchet ready.

It was time.

The battle was over, whether or not Kirsten accepted that. And with that ending came the return of Ezra's thinking mind, the part of himself that Yuri Rauschenbusch had trained and built and molded across a decade of soldiering. The hate for his killer was still there, but capturing her and making her confess would be the only key to the Stealthy Tigers' survival. The emperor's death would be damning, and the Markoja's involvement, but with the truth on his side there was a chance . . .

The *Nightsky* lurched to its feet. His hands triggered his medium lasers without conscious thought, but he was too slow. The lasers missed as Kirsten nearly fell to the side, but caught herself and lunged for him. The *Nightsky* was lame and smoking, and glowed on the *Crusader*'s thermal scanners, but it was still mobile, still a BattleMech. It was still the culmination of centuries of warfare refinement.

Ezra's thumb reversed the *Crusader*'s throttle as she closed, trying to back out of range, but sixty-five tons is a lot of inertia to overcome, even for myomer muscles.

The *Nightsky* fell toward him, twisting, bringing the hatchet around in a backhand that brought the 'Mech's whole motion into the blow.

It took the *Crusader* in the left torso.

The armor there, already weakened, collapsed beneath the blade's crushing weight. It bit deeply, crushing supports and feed lines, power cables, and finally penetrating to the deeply-embedded medium range missile magazines. The depleted-uranium edge broke through the magazine wall and crushed several missiles against each other.

The warheads of those missiles detonated.

Inside the *Crusader*.

Inside the missile magazine—with dozens of their fellows nearby.

The entire magazine went up, and a lot of things happened all at once.

In his cockpit, Ezra Payne screamed as feedback screeched through his neurohelmet. Electricity surged through the delicate connections. The pain was indescribable, but blessedly brief.

The respite was less than a hundredth of a second, though.

Like many modern 'Mechs, the *Crusader*'s ammunition bins were encapsulated in cellular ammunition storage equipment, specially-built blowout panels that channeled the main force of the explosion out the back of the 'Mech. On some 'Mechs, that let the MechWarrior keep fighting, or at least hobble his 'Mech off the field.

However, butted against the CASE bay was nearly a third of the *Crusader*'s massive extralight fusion engine. The destruction annihilated the engine's magnetic shielding, forcing it into emergency shutdown.

It also triggered Ezra's automatic ejection sequence.

The *Crusader*'s head disintegrated as explosives cleared a path for his command couch to fling him up and back on rocket motors. The acceleration was crushing, many more gravities than Ezra could think about with the aftermath of the surging pain of feedback still muddling his brain. He was aware of the hammer blow of ejection, the feel of blessedly cool air rushing past his skin, but then there was the most brilliant white flash he'd ever seen from below, and a wall smashed him into unconsciousness.

"We're getting confirmations now, across several sources, that William Baranov, emperor of Hall and architect of our annexation into the Free Worlds League, has been killed in combat by the 'Mechs of Burton's Brigade. One eyewitness tells us the mercenaries lured the emperor into a trap, drawing him away from his guards and near a warehouse that had been rigged with explosives.

"No officer of the Fourth Oriente Hussars can be reached for comment, due to ongoing combat operations, but our own military correspondents tell us the Dismal Disinherited have begun withdrawing back into the Helmand, pressed hard by the Fourth Oriente Hussars and elements of the Stealthy Tigers.

"We'll be back on the air as soon as we have more information. In the meantime, our hearts and prayers are with every citizen of Hall, for if we've lost our greatest champion on the eve of his greatest triumph, our entry into the League will be forever marred by tragedy."

–From the *Harney Morning Edition*,
Hall HV Channel Six, 11 October 3067

CHAPTER THIRTY

OVERLORD-CLASS DROPSHIP *TIGRIS*
HALL
THE CHAOS MARCH
19 OCTOBER 3067

Ezra couldn't open his eyes, and his throat burned with the sensation of too much dry air for too long. When he tried to blink, his entire head shivered with sympathetic pain, which made his whole body flinch. That was a mistake, a wash of pain all over that would have made him scream if he could do more than croak.

"He's coming around," a woman's voice said.

"Slow," a different voice said—a man's voice. "Ezra, slow."

Ezra grit his teeth and clenched all his muscles, trying to feel if there was any part of his body that didn't hurt. He squeezed his eyes closed and tried to open them, squeezed and opened, over and over again.

"Hold on," the woman's voice said. He felt a warm, wet cloth on his eyelids. After a moment he pried one eye open, then the other. Then he immediately closed them as the low light overhead sent flashing pains through his head.

"Slow," the man's voice said.

Ezra cracked one eye again and squinted, letting it adjust. Then the other.

Three people stood in the small room with him. The room had lights on the wall and the ceilings and the walls were made of metal. Ezra recognized DropShip walls when he saw them. He made a fist, grimacing at the pain shooting up his arm, then opened it and gripped the steel bar near his hand. It was vibrating.

"Where are we going?" he asked, or tried to. It came out like "W'ging?"

"The jump point and out of here," a familiar voice said. Sergeant Major Halleck leaned in close, until Ezra's eyes focused on him.

"It's been most of a week," the woman said. Ezra twisted his head and looked at her. Then he blinked. It was Nathalie Ortiz.

"How're you here?" he whispered. It was easier to half-mumble, half-whisper.

Nathalie frowned and looked at the third man—the man who'd told him to go slow. He wore a ship's crew uniform. Ezra knew his name, or thought he did. He was a doctor on one of the Tigers' DropShips . . . he blinked. Of course he was. He was on a DropShip, wasn't he?

"You've been under for four days," the doctor said. "You suffered significant heat flash and shock trauma when your BattleMech's reactor cut loose. Your parafoil only half-deployed due to damage, and you hit the ground hard."

"Damn hard," Halleck said.

Ezra looked at him. "Kirsten?"

"Dead," Halleck said, nodding.

Ezra exhaled. He hadn't realized he was capable of holding in any tension, but he felt it lessen nonetheless. "Mason?"

Halleck looked away. "You should get some rest, sir," he said.

"Sar'nt Maj'r?"

Halleck glanced at the doctor and Nathalie, then looked Ezra in the eye. "He's still alive."

Ezra licked his lips. He already felt weak, like he'd been fighting for a day and a night straight. "Capt'rd?"

Halleck shook his head.

"But—" Ezra looked around at the DropShip walls, then at Halleck. He raised his eyebrows in question. That hurt, too.

"We left him on Hall," Halleck said. He frowned. "Him and the others."

"Others?"

"Later, Ezra," Nathalie said. She reached out and patted his shoulder through the blanket. He looked at her, then back at the sergeant major, then back.

"How are you here?" he asked again.

"I came across in a shuttle," she said. "From my DropShip."

"She's been here every day," the doctor said. "Until I run her out."

"But . . . how?" Ezra asked. He wanted to put some force into it, to project it as the colonel had always taught him—the colonel.

The old fresh pain came back, deep in his chest. Old gods and new, he'd forgotten about the colonel . . .

"Rest," Nathalie said again.

"*How?*" he demanded.

"We lost," she said flatly. Her eyes flared as she said it, as if she hadn't expected to. But, the gaffe committed, she plowed on. "We boosted after Baranov died, under fire from the Oriente Hussars. It's over—Hall is part of the Free Worlds League."

Ezra tried to concentrate, but it didn't make sense. He recognized the doctor. "This is a Dismal D ship?"

Nathalie shook her head. "This is *Tigris*," she told him.

"What?" *Tigris* was a Stealthy Tiger DropShip, the usual transport of Panther Battalion. *Tigris* was where Colonel Rauschenbusch had flown his flag when embarked between contracts. "But—"

"Rest," she said again.

"That's good advice," the doctor said. "I think this has been enough."

"But the regiment . . ."

Halleck stood up. His face was cut with anguish, but Ezra saw him fighting with himself. He'd seen that look any number of times, while the old NCO fought with himself to say something he thought he shouldn't.

"The regiment is gone," Halleck said. Then a rush of words. "Markoja hit us just after you killed his sister, and most of the regiment—" He swallowed. "Most of the regiment backed him. We got away, me and your Jaguars, and the few Raiders who'd survived. We went back to Bravo. It was burning—the tech staff had chosen sides, too. We put you on *Tigris* and lifted. We met the Dismal Ds in orbit."

Ezra stared at him. His mouth opened and closed, but it was too much. He was cold and hot. His fingers tingled and felt numb. He wanted to thrash his legs, but he couldn't make them move.

"There's still a group on Hall calling itself the Stealthy Tigers," Halleck said, his face working. His eyes were wet. "But it's not our regiment. It's not the regiment we spent a lifetime building. It's something else. Something worse."

Ezra struggled to breathe. It had to be a lie.

It had to be.

He hadn't fought to lose. He hadn't husbanded his knowledge, protected the regiment's reputation, kept it out of the fighting for so long, to lose it. He hadn't spent a decade of his life with

Yuri Rauschenbusch, building the Tigers into something he could be proud of, just to lose it all.

"We'll come back tomorrow," Nathalie said. She stood also. Ezra tried to stop her, to reach out for her, but his arm wouldn't rise. He raged at it, but it refused. Gray appeared at the edges of his vision, and he felt like he was falling.

He fell, no matter how hard he fought, until the darkness overcame him.

"Elly Burton is dead," Jacob Brim said. "I don't know if anyone told you."

Ezra turn his head to look at him. Then he looked back at the hulking 'Mech in front of him. The *BattleMaster* had been the colonel's. It was nestled in its transport cradle. Its red and brown desert camouflage was immaculate; as it should be. The 'Mech hadn't fired a single shot in anger on Hall.

"With Baranov," Ezra said. "Nathalie told me." He shifted his weight, leaning on the cane less. Doctor Howe had let him out of sickbay only on the condition that he take the cane. Weakness, the doctor had told him, would sneak up on him when he wasn't paying attention.

Ezra thought there was a lot of that going around.

Tigris felt empty, and not just because most of Panther Battalion had stayed behind with Mason Markoja. There were fewer than twenty MechWarriors aboard, and twice as many technicians, electricians, and dependents. The ship's crew felt solid, and Captain Ames had come to sickbay to tell Ezra that he, Ames, considered Ezra to be the rightful successor to Yuri Rauschenbusch.

"You were like a son to him," Ames had told him. "I know what he had planned for you." He'd shaken Ezra's hand and slipped out of the compartment without another word.

"You want to sit down?" Brim asked.

"No," Ezra told him. "I need to get my strength back." He turned his back on the *BattleMaster*. "Tell me about Estwicke and the Word." He took a halting step, placed the cane, and took another step. One after the other. It was a good plan.

"We got her," Brim said. His voice was tight. "Right there at the end. I found enough in her warehouses and her files at the safe house to pin the whole thing on her." He laughed bitterly. "It might be the only thing that saves us on this one."

"What do you mean?"

"I mean we lost," Brim said. "The Hussars kicked our asses off-world, and Mason's people . . ." Brim had been very careful never to say "your people" or "your regiment," since he'd come to see Ezra. It was a small thing, but Ezra appreciated it. He was still coming to grips with it.

It felt wrong, but Halleck and the others had made the right decision. Ezra had done little else but study the recording of what had happened after he had ejected. Mason Markoja and his battalion had arrived almost immediately. Finding his sister dead, he hadn't even considered anything else—he'd just ordered his forces to attack. It had been all Halleck and the others could do to scoop up his ejection seat and run for it, and even that had cost them.

Aurel Hicks had given her life to slow the Tigers enough for the rest of them to escape.

Ezra took his Raider pin out of his pocket and held it, rubbing it between his forefinger and his thumb. He'd realized earlier that morning that he was thinking of them that way: that those that had stayed were still the Stealthy Tigers, and those that had come away with him were something else. They weren't Raiders—there was only six of those left—and they weren't Tigers or Jaguars. He didn't know what they were.

It had sickened him, when he'd realized that. He would have thrown up, had there been anything but bile in his stomach. Now, looking at the pin in his hand, he wondered if he'd helped cause the destruction the Markojas had wrought.

The Raiders had been the best of the Stealthy Tigers, but they were an exclusive group. He wondered if their very existence had made it easier for Markoja to turn the regiment against them. The Raiders were the best.

And now most of them were dead.

"Marik-Johns will go back to Outreach and tell the commander that we found evidence of the Word's complicity." Brim shrugged. "The evidence is good, but I don't know what we can do with it."

"What do you think will happen?" Ezra asked. He wasn't ready to think about it himself.

"I don't know," Brim allowed. "Technically, we could be coming back. Our charter is to fight the Blakists where they interfere with the sovereignty of independent worlds, and Hall's was pretty well interfered with. The Wolf might decide to gather the regiments and push the Free Worlds League back off Hall until its people can decide in honest elections."

"You really think so?"

"No," Brim said. "I don't. I think we lost this one, and it'll go in the loss column and we'll move on. There's no upside to declaring war on the Free Worlds League." He grinned and raised his arm to slap Ezra on the shoulder, but thought better of it. "I think we'll rebuild, repair, and move on to the next contract."

"Yeah," Ezra said. "The next contract."

Brim looked at him. "You could come with us, you know," he said quietly. He stopped and turned back toward the *BattleMaster*. "It's not just me and Nathalie saying that. The colonel—" he meant John Marik-Johns, "—would take you in a heartbeat. He's seen the tapes."

Ezra licked his lips. Brim meant the tapes of him killing Kirsten Markoja. He hadn't done it for the Allied Mercenary Command or for the Dismal Ds. He'd done it for Yuri Rauschenbusch, and for the regiment. And because it was the right thing to do.

But now he was dead, and the regiment was gone. He looked at the colonel's *BattleMaster*.

Everything left that he cared about—the people, the *ideas*— was on this DropShip.

"To do what?" Ezra asked.

"Join us," Brim said. "The AMC. Hell, the Dismal Ds, if you want. I can probably get you a billet in the Dragoons if that's what you want. Help us keep what happened on Hall from happening again."

Ezra looked at the *BattleMaster*. He heard what Brim was asking. He heard the ideology behind it. It was a *mission*. It was a *calling*. It was a lot more than a contract. Rauschenbusch had always taught him the contract came first. That honoring the contract was a calling in itself.

"Sixty-eight," he whispered. He hadn't made it to 3068. None of them had.

And their contract—their sacred, inviolable agreement—was broken. One of its signatories was dead, his government subsumed into the bureaucracy of the Free Worlds League. The other was shattered; it still existed in name, but the people filling its roster weren't at all the equal of those that had come before them.

He sniffed against thickened sinuses as his eyes wetted.

"Your people are looking to you," Brim said. Ezra looked at him. The Dragoon nodded and spread his hands. "You're the only officer to come off Hall."

Brim was right. None of the other Raider officers had survived; Roth had been cut down during one of the opening skirmishes with the Dismal Ds. Kirsten Markoja had killed Charles Monet, and her brother had seen to every Raider, officer or enlisted, in Panther Battalion. There was only Ezra and Robert Halleck to provide leadership to the mix of Raiders and Jaguar Company MechWarriors who'd come off-world with them. He owed them something—if they still wanted to follow him.

He surprised himself with the realization that he still wanted to lead.

He looked at the *BattleMaster* again, and almost smiled. *You taught me well,* he thought.

Ezra turned away from the 'Mech and back toward Brim, but before he could open his mouth, a hatch slid open a few meters behind them. Nathalie Ortiz stepped out quickly, already turning toward the *BattleMaster*. She saw them out of the corner of her eye and switched directions quickly.

"What is it?" Ezra asked, when he saw her expression.

"You have your comm off," she scolded him.

"It's back in my room. What is it?"

Nathalie frowned at him and then looked at Brim. "Jake—your comm?"

Brim fished the small device out of his pocket and looked at it. "It doesn't work in here," he told her. "It's not on *Tigris'* systems."

Nathalie shook her head. "It doesn't matter. We just got a signal from Hall—relayed from Hall, I mean. It's a Dragoons code." She handed Brim a noteputer. "It needs your authorization, but the AMC keys indicate highest priority."

Frowning, Brim took the noteputer and manipulated the screen. He entered a code, then another one. He grunted, then held the noteputer close to his face so it could read his retinal scan. Blinking, he lowered it and looked at Ezra and Nathalie.

"It's a delta call," he told them. At their blank stares, he grimaced. "Highest priority, okay?"

"Ah," Ezra said. "What's it say?"

Brim looked down and his eyes skimmed the newly-revealed text. He frowned. Then he blinked. Then he looked up.

"Jake?" Ezra asked. All the blood had drained from Brim's face.

He looked dazed. Ezra didn't know what the message read, but it was bad. "Jake?"

"It's Condition Feral," Brim said. His voice was listless.

"Feral?" Nathalie asked. "Jake, what is it? What's happened?"

Brim handed her the noteputer. He took a step back, half-turning, and tripped and fell. Ezra stared at him for a half-second, then lurched forward, cane forgotten. "Jake!"

Brim was sitting on the deck, staring. "He's dead," he said, as if tasting the words. "He's dead?"

"Who's dead?"

"Oh, Christ and his saints," Nathalie said in a small voice.

Ezra twisted to look at her. "Who?"

"Jaime Wolf. He's dead."

Ezra looked back at Brim. He reached out, but stopped, afraid. "Jake . . ." He closed his mouth. He knew what Brim was feeling. He knew what it was like to lose the man you looked up to most in the world.

Jaime Wolf had commanded Wolf's Dragoons since they appeared in the Inner Sphere more than sixty years earlier. He was recognized, even by his enemies, as one of the finest—if not *the* finest—military commander alive. His Dragoons hadn't always won, but they had been the *créme de la créme* of the mercenary market for more than half a century. He was an icon in the mercenary community.

And now he was gone.

"There was an attack," Nathalie said, still reading. "In Harlech, on Outreach." She slid down to her knees next to Ezra. "Mercenaries attacked the Dragoons. Most of the city is in ruins. And Jaime Wolf is dead."

Ezra looked from Brim to Nathalie. "Condition Feral?"

"It's a code," Brim said, as if he were reading from a script. "It means Harlech is now a closed zone. No one—maybe the AMC, maybe—is welcome in the city except Dragoons. It's never been called before."

"Who did it," Ezra asked Nathalie. She looked back down, then hissed.

"According to the Dragoons, the Word was behind the hirings."

Ezra sat down. He had been kneeling, but this was too much. First the Tigers, and now the Dragoons. The Word of Blake had tired, apparently, of being at war with the Allied Mercenary Command. It had decided to deal with the threat at the source, in the most ancient way possible.

Cut off the head, and the snake dies. It had been an aphorism for as long as there had been words.

He swallowed bile. Over Brim's shoulder, the hulking shape of the colonel's *BattleMaster* caught his eye.

"I wasn't there," Brim said. "I—" he stopped speaking, and frowned. Ezra looked at him. He was clearly in shock. "I—"

Ezra gathered his feet under him. "Come on," he said, offering Nathalie his hand. Once she was on her feet, both of them reached down and pulled Brim upright. Then they started for the hatch.

"Where are we going?" Nathalie asked as Ezra keyed the hatch open.

"The bridge," he told her. "We're going to Outreach."

Behind him, the cane lay on the deck where it had fallen.

ABOUT THE AUTHOR

Jason Schmetzer is an award-winning author and editor who has written more than 50 short stories and novellas. His work has appeared in more than 25 products across many properties, both online and offline. *Embers of War* is his first published *BattleTech* novel. When not writing in other peoples' worlds, he is one of the founders of the publisher Warning Label LLC, and works in self-publishing as an online marketing professional.

SHADOWS OF FAITH

BY LOREN L. COLEMAN • COMING SOON!

A CONSPIRACY OF DARKNESS

Despite internal power struggles, the techno-disciples of the Word of Blake continue their relentless march to bring the worlds surrounding Terra under their control. Each planet that falls under their influence brings them one step closer to full dominion over the birthplace of the Inner Sphere.

Meanwhile, during the uneasy peace after the Second Civil War, Victor Davion and his allies struggle to bring another Star League conference together to confirm the next League. But with two Great Houses rebuilding after the fight, and a third nowhere to be found, his fears that the summit may fall apart seem to be coming true. This alarms the Word of Blake representatives, who attempt to force the remaining leaders back to the table—and allow them to keep working in secret—by any means necessary.

And on Outreach, Wolf's Dragoons, reeling from the loss of their founder, launch a blood-soaked mission of vengeance against the Blakists. But as they scream toward Mars to deliver retribution against those responsible for their leader's death, the secretive and enigmatic "Master" of the Word of Blake executes the next phase of his own plan to bring the Inner Sphere under his control—culminating in a devastating strike at its very heart...

PROLOGUE

WORLD CATHEDRAL
HILTON HEAD, TERRA
12 SEPTEMBER 3067

"Something must be done!"

Cameron St. Jamais smiled, hearing the strong voice of Alexander Kernoff rise above the din of the various arguments. He hid his grin behind a hand, smoothing down his thin, dark goatee as Kernoff's powerful command swept through the dimly-lit Spire, reverberating in power not wholly natural. Its sheer volume shook the five crystalline podiums rising from a translucent floor, but an undercurrent of angelic harpsichord and some time-delay echo gave Kernoff's voice its real strength of conviction and god-like authority.

Precentor ROM had broken the safeguards restricting use of behavior modification synthesizers within the Spire. Again. Or he'd subverted the latest True Believer tasked with maintaining those encryption algorithms.

Either way, Cameron counted it another victory for the Toyama. Someone, after all, must bring order. Especially as this latest gathering of the Ruling Conclave had gone the way of so many before it. A tug-of-war between Word of Blake's two strongest factions. Power brokering. Agendas to promote. Plans laid against the future. And, always, a wealth of resources to divide.

Hilton Head Island was no stranger to such activity, of course, having been so long under the aegis of ComStar. And here as well was where Word of Blake chose to return their own seat of power, constructing their World Cathedral over the ruins that once housed the First Circuit. A grand edifice, unlike anything conceived or built by Terra's former tenants, the cathedral was a perfect wedding of state and church, historical tribute and technological advancement. Brilliant, white marble façade set over strengthened ferrocrete and coated with a laser-refracting glaze. Wide, columned portico, its thick pillars cored with electronic countermeasures. And a functional space-defense system—capital class lasers and particle cannons—hidden within several tall spires along the roof.

Inside, such devotion to "militant aestheticism" was just as complete. Walls of the nave and chancel were paneled with holographic plates, able to create the illusion of a woodland setting, a star-lit spacescape, or battle-scarred plains (among many other choices) at a command from any one of the Conclave leaders. An eight-bay transept, each station fully shielded and capable of assuming full local control over Terra's hyperpulse generators and—with careful coordination—the HPGs of several neighboring star systems as well, was also housed within the building.

And atop the Genius Loci Tower, the presiding spirit of the cathedral, was the main Spire, where only a member of the Ruling Conclave could be admitted.

A domed observatory with full holographic control of its environment, currently the five senior precentors manned their individual stations beneath a nighttime sky filled with bright, bright stars. Arranged equally around the circular arena, each crystalline podium was alive with a soft, golden glow radiating from deep within. And as the three men and two woman traded glances with each other following Kernoff's excited (and excitable) outburst, a backwash of light splashed up against expressions of annoyance, concern, and not a little anger.

The bickering faded. Though more, Cameron suspected as the others quickly adjusted their own filters, to prevent Precentor ROM from wielding undue influence.

As he himself did, sliding his fingers across the holographic controls displayed above his podium's glowing, faceted surface. The dim light played little against his dark skin, and the gold striations radiating at the heart of his podium—"god stars," Precentor Willis had once called them—dimmed even further beneath a strong, blood red tint. A not-so-subtle hint at the processing power being used by the Precentor Martial. More than any others among the Conclave.

"Something is being done, Alex," Precentor William Blane finally answered Kernoff's demand. "The Allied Mercenary Command is being slowly marginalized."

Precentor Blane stood to Cameron's left. Leader of the True Believers faction and a friend of Captain-General Marik, Blane was often the public face of Word of Blake. As usual, he leaned lightest on his podium's resources. His "heart" was pure and golden. The backwash of light turned his white, brocaded robes a soft, buttery gold. His eyes looked like sunken pits, however, and his face was drawn and haggard.

Too many days spent fasting? Or too little sleep?

Blane passed a shaky hand over his podium, activating a pre-set program. Overhead, the holographic representation of a Milky Way spacescape faded to black, replaced by a much more basic map of the Inner Sphere. The five Great Houses. The minor powers, including what was left of Rasalhague. The Clan holdings. Thousands of star systems representing billions upon billions of lives, all paying homage to their petty, nationalistic governments.

Two systems in that backdrop glowed unnaturally bright. Terra. Birthplace of humanity and seat of power for Word of Blake.

And Tharkad.

"It is a time to tread cautiously," Blane said. "The third transfer of power is upon us. In just over two months, the Star League convenes its fourth triennial conference. The first order of business will be a motion to elevate Word of Blake from probationary status within the new Star League to active membership with full voting rights." He looked about. "We do not want to tip our hand ahead of time."

"Nothing is more important," said Precentor Laura Chang on Cameron's right. A tall, slender woman with military bearing, towering above her podium, and another True Believer, if only by default. One of the few Expatriate leaders to survive the last two years of purges, she kept a strong core of her followers under Blane's guidance to help balance out power within Word of Blake.

"Of course you would agree with Precentor Blane." Dampening fields dropped Kernoff's voice to an acceptable level, though a slight, off-focus timber had Cameron wondering if Word of Blake's spymaster had still slipped behavior modification undercurrents into his tone. "It took Victor Davion's ascension as ComStar's Precentor Martial to open your eyes to the light."

Chang leaned away from St. Jamais, toward Kernoff on her other side. "My eyes have remained always open, Precentor ROM."

Still, Cameron did not miss the shadow that drifted across her face. Similar to the one that darkened the "god star" shining in the heart of his podium. Again, Cameron stroked the thin goatee shading his chin.

What was Chang hiding?

Not her aversion to Alexander Kernoff or the Toyama faction, that much was certain.

Cameron pushed his hood back, laying it down across his shoulders, then returned his hands aside the podium to grip the cool, faceted edges. "Precentors," he said. "We've no time to quarrel."

He let a soft touch to his voice carry where shouting might have been ignored. As the man who commanded Word of Blake's military arm, he had no need to run roughshod over the Conclave. No one could afford him as their enemy. There were still whispers about Willima Willis. "God stars," indeed.

"If Precentor Blane has new concerns about the Star League summit," he said, "I would like to hear them. Perhaps the ComStar audit has been more successful than he let on?"

An attack, but a subtle one. And not without merit, his concern. The resurrection of the Star League in 3058 was, by one way of thinking, mankind's first enlightened step in more than three centuries. Three hundred years of deprivation and depredation—as the Blessed Founder, Jerome Blake, had forewarned. Now, possibly, humanity was on the verge of recovery. At the last conference, Blane working closely with the Free Worlds League's Captain-General, the Word of Blake had been admitted to the august body as a probationary member. But there had been . . . concerns. Mainly that the Free Worlds League enjoyed undue influence over Word of Blake due to their close political and economic ties. ComStar had been charged with the investigation.

If the light flickering so uncertainly on Tharkad—host to this year's conference—was indeed Blake's promised beacon, it would not do to be caught unawares.

Especially by the heretics.

"No." Blane waved a thin hand. "Nothing so terrible. ComStar's lack of faith makes it easier to blind them to the truth. They could never believe a pack of 'zealots and misguided faithful' could possibly hide anything from their 'all-seeing' eyes."

Which summed up the difference between Word of Blake and their false brothers quite well. Both believed in the safeguarding of technology, though it was a divine charge for the Blakists. And both organizations still oversaw portions of the vast interstellar communications network that tied the systems and worlds of the Inner Sphere together. But just as ComStar's secular changes under the Mori Heresy, led by the devil Anastasius Focht, had caused an irreparable schism, they'd also wrapped the heretics in self-righteous agnosticism and logic.

They'd forgotten the strength of true faith.

They'd forgotten how to keep the real secrets.

"A copy of ComStar's audit has been forwarded to your personal attention," Blane promised. "They found no more than point-eight percent discrepancy against our original declarations."

"We could have done better."

This last came from Precentor Anuska Brezhnic, the fifth of the Ruling Conclave precentors. She sat on the far side of Blane in her powered chair, shattered legs bumped up against her shortened podium. Once a part of the Counter-Reformists, smallest of the ruling factions within Word of Blake, she now led them in place of the late Willima Willis as a splinter-group of the Toyama; in the same way Cameron St. Jamais led the revolutionary 6th of June and Alexander Kernoff the growing One Voice movement. She rarely spoke unless asked a question, and even more rarely voted, preferring to abstain. It was how the Toyama and True Believers kept the peace now that they had split the Conclave between themselves.

"I say we could have done better!" When she did voice an opinion, Anuska Brezhnic would not be gainsaid or ignored.

"We could have," Blane finally said. "But anything less would have looked suspicious in the absence of corruption. Even one full percent in graft, kickbacks, and payoffs would be considered light by way of the Successor Houses."

She pounded a fist against the arm of her powered chair. "We are *not* a Successor House!" Cameron nearly smiled again, thanking her for the continued attention leveraged at Blane, but did not.

"We are Blake's shepherds," she continued. "Though we may not always know his will, we continue his work."

"We all continue the Blessed Blake's work," Kernoff said, careful not to patronize her, "in whatever way we must." A pause. His bright blue eyes found each precentor in turn. "And I still argue that we must not let a pack of filthy mercenaries challenge our divine cause."

Back to Wolf's Dragoons and their Allied Mercenary Command.

It put Cameron in a difficult position, with Kernoff leading the Toyama these days, and the fact that he shared the other man's frustrations with the meddling mercs. In the last year, especially, the Dragoons and their allies had thwarted military and political operations on Hall and Helios, and made difficult further undertakings on another half-dozen worlds surrounding Terra. Undertakings aimed at the establishment of a new Terran Hegemony.

But by making it an issue among the Conclave, Kernoff opened the door to an internal investigation of the Precentor Martial's methods. His effectiveness. Precentor Blane had opened too many such doors himself in the last few years; it didn't do to give him a standing invitation.

"Outreach," Cameron said, naming the Dragoons' world. Turning it into a sneer of distaste.

A few quick-keyed commands made the system glow brighter on the overhead star map as well, flashing a dangerous, glaring red. Only two jumps from Terra. The world responsible for more than sixty percent of all mercenary hiring within the Inner Sphere. Seat of the Mercenary Review and Bonding Commission.

"Our on-planet agents make a convincing case for a preemptive move." Were incredibly strident on the subject, in fact. "Perhaps it is time to . . . review . . . our failsafe position." Said in such a manner to promote action, not more administration.

And as he'd suspected, Blane wanted no motion brought forward to actually *do* anything. Not so close to the third transfer of power. Not when everything they'd waited for all seemed ready to land in the lap of Word of Blake.

"We can entertain that at our next meeting," Blane said. "Perhaps. Any application of hidden assets, do not forget, will set off a flag against ComStar's completed audit."

Stressing once more the value of the fast-approaching Star League summit.

Oh yes, Blane had his own agenda to promote. Or, more to the point perhaps, he had Captain-General Marik's agenda to promote.

The ruler of the Free Worlds League would likely be the next First Lord of the Inner Sphere. He and Precentor Blane relied much on each other, and no doubt Blane saw their alliance giving him power to break the Conclave and assert himself—finally—as Primus. Formal director over Word of Blake.

Was that blood Cameron smelled? A vulnerability?

"A wise decision." He folded arms across his chest. His dark, voluminous robes draped easily along his lean frame. "I should, naturally, undertake a personal review of all contingency plans before making any recommendation. And any course of action would be precipitous, considering our lack of strong intelligence concerning the Dragoons' movements."

He would seem to be capitulating to Blane, and scoring fresh blood against the leader of his own faction at the same time. But if the True Believers' leader saw it coming, he had the sudden steel to not let it show on his face.

"Of course, I would then submit that Precentor ROM be given access to further resources in order to investigate any possibility of threat from a mercenary action."

Kernoff did not bother to hide his smile. Even went so far as to nod his encouragement to St. Jamais. "Did not Blake once say, 'information is ammunition?'"

Blane hesitated, then nodded. "And whose resources do you propose we gift Precentor ROM?" he asked with a shrug, as if the question hardly concerned him. No doubt girding up for a battle over shared resources between True Believers and Toyama.

Blood. Oh, yes. Salty and warm. "We still have unallocated forces and material resources stemming from last week's decision to pull our support from Sian. Sun-Tzu's decision will not to be without repercussions, after all."

There were several thin smiles. Even from Chang, though likely everyone in the room knew very well that Blane had already marked those "freed and unallocated" resources for his continuing efforts within the Free Worlds League. Not that he could admit to it, however.

"It is a simple shift to task those resources to support our efforts in the Chaos March and against Outreach," Kernoff said, assuming there would be no objections.

There would not be. Precentor Blane was cagey enough to poll the room on his own, see that there were three obvious votes in favor, and even Chang would have trouble arguing against the allocation. Cameron watched the argument play out over Blane's face. Saw him nod. "Very well. Shall we meet again to discuss what these resources have purchased us? In . . . one week?"

"I shall need at least three to begin new operations."

"We seem to have settled on two."

Two weeks. The outside limit before Cameron and Blane had to leave for Tharkad. For the summit. As it was, they would rely on a partial command circuit of JumpShips, relaying from one star system to the next, before splitting up to join their WarShip escorts already en route.

Which meant any oversight of Kernoff's actions would be slight, at best.

It worked nicely.

"Blessed be those who walk along Blake's shining path," Blane said, offering a quick prayer for the end of the council, and their continuing efforts to prepare. "May they avoid the shadows of desolation, and be ever ready for the darkness ahead."

"Blessed be," the others said. Including Cameron.

And then he was rudely disconnected from the Spire's interface.

To others in the room, physically there, he knew his body had slowly faded away before their eyes. But for him, the Spire suddenly blinked out of existence, replaced by a swimming feeling of vertigo as the neurofeedback loop which had kept him connected between Mars and Terra suffered complete degenerative failure.

Darkness. Falling. A cold, metallic taste at the back of his throat.

And then the world came crashing down on him from all sides in a riot of color and sound and labored breathing. A world turned one hundred eighty degrees from what he had believed only seconds before.

In theory, it was an elegant solution for when Cameron or Kernoff visited the Mars Research Station. Point the MRS hyperpulse generator at one of the Terran stations and create a real-time link. No appreciable time delay. Devote high bandwidth to carry a full-sensory virtual reality signal, and link his podium within the Spire to the replica built here within the simulation chamber.

In fact, the local technology was so very similar to what Cameron had once used in MechWarrior training, though advanced far beyond a simple combat simulation.

The ultimate in telecommuting.

But while his consciousness had never been truly transferred earth-side, the illusion had built up momentum. Similar to the way a man on a treadmill, running in place for any length of time, can step off the track and then suddenly reel back as his mind was torn between the idea of running without moving, and then not moving without running.

Here, his reality had been stretched for so long within the illusion, it truly felt like a rubber band snapping back into form, or nearly so.

Cameron St. Jamais sagged to his knees. Pounded a fist against his leg, using the pain to help focus his thoughts.

With care, he stripped the sim-gear away: a cloth cap wired with electrodes that fit snugly over his head, and the wired gloves. Then he laughed, dry and brittle, and slowly hauled himself back up the podium.

Gone was the darkened arena of the Spire. The simulation chamber had reverted back to displaying the MRS lab, relying on the same image-transference technology used in the mimetic armor of a Purifier battlesuit. Not quite perfect. A watery distortion blurred his surroundings.

He ignored this and checked the logs still displayed on the podium's holographic screen, confirming his suspicions.

Then he cracked the seal on his chamber, and stepped out into the real lab, with its stainless steel fixtures and white porcelain countertops. A static charge in the air made the hair on his arms and the back of his neck immediately stand up, bristling. The ozone scent of warm electronics left an acrid taste in his mouth. Reels of fiber optic micro-cable lay strewn about the room, along the walls and spooling over the floors, connecting the large computer core resting within one workstation bay to various stations filled with diagnostic equipment.

CSDI-2103 was stenciled on the block-shaped core.

Two doors led from this room. A double-wide sliding door of brushed steel. And a much smaller personnel access hatch recessed in the back wall of the lab. Not secret, the smaller hatch, but definitely not for just anyone's use. Cameron paused near the hatch to thumb his DNA onto the small control panel. The hatch irised open, and he activated the communications circuit as well.

"Lab A-14, cleared for use," he said. The technicians could return now, and complete their latest analysis.

Then he stepped through the hatch, which whispered shut behind him.

Cameron stood in a long corridor hewn through solid rock, fused and polished until the walls gave back a dark reflection. Glowing runners along the floor and ceiling provided enough light to see by, just.

He turned left and pushed off in a gliding walk, perfectly at ease in Mars's point-three-eight gravity. His boots scuffed the floor between long, casual strides. His formal robes would have been impractical, and so had also been a construct within the virtual reality illusion. Instead, he wore a uniform jumpsuit of light gray, with a high, dark collar, and a simple cloak weighted at the hem to flow more naturally in the light gravity environment.

"There was a problem?"

The voice whispered from hidden speakers throughout the corridor. It had a scratchy sound to it, as if it had been poorly scrubbed by filters to prevent identification. Though Cameron knew such was not the case.

"Nothing but a small demonstration of ability," he said.

He directed his comment in no particular direction. The corridor—the entire research station—was wired with thousands of omnidirectional mics for sound pickup. He knew this as well.

"Precentor Blane has broken our safeguard locks on the Cathedral's priority override system." He anticipated the next question. "It would be a waste of resources to try and rebuild them. If he's willing to let us know of his progress, it is because he's sure of himself."

"Circles within circles," the bodiless voice said.

More like boxes within boxes. Blane had yet to figure out that he was hardly tunneling through security walls. No doubt the True Believer thought himself digging deeper into the mysteries of Word of Blake. Certainly he still believed himself in a position of true power.

The truth would be made clear to him, to them all, very soon now.

A four-way junction. Cameron caught himself at a handhold, looked left and right out of habit. He saw one of the trusted adepts hauling a large sled of components down the right-hand corridor. Ahead, he knew, the corridor bent around toward an underground hangar bay. He turned left again.

"And Kernoff?" asked the voice.

"Is frustrated by the Dragoons' efforts to camouflage their next move. The mercenaries are shuffling around their regiments and independent battalions. Two of them, he is certain, are registered incorrectly with the Mercenary Review and Bonding Commission. They will claim it was an oversight, and pay a small fine. But now that the Northwind Highlanders have activated escape clauses in their current contracts to head home . . . it is suggestive."

"Or it may be nothing but shadows," the whispers said, chasing him along the corridor. *"To err is not merely human, Cameron. It is often an imperative of the species. In the absence of knowledge, or faith, ignorance rears a dark and terrible head. But who errs? Is it Kernoff? Or do the mercenaries truly tempt our wrath so close to the third transfer of power? The agents of chaos and subversion, challenging Blake's light?"*

Cameron recognized the rhetorical questions. Knew the way his master often thought out loud, even in the abstract. He came to another hatch. One of several along the corridors, and no different than any of the others. Not at a glance.

But it was different. Oh, yes.

Beyond this hatch, the mysteries of the universe were often challenged, wrestled with, and thrown down. It was where Blake's shining path truly began.

He placed his thumb against the control panel, and waited while a DNA sample was checked against the security clearances, the time, and the whims of the man who was the true strength behind Word of Blake.

It irised open, and Cameron slipped into the large underground workshop. Dropped immediately to one knee. His cloak billowed behind him, as if stirred in a breeze.

He kept his head bowed, though his gaze was up and searching the shadows. There was the computer center rotunda at which he'd already logged thousands of hours, combing through rosters and force strength estimates and countless communication logs. And the holographic imaging table, capable of working with new technology simulations or battlefield displays or anything in between or in combination.

The sensory deprivation tank, now wheeled back against the nearby wall, lid standing open as if waiting for its next victim. Perhaps an Inner Sphere leader next time. Perhaps St. Jamais. Again.

The sounds of motion came far back in the dimly-lit space. Cameron had no way of knowing if the sounds came from Him, His automatons, or His protégé.

No way to detect his master's presence at all, until the shadows parted and a man shuffled forward. Not a giant of a man. Not even a great deal of physical strength in the way he moved, or stood, or occasionally shifted from side to side, as if he might change his mind at any moment to return to his all-encompassing work.

But power—true power—was rarely measured in such small-minded details. This had been the greatest lesson to learn of them all. Strength of will. Strength of thought. Strength of faith. These were what mattered. These were the blades capable of slicing clean through those knots tied into the fabric of the universe by the actions of unenlightened men.

Someone, after all, must bring order.

"We have many plans to set in motion," that same voice whispered.

And raising his head, Cameron St. Jamais smiled.

CHAPTER ONE

HARLECH
OUTREACH
18 OCTOBER 3067

"Gray One to all Dragoons. Wolf Actual—down! Wolf Actual is down!" A crackle of static. Then, "Set Condition Feral."

Wide swaths of Harlech still burned. Entire city blocks lay in flame and ruin, and dark, roiling smoke scorched the sky, blotting out the sun for the third straight day. Fires baked the air so dry it stole the moisture from a man's body the moment he cracked his cockpit hatch. As if Hell itself had come visiting.

Yet Captain Jason Williamson of the Dragoons' Home Guard felt ice spike into his gut at the transmission. A thick, frozen blade digging around inside him, then ripping its way up his spine. For an instant—one incredibly long and painful heartbeat thundering in his ears—he was back on the high, frozen plateau of Jolo Island, on the world of Elgin, listening to his comms sergeant relay another damning message. Another defeat.

Another commander lost.

A single heartbeat was all the time he had. The rogues weren't above striking while his guard was down. Caught in a crossfire between an ancient -3U *Clint* and a fresh-from-the-factory Earthwerks *Thunderbolt*, his *Gallowglas* shook desperately as the *Clint*'s particle cannon carved into one side and the *T-Bolt*'s light Gauss hammered a hard-edged blow on the right. Ruby lances and emerald darts slashed in behind, the lasers scarring and scoring deep, deep into his BattleMech's armor.

The *Gallowglas* stumbled backward, out of the intersection Jason had been holding. Thin-poured concrete on the street's sidewalks cracked and caved in beneath his feet.

It took him out from under the *T-Bolt*'s crosshairs—not a small favor—and all that prevented the seventy-ton machine from going down was the five-level parking garage he fell against. He caught one of the metal guardrails with his BattleMech's left hand, tearing the steel rail half out of its concrete foundation, twisting it into a crumpled ruin.

Leaning forward, putting his own balance to the test, Jason dug in with throttle and foot pedals to lever his *'Glas* back into the fight. Large hands wrenched at the BattleMech's control sticks. Already his finger tightened down on the main trigger.

Dragging his targeting crosshairs up and over, he found the *Clint* advancing at a run, coming right at him down the double-wide street, and centered the target crosshairs right dead-center across the other BattleMech's square-bodied torso. In a crackling, violent discharge, the PPC on the *Gallowglas*'s right arm struck with a twist of hellish, blue-white energies. It cored through all that was left of already too-thin armor. Burning. Gouging.

Then Jason thumbed the firing stud mounted on the upper ridge of his control stick and added both lasers from his right-side chest to the injury.

One sliced deep into and through the *Clint*'s right arm, dropping a severed hand to the ground.

His second laser punched a bright-red lance into the gaping wound already burned through the 'Mech's chest. Through the *Clint*'s gyroscopic stabilizer. And right out the back.

Forty tons of upright, walking war machine relied on many critical systems, not the least of which was a highly-skilled, highly-trained pilot. But a MechWarrior was more than a simple throttle jockey. Through the heavy neurohelmet all MechWarriors wore, his sense of balance—his "inner ear"—was translated into a regenerative feedback signal which worked with the gyros, fed it information, and strained against gravity.

Jason had just cut that particular cord.

The *Clint* staggered and sprawled out across the street, grinding sparks beneath it as it slid across the intersection. It ground to a halt not ten meters in front of Jason's *Gallowglas*. Struggled to right itself.

Sweat burned in Jason's blue eyes, and his breathing came in careful, shallow gasps as the waste heat from the 'Mech's fusion reactor bled up through the cockpit deck. His temperature gauges, never good to begin with as he fought his way through the burning city, spiked hard through the yellow and edged into the red.

Condition Feral.

Elgin.

Jason chopped back on his throttle, and sidestepped his machine toward the *Clint*'s head. He brought one large foot up, and then crashed it down once . . . twice against the side of the angular "face."

After the second stomp, there wasn't much left but a tangle of metal and ferroglass and (somewhere inside) mangled flesh.

"On your right, Captain!"

The warning very nearly came too late. As it was, it barely gave Jason a second to think before the warning screams of a missile lock pierced through the cockpit's tight confines. But a lot could be done in a second.

Enough time for a glance at his heads up display, to see the golden icon of friendly forces moving up behind and that bright, burning red of an enemy target as the *Thunderbolt* cleared the corner and took the intersection.

More than enough to shove down hard against his foot pedals, cutting in his jump jets.

The thrusters lifted his *Gallowglas* on fiery jets of plasma, rocketing up, up over the street as the *T-Bolt*'s missiles slammed into the ferrocrete and blew a few extra holes in the *Clint*'s hapless corpse. The light Gauss slammed out another of its nickel-ferrous slugs, taking down a street lamp and bowling over a parked car.

Committed, there wasn't much the *Thunderbolt* could do except throttle back and try to make Jason's jump a hard reach. But too late. City fighting favored close-in scraps and brawling tactics, and the rogue mercenary had been too eager for the kill.

Leaning to one side, working his own sense of balance against the already-overtaxed gyros, Jason turned the *'Glas* though an almost-graceful jumping spin. Timing the short "flight," he feathered back on his thrusters to dip low, as if ready to crush the *T-Bolt* beneath two shovel-bladed feet in much the same attack he'd executed against the *Clint*. One last goose on the jets, though, and he cleared the wide-shouldered BattleMech with a half-dozen meters to spare—and then cut the burn completely to drop in a bone-jarring crouch just behind the sixty-five ton enemy machine.

Speared his targeting reticle dead-on over the *T-Bolt*'s wide back.

Wolf Actual is down!

Saw the crosshairs burn a deep gold.

Set Condition Feral.

Tied every weapon into his master circuit with a quick toggle and a yell of blinding rage. Yanked on the trigger. Again. And again. *Elgin.*

And again.

His particle cannon worked the most devastating damage against the stricken *Thunderbolt*, flailing at the other 'Mech with a scourge of manmade lightning. Deep, raw-edged rents carved down the back of the machine's powerful outline. Shards and splatters of molten composite rained down over the street's black ferrocrete.

He had little but a guess that his first PPC blast might have cut into some of the struts that helped support the *Thunderbolt*'s massive gyro. He knew that his first combination of scarlet lances and flurry of emerald darts cooked away at least a ton to a ton and a half of armor spread across the back and legs of the *T-Bolt*.

The impact. The armor loss. Before Jason's second furious salvo, the machine staggered forward, dropping to its knees, then sprawled full length to pile up against the dead *Clint*.

His second blistering assault carved away more armor, and chewed in behind a knee to ruin the joint. Power spikes put a strain on the reactor, and his temperature gauge pushed heavy into the red. Jason slapped at the shutdown override.

His third salvo (maybe) was the one that put a laser beam into the back of the *T-Bolt*'s head. His fourth certainly found the ammunition bin housed in the struggling 'Mech's right side. It erupted in a tall gout of fire and smoke and debris, blowing out through special blast-directed chambers to preserve the BattleMech and the Mech-Warrior's life. Whatever was left of either.

Not a great deal. From further down the street, an assault-class *Annihilator* stalked forward, leading a short column of armored vehicles and tanks, including a pair of Badger tracked transport vehicles.

As Jason beat against his overrides, preventing a heat-induced shutdown, the *Annihilator* raised one double-barreled arm and blasted what was left of the *Thunderbolt*'s head clean away.

An abrupt lull after several frantic moments. Jason stared down at the two dead machines, at mostly his own handiwork, and found he did not have a great deal of pity left to spend on these rogue mercenaries. Not after three days of slaughter and setbacks and non-stop battle. He barely remembered the three hours of sleep he'd been forced to take before getting back in the cockpit again. Nor would he accept another forced rest period. He might be a battlefield orphan, adopted by Wolf's Dragoons after his abandonment in the Chaos March, but Outreach was his home as much as he had one.

And that home was in danger.

It no longer mattered to him who the attackers were, even. He knew the Fifty-first Dark Panzers were in on it. Some said Smithson's Chinese Bandits as well. Everyone talked about Colonel Waco: his *BattleMaster* had been caught on battle ROM footage leading the charge from TempTown. And many suspected Word of Blake. Especially after one of their Bloody Hand creations had been hauled out of the rubble at the power generator station.

But these two? The *Clint* and the *Thunderbolt*? They were simply his enemies. Same as the ones who had detonated fuel-air explosives in the Home Guard barracks three days before. Same as those who led the first assault, or the second, or the third. All the same.

Jason was past putting a name to the machines. No member of Wolf's Dragoons had that luxury today. Not now.

Not anymore.

He stepped back from the wreckage, panting heavily as he sucked at the scorched air in his cockpit. Every breath pulled white-hot coals down into his lungs. Sweat burned with a salty taste on his upper lip. Stung his eyes.

Blinking to clear his vision, he surveyed the approaching forces. The information on his HUD tagged them as Home Guard, as did the insignia on the *Annihilator* and both Badgers. But the way the 'Mech had moved, and continued to move, said something else entirely. As did the casual skill with which the other MechWarrior had decapitated the *T-Bolt*. Targeting systems could line up such a shot. But it took a natural touch to handle a one-hundred-ton monster that way.

Then one of the Badgers rolled up ahead of the *Annihilator*, and Jason saw that some soldier had slashed red paint across the nose in a blood red "Z." And he knew.

Zeta Battalion! In whatever machines they could salvage or scrounge, nothing kept them from the battle.

"We're stuck near Gateway Bridge and the spaceport is still a loss," said a female voice. The same one that had warned him earlier. "But we've got a thin line held against the rogues boiling up out of TempTown. Go, Captain! We have your back."

No matter the hand on the stick, an *Annihilator* was never going to set any records at a top speed of thirty-odd kilometers per hour.

Jason's *Gallowglas* might double that, though not at the moment as gray smoke seeped from every joint, and the heat-stricken 'Mech could barely turn in place without its actuators locking up.

The lead Badger rolled to a stop and deployed a light star of Elemental infantry. The *Annihilator* never slowed. And the MechWarrior inside, whatever her rank, was not one to let a heartbeat be wasted.

"It might be a mistake!" she warned. Jason heard the plea in her voice, even over the static of transmission and however much she might prefer to hide it. Or not. Her *please great father, let this be a mistake.* "Get to Wolf! Go go go!"

His first step was shaky, with the *Gallowglas*'s heat-addled control circuitry having trouble. He swallowed dryly. Painful. His vision swam again for a moment. If not for his cooling vest working to keep his body's core temperature down, he would likely have passed out somewhere between his third and fourth salvo, no doubt.

But he hadn't, and his commander might need him. The Dragoons certainly needed him somewhere. Citizens in Harlech—those who were left alive—needed them all.

His second step was stronger, and came with greater speed. He slammed his throttle against the forward stop, watching his indicators climb past twenty kilometers per hour. Then thirty, and forty.

Breathing became easier as he pushed up again near his maximum speed of sixty-five kph. By the end of the next block he had blinked his vision clear. Another block, he saw the sweat already starting to dry into a white scale on his forearms.

Another block. Then another. Always heading toward the city's center.

Heading there, and not wanting to look.

At least Jason had company. A lance of Kestrel attack VTOLs that had taken up station above and to his left. Then a pair of struggling Partisans. A lone *War Dog* limped along, Beta Regiment's insignia still visible on the left shoulder. The wolf's head crest of the Dragoons had been burned away. Along with most of its armor.

A *Vulture*. A *Highlander IIC*.

Only two rogues made the mistake of crossing paths with the scattered Dragoons. A *Phoenix Hawk* and a *Caesar*, both bursting out of concealment from a large commercial office building.

They shouldered their way through a wall of steel girders and concrete to challenge the *Vulture*. It was the last mistake of their lives as six Dragoon BattleMechs, as many tanks and the four attack VTOLs fell on them like a starving pack. Lasers slashed and stabbed, and cannon fire thundered across the cityscape in a new storm of destruction.

There was no call for mercy.

No thought of giving quarter.

Condition Feral was a code all Dragoons knew, though no one had ever thought to hear it. Certainly not in the heart of the Dragoon home. Even Jason, an adopted orphan, was well drilled in its execution.

To meet all resistance with overwhelming and deadly force.

To treat as the enemy any military force not showing Dragoon codes or colors. Even "friendly" units from within the Allied Mercenary Command were to be given one warning, and one only, to stand down. Or they would be put down with extreme prejudice. Hard lessons learned on New Delos, on Hephaestus.

Simply put: if it moved, and could even remotely be a threat, it died.

The *'Hawk* and the *Caesar* died. The Dragoons rolled over them as if they were little more than an annoyance as all able machines streamed in toward city center. Converging on the great hole in the skyline where six (six!) twenty-story buildings had once stood. A wound nothing could heal, and a battle that simply could not be won no matter how fast the Dragoons moved, how accurately they shot, or how bravely they stood their ground.

Hiring Hall. Jason did not even need to close his eyes to picture it as it had been. The well-kept grounds. A ten-story dome surrounded by the tallest buildings of Harlech. It was the entire reason for Outreach. Pride of Wolf's Dragoons, in a way. The center for most mercenary hiring throughout the entire Inner Sphere, and once the brilliant jewel in Harlech's crown.

It was gone.

And as Jason worked his *Gallowglas* around a corner, breaking into the open, he saw as well that there was nothing more to be done here.

The Wolf Spider battalion—what was left of them—had cordoned off the area with lances stationed at the four cardinal points and patrols of two 'Mechs each walking a wide perimeter. They allowed no one to approach. Not even other Dragoon 'Mechs.

All they had left to watch over, however, was a graveyard.

Huge piles of rubble several stories high loomed over a terrible battlefield. The debris continued to smolder. Ash and dust lay in a thick cover over everything, including the killing fields where BattleMechs lay strewn about like fallen soldiers at a massacre, the accumulation of three days' fighting.

Pieces and parts. Some near whole. Others blasted into scrap by an artillery strike, or even a fusion reactor letting loose in a small but powerful explosion. Those areas were more obvious, as the ground would be blackened and cleared for several dozen meters to any side, where a blast had swept everything clear.

Jason saw the *BattleMaster* as well.

Collapsed over two other 'Mechs. Forward-most among many—so many!—recent kills which still burned or smoked or smoldered on the corpse-riddled grounds. The dun color. Rust red accents. The red and blue star painted on the outside shoulder, still visible, with the white "W" emblazoned over it. Waco's Rangers. Seeing Colonel Waco's BattleMech there, among the fallen honored, was hard. Even for Jason, who knew the stories second and even third-hand.

But the worst was still not over. Not for the Dragoons.

That came with the 'Mech waiting alone on the battlefield; the last machine left standing. An old design, and a true veteran of many wars. Blocky shoulders that housed its twin LRM launchers. The forward-thrust cockpit—now smashed and breached in a half-dozen places, at least.

The classic *Archer* profile. Still painted with the blue and gold scheme he had made famous—or infamous—throughout the Inner Sphere.

For just that moment, Jason hoped. The *Archer* still stood, after all. The only machine left on its feet. He could be wounded. Unconscious. Many things, in fact.

Then he saw it.

The only body the Wolf Spiders had bothered to remove from any of the destroyed machines. Resting between the *Archer*'s feet, covered in a flag bearing the Dragoons' crest.

His crest.

And there was now a wound torn through Harlech, and Outreach, worse than the loss of the Hiring Hall. Knowingly or not, someone, somewhere, had made a very, very terrible error.

Because it was true. And no mistake.

Jaime Wolf was dead.